Cybercrime scholarship is moving from the descriptive to the analytical, with a rapidly accumulating evidence base. This book contains a valuable overview of major issues in cybercrime research, from theory testing to practical preventive measures. Informative, eminently readable, and richly documented, its impressive compilation and ordering of research findings will enlighten a generation of cybercrime students.

Peter Grabosky, *Professor Emeritus,*
Australian National University, Australia

Cybercrime in Progress is by far the most comprehensive yet incisive book on cybercrime available anywhere. It is written with clarity, authority and vision, so well written, in fact, that it would be an appropriate text for any undergraduate or graduate class. The title *Cybercrime in Progress* captures the essence of cybercrime: it is a moving and fluid target, changing constantly, creating new opportunities for offenders; new challenges for society's traditional responses to crime. Many people may think that cybercrime is too technical to understand. This book will change all that. Holt and Bossler are masters of their craft: they succinctly sum up the short history of cybercrime, point to the gaps in our responses to it, and tell us exactly what we must do in the future if we are to control it.

Graeme Newman, *Distinguished Teaching Professor,*
University at Albany, USA

Thomas Holt and Adam Bossler have done a really great job in locating cybercrimes and the future development of online criminal opportunities within the context of the various criminological debates. This book should not only help students undertake their studies into cybercrime, but also assist established scholars in coming to grips with this interesting, but constantly shifting area of interdisciplinary study.

David S. Wall, *Professor of Criminology,*
University of Leeds, UK

Cybercrime in Progress

The emergence of the World Wide Web, smartphones, and computers has transformed the world and enabled individuals to engage in crimes in a multitude of new ways. Criminological scholarship on these issues has increased dramatically over the last decade, as have studies on ways to prevent and police these offenses. This book is one of the first texts to provide a comprehensive review of research regarding cybercrime, policing, the enforcement of these offenses, and the prevention of various offenses as global change and technology adoption increase the risk of victimization around the world.

Drawing on a wide range of literature, Holt and Bossler offer an extensive synthesis of numerous contemporary topics, such as theories used to account for cybercrime, policing in domestic and transnational contexts, cybercrime victimization, and issues in cybercrime prevention. The findings provide a roadmap for future research in cybercrime, policing, and technology. Holt and Bossler discuss key controversies in the existing research literature in a way that is otherwise absent from textbooks and general cybercrime readers.

This book is an invaluable resource for academics, practitioners, and students interested in understanding the state of the art in social science cybercrime research. It will be of particular interest to scholars and students interested in cybercrime, cyber-deviance, victimization, policing, criminological theory, and technology in general.

Thomas J. Holt is an Associate Professor in the School of Criminal Justice at Michigan State University, specializing in cybercrime, policing, and policy.

Adam M. Bossler is an Associate Professor of Criminal Justice and Criminology at Georgia Southern University, specializing in cybercrime, policing, and innovative corrections.

Crime Science Series
Edited by Richard Wortley, *University College, London*

Crime science is a new way of thinking about and responding to the problem of crime in society. The distinctive nature of crime science is captured in the name.

First, crime science is about crime. Instead of the usual focus in criminology on the characteristics of the criminal offender, crime science is concerned with the characteristics of the criminal event. The analysis shifts from the distant causes of criminality – biological makeup, upbringing, social disadvantage and the like – to the near causes of crime. Crime scientists are interested in why, where, when and how particular crimes occur. They examine trends and patterns in crime in order to devise immediate and practical strategies to disrupt these patterns.

Second, crime science is about science. Many traditional responses to crime control are unsystematic, reactive, and populist, too often based on untested assumptions about what works. In contrast, crime science advocates an evidence-based, problem-solving approach to crime control. Adopting the scientific method, crime scientists collect data on crime, generate hypotheses about observed crime trends, devise interventions to respond to crime problems, and test the adequacy of those interventions.

Crime science is utilitarian in its orientation and multidisciplinary in its foundations. Crime scientists actively engage with front-line criminal justice practitioners to reduce crime by making it more difficult for individuals to offend, and making it more likely that they will be detected if they do offend. To achieve these objectives, crime science draws on disciplines from both the social and physical sciences, including criminology, sociology, psychology, geography, economics, architecture, industrial design, epidemiology, computer science, mathematics, engineering, and biology.

Cybercrime in Progress

Theory and prevention of
technology-enabled offenses

Thomas J. Holt and Adam M. Bossler

Routledge
Taylor & Francis Group

LONDON AND NEW YORK

First published 2016
by Routledge
2 Park Square, Milton Park, Abingdon, Oxon OX14 4RN

and by Routledge
711 Third Avenue, New York, NY 10017

Routledge is an imprint of the Taylor & Francis Group, an informa business

© 2016 Thomas J. Holt and Adam M. Bossler

British Library Cataloguing in Publication Data
A catalogue record for this book is available from the British Library

Library of Congress Cataloging in Publication Data
Names: Holt, Thomas J., 1978- | Bossler, Adam M.
 Title: Cybercrime in progress : theory and prevention of technology-enabled offenses / Thomas J. Holt and Adam M. Bossler.
 Description: First Edition. | New York : Routledge, 2016. | Series: Crime Science Series ; 17
 Identifiers: LCCN 2015025494| ISBN 9781138024168 (hardback) | ISBN 9781315775944 (ebook)
 Subjects: LCSH: Computer crimes. | Computer crimes–Prevention. | Criminal investigation–Technological innovations.
 Classification: LCC HV6773 .H6485 2016 | DDC 364.16/8–dc23
 LC record available at http://lccn.loc.gov/2015025494

ISBN: 978-1-13-802416-8 (hbk)
ISBN: 978-1-315-77594-4 (ebk)

Typeset in Times New Roman
by Taylor & Francis Books

Contents

Acknowledgement

There are a number of people who we must thank for their assistance in making this work possible. First and foremost, we would like to thank Tom Sutton, Heidi Lee, and the production staff at Routledge for their dedication to this work. Their assistance and patience with us at all stages of the process were greatly appreciated. We would also like to thank the scholars whose work forms the basis for our evaluation and discussion throughout this book. The continuous developments in cybercrime research suggest the state of the field is improving, leading to new insights every year. Finally, we would like to thank our families for their support and patience during the months we spent developing this text.

1 Technology and cybercrime

Chapter goals

- Explore the evolution of technology in society
- Define cybercrime and deviance
- Utilize a cybercrime typology to categorize various forms of cybercrime
- Consider how changes in technology influence digital evidence
- Examine the different levels of law enforcement that police in the Digital Age

Technology has become an integral part of our everyday lives. It has been over 30 years since Pac-Man (1980) made its big splash in arcades, and middle-class families were bringing home the Commodore 64 (1982) and Apple IIC (1984) personal computers. Today, the technological landscape is littered with devices of all shapes, sizes, and utilities, including mobile phones, tablet computers, iPads, Kindles, MP3 players, smart watches, and peripheral devices that track daily activities. Most of these devices can either be connected to the Internet via wireless network or share data via Bluetooth to an Internet-enabled device. In addition, televisions, appliances, HVAC (heating, ventilation and air-conditioning), and even automobiles, are now Internet enabled, creating the Internet of Things. In a relatively short period of time, our relationship with technology has transformed from being infrequent and one of convenience to an omnipresent necessity in almost all of our lives.

These changes have dramatically affected the nature of crime and deviance in the modern world, giving rise to cybercrimes, or offenses enabled by technology. The criminological scholarship regarding technology and offending has expanded substantially over the last two decades, incorporating a range of both qualitative and quantitative methods and theories to account for victimization and offending. The findings demonstrate that cybercrime is a complex and diverse problem, though the nature of studies and methods make it difficult to truly assess the totality of the field.

To understand the state of the field, a roadmap is necessary to identify not only what we know, but how to improve our knowledge of the causes of cybercrime, and how best to investigate and prevent these offenses. The purpose of this work is to present a roadmap of the current state of the field, as it is a body of research in progress, taking shape in part from the technologies that affect our lives. We intend this book to spark a debate on how best to move our understanding of cybercrime forward. We provide summaries of the literature as well as research questions that we believe are necessary to better identify the causes of and responses to cybercrime. The specific areas that we have chosen to cover in this book include: how we as a field have studied cybercrime and how to improve our knowledge (Chapter 2); the theoretical causes of a variety of cybercrimes and the gaps that still exist (Chapter 3); the capabilities of law enforcement and government agencies to respond to cybercrime and how to improve this response (Chapter 4); the implications of using a situational crime prevention framework to better understand how to decrease cybercrime victimization (Chapter 5); and the future of cybercrime, including trends and the impact that technology may have on these developments (Chapter 6). Throughout the book, we do not mean for our comments to be the final word on any issue or research question. Rather, it is a crucial starting point based on our summary of the literature, demonstrating gaps in our knowledge, and how we may best move the field forward.

In this chapter, we introduce the reader to the ways that technology has: (1) evolved over time; (2) affected all components of society and human behavior; and (3) created new forms of crime while also modifying old forms. The chapter provides clear descriptions of cybercrime and cyber-deviance using Wall's (2001) classic typology of cybercrime. This discussion provides definitions, explanations, and examples of each type. The chapter also illustrates that while technology has caused further dangers in the forms of new and modified crimes, it also has provided benefits and challenges for law enforcement as a result of new techniques and forms of evidence to investigate crimes. The chapter concludes with a discussion of what "policing" looks like in this new digital age, including which agencies are primarily responsible for investigating these crimes and how their roles have evolved due to these new technologies.

The impact of technology in society

It is staggering to contemplate how technology has changed and taken a more integral role in our lives over the last several decades. Less than two decades ago, most individuals in the US did not have cell phones, and they surely were not texting. A personal computer was still quite expensive and economically out of reach for many families. For those who did have home computers, most individuals had to use dial-up modems to connect to the Internet—literally paying by the hour for access to the web. The Internet was used more for "web surfing" for information or curiosity purposes. Email, online banking, and buying products online were still uncommon. In what today's youth might find foreign, video game systems used 16-bit graphics or less and did not connect to other devices. Playing video games at home was only a social event if other individuals were physically present with you in the same room. If you were not in the military, you probably were not using GPS either.

Today, computers, the Internet, and various mobile technologies have reshaped modern society. There are now over 2.8 billion Internet users worldwide, with 641.6 million users living in China and a quarter billion in the US (Internet Live Stats, 2015). These two nations have the highest populations of users of all nations worldwide, though individuals in virtually every nation around the world have some presence online (Internet Live Stats, 2015). It is not uncommon for most individuals in the US to have personal laptops or notebooks, cell phones, and video game systems that are all connected to the Internet via Wi-Fi. Many individuals have multiple presences online as indicated by several email accounts for both personal and business use and social networking profiles on different sites like Facebook and Instagram. Consumers are also increasingly discarding the use of print media and opting for e-readers or digital book formats (Wray, 2014). In addition, the cell phone, particularly text messaging, has become the preferred method of communication over other traditional means, including in-person conversations, letters, phone calls, and even email. In fact, individuals under the age of 20 are the age group most likely to send texts rather than to make phone calls (Zickuhr, 2011).

This proliferation of technology has not just simply affected all aspects of our lives; it has transformed how we *engage and view* the world around us. Shopping, communicating, and sharing information occurs increasingly in digital environments, even to the point where consumers are being directed to use their devices while in physical environments. For instance, retailers have created applications that customers can use while in the store to scan items and get immediate coupons or discounts that can be applied upon checkout (Wahba, 2014). Our behaviors will continue to evolve as technological innovations occur and are implemented widely.

The ways that technology influences our actions can be understood through sociological research. For instance, the behaviors in which we engage throughout our daily lives are structured by **folkways**, or norms for routine social interactions (Odum, 1937). Sociologist Howard Odum (1937) recognized early on that technology affects our day-to-day lives, simplifying some aspects of our lives and changing how we may behave. He referred to the process of behavior change in response to, or as a consequence of, technological innovation as **technicways** (Odum, 1937; Parker, 1972; Vance, 1972). Though Odum's (1937) work focused on evolutions in farming technology, this concept has clear utility in a modern context. Essentially, technologies change our folkways by replacing existing behavior patterns, such as how we communicate or conduct business, and force fundamental institutional changes in society (Vance, 1972). For example, instead of walking over to the neighbor's house or calling them on a phone to chat, technology enables individuals to send a hasty text or post commentary on social media to communicate.

Although specific technicways may affect one population group more than others, they may eventually alter societal interactions as a whole, regardless of age, sex, race, and economic status. For example, the wide availability of broadband Internet connectivity across the US, coupled with increased ownership of personal computers, smart phones, and other mobile devices, has led to the strong use of video-sharing sites. Some 71 percent of Americans, including racial and ethnic minorities who historically have had limited access to technology, now use video-sharing sites (Moore, 2011). Over 80 percent of adults in the US own a cell phone; approximately one-third of those cell phone owners have smart phones on which they can connect to the Internet (Smith, 2011). The percentage of technology ownership in other nations is lower than that of the US, but the fact that device access is still prevalent globally indicates that a substantive portion of that population possesses newer communication technological devices. For example, in the UK, 42 percent of households have fiber optic or cable broadband Internet connections (Office for National Statistics, 2013). A larger percentage—61 percent—of individuals in the UK owned a smart phone that could connect to the Internet (Office for National Statistics, 2013).

Contemplating how technology has changed our lives over the last several decades is a challenging assignment for youth who have never experienced life without the Internet and **computer-mediated communications (CMCs)**, such as email and texting. Asking a teenager to consider life without a smart phone or the Internet is akin to asking many adults to contemplate life before automobiles. Although we can appreciate some of the challenges that previous generations must have experienced, it is impossible to truly grasp what life was like without these innovations. For today's youth in the US, they generally acquire their first cell phone between the ages of 12 and 13 (Lenhart, 2010). In addition, three-fourths of them own either a laptop or desktop computer; 15 percent own both devices (Lenhart, Madden, & Hitlin, 2005). Furthermore, nearly all American youth—93 percent—between the ages of 12 and 17 use the Internet. In fact, they frequently access the Internet. Almost nine out of ten children (88 percent) who go online do so at least once a week (Lenhart & Madden, 2007). More astonishing, Wolak, Mitchell, and Finkelhor's (2006) analysis of a national sample found that half of children were online between *five and seven days* each week.

Technology does not simply shift the behaviors of youth; it molds their behavior and shapes their world view from the very beginning. Individuals born in the late 1980s have never lived without the Internet, computers, or cell phones and therefore do not know what their lives would be like without these devices. These youth therefore can be considered **digital natives** since they were born and raised in a digital world, spend as much time if not more interacting in the virtual world than the physical one, and utilize technological devices to satisfy many of their daily wants and needs (Prensky, 2001). These individuals, particularly those between 18 and 34, possess the most technological resources and are the heaviest users of the Internet (Lenhart,

Purcell, Smith, & Zickuhr, 2010). In the US, two-thirds of adults use the Internet, while 87 percent of teens use the Internet (Zickuhr, 2011). Therefore, approximately 18 million youth are online every day (Lenhart et al., 2010). Not surprisingly, this age group also comprises half of the entire population of Facebook users in the US (Socialbakers, 2011).

By contrast, **digital immigrants** are those individuals who were born before the advent of digital technologies and the Internet (Prensky, 2001). As a result, digital immigrants are required to adapt to the digital environment and allow technology to alter their behavior patterns if they decide to participate in this technologically evolving world. In some situations, these technological advancements and subsequent technicways require more rapid changes than some are prepared to make. This can be especially problematic for older individuals who may have been born several decades before these innovations and have already made several adaptations to technology throughout their lives. They may be less willing to spend the resources, including time, energy, and money, to adopt these new technological tools. For example, less than half (45 percent) of adults in the US over the age of 65 own either a laptop or desktop computer (Zickuhr, 2011). They also receive on average 14 or fewer texts per day than other age groups (Zickuhr, 2011). In the UK, less than one in five (17 percent) individuals over the age of 65 possess a mobile phone (Office for National Statistics, 2013).

In addition, some newer technological resources ask individuals to provide personal information in ways with which many middle-aged and older individuals do not feel comfortable because they perceive it as a violation of their privacy. This is an issue that clearly does not affect youth as much, as they have been raised on social media that reward individuals who share all important and unimportant information about their lives, regardless of how personal. Therefore, some technological resources, such as social media (e.g. Facebook), are difficult for many digital immigrants to understand because they require users to provide information regularly about themselves and their interests, which strikes at their sense of privacy. It might not be too surprising, then, to discover that people over the age of 55 constitute only 13 percent of the entire population of US Facebook users (Socialbakers, 2011). Thus, digital immigrants' experiences with the adoption and use of various technologies differ greatly from those of digital natives.

In summary, the ubiquity of technology in modern society has had a significant impact on human behavior, regardless of who we are. Technology has altered how we communicate, interact with other individuals and entities, shop, recreate, and simply live. At the same time, a technological divide exists between generations based on the ways they choose to adopt and adapt to various technologies. As the next section illustrates, some individuals' adoption of technology includes behaviors that subvert the original beneficial designs of the technology into negative gains for themselves.

Defining cybercrime and deviance

The substantive societal changes stemming from the development of computers, cellular telephony, and the Internet require clear definitions of what constitutes the abuse and misuse of technology. The definitions for such activities have evolved in tandem with technology itself to create a somewhat complex terminology. As early as the 1970s, individuals used the term "computer crime" to refer to the misuse of computers and data (Parker, 1976). During this same decade, one of the first computer crime laws in the US was passed in Florida in 1978, making all unauthorized access to computer systems a third degree felony (Hollinger & Lanza-Kaduce, 1988). The Internet existed at this time, though it was not well known or used outside of government, corporate, and university environments. Individuals who had the capacity to engage in computer crimes were generally employees working within a regulated environment who already had access to computerized data (e.g. Parker, 1976).

The term computer crime was most commonly used to refer to virtually all criminal activity involving computers until the late 1990s. The terminology began to change as technology use and access fundamentally transformed society. The development of the Windows 95 operating system made computers much more user friendly, as did the ease of access to Internet connectivity. Similarly, the creation of the web browser in the early 1990s, such as Netscape Navigator and Microsoft's Internet Explorer, allowed the home user to go online and experience content in a visual fashion through integrated images, text, audio, and video files. Dial-up Internet service providers reduced the price of their services, and personal computers were sold with integrated modems and connection ports for phone lines or Ethernet cables for high-speed connections. The global expansion of and connectivity afforded by the Internet led to the digitalization of sensitive financial and government information and massive accessible databases online. Financial service providers, social networking sites, and business platforms moved to online environments to offer services directly to home computer users, offering convenient modes of communication and shopping.

As technology use patterns changed, researchers such as David Wall (1998) began to use the term "cybercrime" to refer to crimes performed online. Grabosky (2001), however, used the term computer crime to refer to computer misuse. These terms were used relatively synonymously by researchers and journalists working during this period (e.g. Furnell, 2002; Jordan & Taylor, 1998; Taylor, 1999), though they technically recognize differences in the role of technology in the course of an offense. Specifically, **cybercrime** refers to crimes "in which the perpetrator uses special knowledge of cyberspace," while **computer crimes** occur because "the perpetrator uses special knowledge about computer technology" (Furnell, 2002: 21; Wall, 2001).

By the mid-2000s, criminological researchers appeared to have adopted the term cybercrime to refer to technology-enabled offending. This is sensible as virtually all forms of computing, from mobile phones to MP3 players, are now Internet enabled. If all these devices can access the Internet, the potential for misuse in cyberspace increases dramatically. As a result of this technological change, we use the term cybercrime throughout the course of this work to refer to offenses that can occur in online environments. It is important to note that these terms are rather vague and are not the only definitions used by academics and practitioners alike. Within academia, for example, McGuire's (2007) concept of "hypercrime" (p.7) addresses the distinct interactional nature of online environments coupled with their mutability and coexistence with other spaces, real and imagined. The presence of multiple webpages, online communities, and operating environments transforms the nature of cyberspace into a milieu of different but intermingled environments existing all at once. Thus, crimes in online spaces transcend singular environments to create a complex form of offending that has analogues to, but distinctions from, traditional crime in physical spaces.

Within the law enforcement community, there are further segmentations used to specify how technology is used in the course of an offense. For instance, the National Incident-Based Reporting System (NIBRS) in the US is designed to capture and record incidents made known to the police at the local level. A single category is included in the NIBRS to identify whether a computer was used in the course of the offense. This unfortunately does not provide much utility when viewed separately from all other items that are captured in the data.

The UK police and policy-making bodies use a more specific typology that distinguishes between "**computer-assisted crimes**" and "**computer-focused crimes**" (Furnell, 2002: 22; McGuire & Dowling, 2013). "Computer-assisted crimes" involve computers acting in a supporting role in the commission of a crime, such as the use of email as a means either to send fraudulent messages and scams or to post harassing messages via social media. By contrast, "computer-focused crimes" are a direct result of and cannot exist without computer technology, such as hacking into a sensitive network or the utilization of computer viruses to acquire information (Furnell, 2002: 22). This typology presents a clearer explication than other current definitions, and illustrates the wide variety of terms used to classify computer crimes.

In addition, researchers have also begun to pay attention over the last several years to the ways that technology may be used as a means to engage in behavior that may not be illegal, but violates norms and beliefs of the larger culture. Though such acts would typically be referred to as deviance, the online environment has led to the adoption of the term **cyber-deviance**. Though cyber-deviance encompasses a wide range of behavior, there is a substantive focus among criminological and sociological researchers on sexual activities online, including viewing pornography and engaging in sexual conversations with strangers (e.g. Quinn & Forsythe, 2013).

The focus on sexual deviance online may stem from two factors: (1) the Internet has made it exceedingly easy for individuals to create, share, and view pornographic images and videos across multiple technological platforms (e.g. cell phones, tablets, laptops, desktops); and (2) there are dramatic differences in national laws pertaining to pornography and sexual activity online. The borderless nature of the Internet allows individuals to access content that may be illegal in their home country if it is hosted in another nation with more permissible laws (Brenner, 2011). Furthermore, individuals can conceal their activities from others and view any sort of content without having to divulge their interests publicly. As a result, technology is transforming the nature of deviance by improving anonymity and accessibility to interested parties who share predilections or attractions.

In addition to cyber-deviance and crime, there is also increasing attention paid to the role of technology in the facilitation of ideologically driven acts of hate speech and violence both on and off-line (Brenner, 2008; Chermak, 2003; Chermak, Freilich, & Suttmoeller, 2013; Corb, 2011; Pollitt, 1998; Weimann, 2011). The preponderance of extremist and hate groups online provides a resource to espouse ideological beliefs and justifications for their beliefs and actions as well as potentially recruit and indoctrinate individuals into movements around the world. In fact, there were nearly 8,000 websites serving terrorists and their supporters in 2010, including all organizations designated "foreign terrorist organizations" by the US State Department (Weimann, 2011: 770). The robust nature of these communities provides what Bowman-Grieve (2009) called "**virtual communities of hate**," where individuals can engage with others who may share their beliefs or foster rapport with those who are already heavily entrenched in a particular ideology.

The Internet creates a unique environment for potential acts of political or ideologically motivated crime and terrorism. The various platforms where individuals can connect and share information online, whether Facebook, Twitter, or YouTube, enable expression of political opinions or beliefs that may be in opposition to larger social norms (Martin, 2006; Schmid, 1988, 2004). Additionally, the spread of messages and content can extend beyond physical boundaries and enable individuals to be exposed to opinions, beliefs, and social causes that may not be otherwise evident in their local community (Ayers, 1999; Chadwick, 2007; Jennings & Zeitner, 2003; Stepanova, 2011). In turn, participation in online extremist communities may foster individuals to action in the real world, whether through traditional forms of political expression such as protests and demonstrations (Chadwick, 2007; Earl & Schussman, 2003; Jennings & Zeitner, 2003; Stepanova, 2011; Van Laer, 2010) or acts of violence against others (e.g. Chermak et al., 2013).

The infrastructure of the Internet and World Wide Web can also serve as an attack vector for actors, ranging from acts of vandalism to more serious forms of harm (Brenner, 2008; Denning, 2011; Holt & Kilger, 2012a, 2012b). In virtual spaces, individuals may engage in similar forms of vandalism to demonstrate political dissent. For instance, a group may use hacking techniques to promote an activist agenda or express dissent (Denning, 2011; Jordan & Taylor, 2004; Taylor, 1999). One of the best examples of such activity is the use of **web defacements** to vandalize websites and post messages of political opinion (Denning, 2011; Woo, Kim, & Dominick, 2004). The attacker replaces the existing HTML content of a website with either an image or message of their own choosing. Many defacements do not result in actual damage to the data stored on the server hosting the site, though they serve as an inconvenience to the site owner (Denning, 2011; Woo et al., 2004).

The most extreme forms of political activity in the real world involve planned acts of violence through the use of explosives or assassinations to promote a social agenda (Schmid, 2004). Such acts are often defined as terrorism, especially if the action is intended to cause political change or produce fear or concern among civilian populations (Martin, 2006; Schmid, 2004; Schmid & Jongman, 2005). Though there is no analogue for a bombing in an online environment, researchers began to recognize the potential that cyberspace may be misused by motivated actors as a mechanism to cause harm or spread fear. As a result, as early as 1998 scholars began to use the term **cyberterrorism** to refer to political or ideologically motivated attacks in online spaces (e.g. Pollitt, 1998).

There are distinct differences in the practical realities of cyberterrorism relative to physical terrorism. For instance, some researchers have argued that an act of cyberterrorism must result in a loss of life or physical harm in the real world, since this is an essential component of traditional definitions of terrorism (Martin, 2006; Schmid & Jongman, 2005). The reality that such an outcome could occur from a cyber-attack is difficult for many to realize, especially since there has been no evidence of such an incident occurring to date (e.g. Yar, 2013). That is not to suggest that it is impossible; such an attack may simply be unlikely given the overall capacities of many terrorist and extremist groups today.

The emphasis placed on physical harm may be misplaced, as other definitions of cyberterrorism recognize that an attack must be motivated by a political or ideological agenda in order to produce fear, coerce, or otherwise intimidate a government or its people (Britz, 2010; Denning, 2011; Foltz, 2004; Pollitt, 1998). These elements are also present in definitions for physical terrorism, and may be more appropriate when considering the possible after-effects of a cyber-attack. Most aspects of modern life, from personal communications to interstate commerce to sewer system functionality, depend on the Internet in some way. A virtual attack that leads to a loss of service or hinders the ability of the population to communicate may generate substantive fear or concern for their safety (Brenner, 2008; Britz, 2010; Brodscky & Radvanovsky, 2011; Denning, 2011). Islamic extremist websites have even communicated the value of cyber-attacks against financial service providers, since an attack lasting "for a few days or even for a few hours … will cause millions of dollars worth of damage" (Denning, 2011: 172).

The economic impact of a cyber-attack may, therefore, be commensurate with the harm caused by a physical attack in terms of both financial harm and fear created within the larger population. While there have been few such attacks to date, a group calling itself the Izz ad-Din al-Qassam Cyber

Fighters began a series of denial of service attacks against major US banks in 2012 (Gonsalves, 2013). The group used compromised computers within the US as a basis for the attacks and was able to interrupt online services for customers of U.S. Bankcorp, JP Morgan Chase & Co, Bank of America, PNC Financial Services Group, and SunTrust, among others. The attacks varied in their degree of success, though at least seven financial institutions' services were off-line for minutes to hours, depending on the bank (Gonsalves, 2013).

The group made a series of posts on the Pastebin website explaining that they were engaging in these attacks as retaliation against the US for its treatment of the Islamic faith in general, and specifically with respect to its refusal to remove from YouTube a set of film clips that disparage the Prophet Mohammed. These posts also indicated that the attacks would occur in proportion to the amount of time the videos remained online and the number of times the videos were viewed. Though the incident was not well publicized, no information has been provided with respect to the economic ramifications of the attack for these financial institutions. As a result, this attack may be one of the first successful instances of cyberterrorism against an economic target in the US.

Beyond attacks against virtual targets, it is also pertinent to recognize that email and electronic communications can serve as a vehicle for fundraising, information management, and communications between extremists (Gruen, 2005; Pool, 2005; Simi & Futrell, 2006). In her review of cyberterrorism, Britz (2010: 197) provides an expansive definition that not only includes electronic attacks, but also takes into account the Internet as a resource to support terrorist plots and actors:

> The premeditated, methodological, ideologically motivated dissemination of information, facilitation of communication, or, attack against physical targets, digital information, computer systems, and/or computer programs which is intended to cause social, financial, physical, or psychological harm to noncombatant targets and audiences for the purpose of affecting ideological, political, or social change; or any utilization of digital communication or information which facilitates such actions directly or indirectly.

The relatively comprehensive scope of this definition compared with others suggests it is a practical framework to examine cyberterrorism. As such, we will use this definition to refer to cyberterrorism throughout this work in discussions of the ways that technology is used to facilitate ideologically driven behavior on and off-line.

The cybercrime typology

In light of the various ways that technology engenders crime and deviance as well as fosters unique tactics for offending, it is necessary to understand the wide range of behaviors that constitute cybercrime. In the current research literature, a variety of activities may be referred to as cybercrimes, leading to different terms, as discussed above, and various typologies to refer to cyber-criminals (e.g. Rogers & Seigfried-Spellar, 2013; Shoemaker & Kennedy, 2009). Offender-based typologies, however, are largely used by their individual creators rather than commonly cited in the literature. In seeking a concise typology of cybercrime, one of the most recognized was developed by David Wall (2001), which encapsulates cyber behaviors into one of four categories: (1) cyber-trespass; (2) cyber-deception and theft; (3) cyber-porn and obscenity; and (4) cyber-violence. These categories reference the wide range of deviant, criminal, and terrorist activities utilizing technology that have emerged across the globe.

Cyber-trespass

The first category is **cyber-trespass**, referencing the act of crossing invisible, yet established, boundaries of ownership in online environments. An owner or system administrator attempting to secure wireless networks, computers, and mobile devices with passwords and other access controls demonstrates that they are restricting the use of these devices to certain individuals. When individuals attempt to use these resources without permission, whether by guessing passwords or more sophisticated means, they are engaging in an act of trespass (Furnell, 2002).

Acts of cyber-trespass are commonly attributed to computer hackers who attempt to gain access to computer systems, email accounts, or protected networks that they do not own (Furnell, 2002; Jordan & Taylor, 1998). While the general public often associates hacking with criminal acts of trespass (e.g. Furnell, 2002), the same hacking techniques can be applied in order to protect networks from compromise (Jordan & Taylor, 1998; Taylor, 1999). In these instances, the hackers typically have permission from the system owners, which neutralizes the potential that it is a criminal act of trespass.

The focus placed on malicious hacks without permission in popular media has led to the perception that hackers cause substantial harm to citizens, industry, and governments around the world. In fact, estimates from the US GAO (2007) indicate that cybercrimes facilitated in part by hacking cost the US economy over $100 billion each year. Much of this economic harm may be associated with malicious software programs, or malware, that automate a variety of attacks and enable hackers to break into computer systems (Furnell, 2002; Symantec Corporation, 2013). There is a range of malware currently circulating online, including viruses, worms, Trojan Horse programs, botnets, iFrame malware, and remote administration tools (Symantec Corporation, 2013). Each form has its own attributes, though they all can be used for different malicious ends, such as degrading network connectivity, gaining access to private files, deleting material, capturing keystrokes, and enabling the computer to be commanded remotely by an attacker (Symantec

Corporation, 2013). Malware therefore makes it easier for cybercriminals to engage in identity theft, fraud, and destruction of sensitive information (Holt & Bossler, 2014; Nazario, 2003; Symantec Corporation, 2013).

Cyber-deception/theft

The second category within Wall's (2001) typology is **cyber-deception/theft**, encompassing all ways that individuals may illegally acquire information or materials online. There is a clear connection between acts of trespass and theft, as hackers frequently attempt to gain access to sensitive financial information or data that can be resold or misused to engage in fraud (e.g. Franklin et al., 2007; Holt & Lampke, 2010; Peretti, 2009). The quantity of sensitive personal information stored in databases and transmitted over the Internet creates substantial opportunities for theft (James, 2005; Newman & Clarke, 2003; Peretti, 2009). For instance, payment systems and databases maintained by major US retailers, including Target, Home Depot, Neiman Marcus, and various restaurant chains including Dairy Queen, Jimmy Johns, and P.F. Chang's, were compromised leading to the loss of millions of consumer credit and debit cards (Higgins, 2014; Pauli, 2014; Seals, 2014).

The substantial quantity of information obtained by hackers and attackers has also led to the growth of online markets where cybercriminals can sell stolen data to others (Franklin et al., 2007; Holt & Lampke, 2010; Motoyama et al., 2011; Peretti, 2009; Wehinger, 2011). Research suggests that actors engage one another via Internet Relay Chat (IRC) or web-based forums whose users communicate in Russian, though a small proportion also operate in English (Franklin et al., 2007; Holt & Lampke, 2010; Motoyama et al., 2011; Symantec Corporation, 2014). These markets facilitate the sale of millions of credit card numbers and personally identifiable information, as well as resources to facilitate various cybercrimes (Holt & Lampke, 2010; Peretti, 2009). The sales process is driven by advertisements posted by interested sellers describing the products they have to offer, their pricing structures, contact information, and any rules regarding the transaction process. In turn, buyers contact the seller and negotiate the terms of sale, and then send money directly to the seller and wait for their products to be delivered (Franklin et al., 2007; Holt & Lampke, 2010).

There are also a range of fraud schemes that are facilitated through email-based spam, including auction and retail-based fraud, stock manipulation schemes, and dating scams designed to attract respondents into sending funds or information (Newman & Clarke, 2003). One of the most prevalent and costly forms of cyber-fraud are advance fee email schemes, sometimes referred to as Nigerian or 419 scams (Holt & Graves, 2007; Wall, 2004). The senders typically state they reside in a foreign country, such as Nigeria or other African nations, and need assistance transferring funds out of their country (Buchanan & Grant, 2001; Holt & Graves, 2007). In return, the sender will share a portion of the sum with the individual who aids them

(Holt & Graves, 2007). Victims of this type of fraud often lose thousands of dollars on average, and may be too embarrassed to report their experiences to law enforcement because of the often obviously false nature of the message to which they responded (Buchanan & Grant, 2001; Newman & Clarke, 2003; Wall, 2004).

In addition to financially motivated fraud, the category of cyber-deception/ theft also includes the theft of intellectual property via digital piracy. The Internet and mobile devices have transformed the nature of media, leading to the digitization, sharing, and streaming of music, movies, television programs, and even games and software. The ability to access digital materials through direct download has enabled a global community of individuals who share illegal copies of media files without proper consent of or remuneration to the copyright holders (Decary-Hetu, Morselli, & Leman-Langlois, 2012; Gopal et al., 2004). In fact, estimates from the software industry indicate that the rate of piracy of various software may be as high as 80 percent in various countries around the world (Business Software Alliance, 2012). As a consequence, companies estimate their financial losses as a result of piracy to be in the billions every year (Siwek, 2007). The prevalence of this problem has led to substantial research by various criminological scholars, making it one of the most commonly studied forms of cybercrime in the literature today (Holt & Bossler, 2014).

Cyber-porn/obscenity

The third category in Wall's (2001) typology of cybercrime is **cyber-porn** and obscenity, representing the entire range of sexual expression possible online. **Pornography**, defined as the representation of sexual situations and content for the purposes of sexual arousal and stimulation (Lane, 2000), can be found online in various formats, including erotic writings, line drawings, photos, video, and audio content (Brenner, 2011). Computer-mediated communications serve as a vital resource for individuals to identify, publish, consume, and distribute sexual materials of any stripe to anyone, regardless of age, sexual orientation, or preferences (Quinn & Forsyth, 2013). The variation in laws pertaining to what is acceptable with respect to sexually explicit materials and content varies from place to place. As a result, some acts may be perfectly legal but considered socially deviant, while others may be crimes depending on local laws (Brenner, 2011). In the US and most Western nations, pornographic content is legal so long as the voluntary participants in the acts depicted and the consumer or viewer of the content are of the legal age for the country. There is also a wide range of sexual fetishes and niche content available to cater to virtually any interest, no matter how unusual or obscene (Quinn & Forsythe, 2013).

The Internet and computer-mediated communications also facilitate a broad economy of paid sexual services which may or may not be legal in a given area. For instance, individuals can perform in live-streaming video feeds which are supported by viewers who pay the person for their time (Roberts & Hunt, 2012). Since there is no actual physical contact between the performer and her clients, it is not technically illegal. The fact that the performers are paid clearly makes this a form of sex work.

Technology also supports traditional prostitution, or paid sexual encounters, in the real world as well. There are now forums and websites designed to connect the prospective customers of sex workers together and facilitate discussion about the practices, quality, and locations of workers in a given area (Holt & Blevins, 2007; Milrod & Monto, 2012; Weitzer, 2005). In much the same way, sex workers use websites, blogs, and email to negotiate with their clients and verify their real identities in order to determine their status as a law enforcement officer (Cunningham & Kendall, 2010).

In addition, cyber-porn and obscenity include the repulsive and significant problem of **child pornography**, or images and video of individuals under the age of 18 (or 16 depending on the nation) engaging in sexualized acts and behaviors (Durkin, 1997; Durkin & Bryant, 1999; Jenkins, 2001; Krone, 2004). Child pornography existed well before the development of the Internet, though the anonymity and global connectivity afforded by this technology has created an environment that fosters the creation and exchange of these materials (Edward, 2000; Holt, Blevins, & Burkert, 2010; Krone, 2004; Quayle & Taylor, 2002). Though there is no single estimate of the quantity of child pornography available online at any given time, evidence suggests there may be at least 20,000 images of child pornography posted online *each week* (Rice-Hughes, 2005). In addition, some individuals use the online environment as a means to solicit children to engage in sexual acts either on or off-line (Durkin & Bryant, 1999; Krone, 2004). As a consequence, law enforcement agencies around the world have invested substantial resources in the investigation and prosecution of child pornographers.

Cyber-violence

The final form within Wall's (2001) typology is **cyber-violence**, referring to the opportunity afforded by technology to create, distribute, or solicit access to injurious, hurtful, or dangerous materials. In this case, harm typically refers to emotional harm to the victim, whether through shame or stigma. Physical harm may result as well if the individual internalizes the pain and commits self-injurious behaviors, such as abusing alcohol and drugs, binge eating, or committing suicide (e.g. Hinduja & Patchin, 2009). Thus, the effects of cyber-violence cannot be summarized as someone simply having their feelings hurt, but rather, it may include emotional and physical trauma, and in rare cases death. In particular, cyber-violence captures two distinct phenomena depending on whether it targets specific individuals or broader populations or groups.

Acts of cyber-violence against individuals typically take the form of harassment through various forms of computer-mediated communication

(Hinduja & Patchin, 2009; Holt & Bossler, 2009; Jones et al., 2012). Juvenile populations increasingly appear to engage in **cyberbullying** behaviors, where an individual sends mean or threatening messages about another person through social media, text, or video files (Hinduja & Patchin, 2009; Wolak et al., 2012). This same behavior occurring in adult populations may be referred to as online harassment or cyberstalking, depending on the severity and persistence of the messages sent (Bocij, 2004; Nobles et al., 2014; Reyns et al., 2012). Though it may seem that experiences with harassing communications could be dismissed by the recipient, a significant proportion report intrusive thoughts, depression, suicidal thoughts, and other negative consequences (Bocij, 2004; Hinduja & Patchin, 2009; Nobles et al., 2014). In addition, victims are unlikely to report their experiences to law enforcement or peers due to perceptions that the incidents may not be taken seriously (e.g. Hinduja & Patchin, 2009; Catalano, 2012), or that they may actually increase the number of messages they receive (Nobles et al., 2014).

Incidents of cyber-violence that target broader populations include behaviors that may also be defined as acts of cyberterrorism, such as web defacements or hate speech in online environments (see discussion above; Wall, 2001). This category also includes the creation and distribution of materials that can be used to cause harm on or off-line, such as bomb-making manuals, guides on how to engage in *jihad*, and tutorials on hacking and fraud techniques (Denning, 2011; Wall, 2001). While the availability of these materials online does not constitute an immediate threat to any one population, the presence of information means that someone with sufficient motivation could use it against a target (Hoffman, 2006). As a result, the use of technology has expanded the potential knowledge base of extremist groups and may enhance their capability to cause harm to populations and targets across the world.

The role of digital evidence in cybercrime

Wall's (2001) cybercrime typology recognizes forms of offending that include both computer-assisted and computer-focused crimes. The difference between these two terms depends on whether the computer was used as a tool to commit an offense that has a similar counterpart in the physical world, or whether it is a newer form of crime that has only existed since the advent of the computer and involves either the system or the data it contains as the target of the offense. In this respect, a computer or mobile device may serve as a through-point for communications between offenders or from an offender to a victim.

Alternatively, a device may itself be a target, becoming the victim of either a compromise or malicious software infection. Finally, there may simply be illicit content stored on the device that implicates an individual in the crime or act of deviance. For instance, the presence of child pornography on a laptop or flash drive suggests that its owner has engaged in some type of crime.

Regardless of the way that a piece of technology may be utilized or affected, any information stored on the device that ties it to a crime constitutes **digital evidence**, defined as information that is either transferred or stored in a binary format (Casey, 2011). Laptops, desktops, mobile phones, tablet computers, Kindles, GPS devices, digital cameras, flash drives, CDs, DVDs, and even video game systems all store digital files in some fashion. Thus, any applications, email, images, video, audio files, browser histories, search histories, user contacts, and other information stored on these devices constitute digital evidence. This information may be used in the course of investigations of both on and off-line crime. For instance, the browser history of an individual's laptop may provide evidence of searches for and attempts to illegally download movies and television shows (Casey, 2011; Ferraro & Casey, 2005). At the same time, law enforcement officers may seize a drug dealer's mobile phone in order to capture text messages, call logs, and contact details to see who they are communicating with, and determine if the device may implicate the individual in drug trafficking or other crime (e.g. Holt, Bossler, & Seigfried-Spellar, 2015).

The inherently social nature of the web and CMCs has also led law enforcement and intelligence agencies to seek digital evidence, or artifacts, from websites and social media that implicate individuals in criminal activity. For instance, law enforcement agencies across the US have begun to arrest students for making supposedly anonymous threats of physical violence against their campuses using the social media application (app) Yik Yak (Svokos, 2014). The app is a short-form shared text-based posting site, similar to Twitter, only the users are shown content based on their geographic location. As a result, users can see content and respond based on the interests of others nearby. The site has a massive following among youth, thanks in part to the fact that the site does not provide usernames, but only the location of the post (Svokos, 2014).

While this appears to promote user anonymity, the site operators willingly share the IP address and GPS coordinates (if possible) with law enforcement in the event that a threat is made that appears credible (Svokos, 2014). This information has proven useful enough to lead to the arrest of students at middle schools, high schools, and universities in Georgia, Illinois, Indiana, Iowa, Michigan, Mississippi, New York, Oklahoma, and Pennsylvania, among others (Svokos, 2014). In all of these instances, the individuals arrested threatened to engage in mass shootings, bombings, or other acts of violence against the student body (Svokos, 2014). Due to concerns over the safety of student populations in the wake of various mass shooting incidents at high schools and universities, law enforcement treats these threats as real and actionable, and are able to generate valuable intelligence leads from the digital evidence made available from the site's security personnel (Svokos, 2014).

The broad range of storage devices that may contain digital evidence requires law enforcement to carefully search any suspect and crime scene to identify all potential pieces of technology that may implicate an individual in an offense. There are major variations in the ways that different devices work, and how they may connect to the Internet. This directly impacts the way that an officer must handle the device to ensure that it is properly maintained and will not be rendered inadmissible later during any court proceedings. Not all officers are aware of the differences in the processes and storage capacities between devices—even those made by the same company. In fact, the constantly evolving nature of technology makes digital evidence handling one of the most complex issues that law enforcement may face in the field.

Policing in the digital age

As demonstrated so far, cybercrimes and advances in technology create unique challenges to our understanding of criminality. The same challenges are evident in the response of policing agencies to cybercrime over the last three decades. While cybercriminals are agile, connecting with offenders in loosely coupled associations and disbanding quickly (e.g. Decary-Hetu & Dupont, 2012; Holt et al., 2012), law enforcement agencies are complex bureaucracies with roles that are limited by jurisdiction. Local agencies are only able to respond to local crimes, while offenses that exceed a certain dollar amount or involve offenders affecting victims across state or national boundaries are typically reserved for national or federal agencies. Cybercriminals, on the other hand, can target victim populations around the world with no prior contact.

In order to identify the key gaps in our knowledge of the law enforcement response to cybercrime (see Chapter 4), we must first have a basic understanding of the structure of policing generally. In most nations around the world, local law enforcement agencies serve as first responders for criminal incidents. Victims of most crimes will contact their local police agency for assistance. Local agencies are responsible for investigating offenses where both the victim and offender reside within their local jurisdiction. These agencies vary widely in terms of the populations they serve, the size of the agency, and its general response capabilities. In the US, for example, most law enforcement agencies serve rural or suburban communities with populations under 50,000 (LEMAS, 2010). In addition, half of all local police agencies had fewer than 10 sworn officers in 2008. A majority of these agencies—75 percent—served towns of fewer than 10,000 total citizens (LEMAS, 2010). In the UK, the majority of police agencies are territorial police forces which are responsible for policing a specific jurisdictional area (Yar, 2013). In Canada, major urban centers, such as Toronto or Montreal, also have their own police forces designated to serve that specific local population.

Although local police agencies comprise the majority of law enforcement agencies, they have a relatively limited role in the investigation of cybercrime (see Holt, Burruss, and Bossler, 2015). The small sizes of both the police agencies and the populations they serve limit their budgets and access to the specialized training and equipment necessary to investigate these crimes.

Furthermore, their geographic jurisdictional limitations minimize their responsibility to only those crimes where both the victim and offender reside in the same jurisdiction. The majority of cybercrimes that are handled by local police appear to involve online harassment, stalking, child pornography, and sexual exploitation cases (e.g. Holt, Bossler, & Fitzgerald, 2010; Senjo, 2004). Even in these cases, they may have to send victims to other agencies with more expertise to aid with the investigation.

The next organizational level of law enforcement with responsibility to investigate cybercrime are state (e.g. US, Australia) or provincial (e.g. Canada) police agencies, depending on the nation. In the US, state agencies may be classified under different names depending on the state constitution. For instance, some states have highway patrols while others have bureaus of investigation, but most have some responsibility to investigate offenses that cross jurisdictions within the state or aid smaller local agencies that are unable to respond properly. In fact, most local agencies do not serve a large enough population to support their own digital forensic investigation units. Thus, state agencies serve as a critical resource for forensic laboratory needs to facilitate local investigations and coordinate responses across local agencies.

The highest levels of law enforcement in the US and Australia operate at the federal level, though in Canada, South Korea, and the UK they are referred to as national police forces. These organizations have the greatest responsibility with respect to cybercrimes as the jurisdictional boundaries of a federal or national agency include their entire country. In addition, they have substantial resources, tools, and training to handle cybercrime cases, over and above local agencies. For instance, in the US there are multiple federal law enforcement agencies with cybercrime investigative responsibilities, including the Bureau of Customs and Border Patrol (CBP), the Federal Bureau of Investigation (FBI), Immigration and Customs Enforcement (ICE), the US Postal Service (USPS), and the US Secret Service (USSS). Similarly, the UK operates multiple forces at the national level including the National Domestic Extremism and Disorder Intelligence Unit, and the National Crime Agency, which operates its own National Cyber Crime Unit.

Cyber-threats that escalate beyond individuals to involve issues of national security will fall under the responsibility of the military or non-law enforcement agencies. In the US, for instance, the Department of Defense's US Cyber Command and the National Security Agency (NSA) respond to cases of cyberterrorism and warfare. The US Cyber Command is tasked with the defense of US cyberspace and critical infrastructure against attacks. The NSA serves as a key resource in both intelligence gathering of other nations' cyber infrastructure vulnerabilities while developing data encryption and protection strategies of nearly all US government computer networks. Other nations have similar agencies, such as Australia's Defence Signals Directorate (DSD), Canada's Communications Security Establishment (CSE), New Zealand's Government Communications Security Bureau (GCSB), and the UK's Government Communications Headquarters (GCHQ) (Andress & Winterfeld,

2013). Specialized military units also engage in offensive and defensive operations in cyberspace. Defensive groups focus on government computer systems and networks, as well as systems maintained by the Defense Industrial Base (DIB) of a given nation (Andress & Winterfeld, 2013). Offensive groups will target the infrastructure and systems of foreign nations in order to engage in espionage and misinformation campaigns (Andress & Winterfeld, 2013).

Though there are many law enforcement agencies focusing on cybercrime, there is generally little research on the law enforcement response to these crimes (Holt et al., 2015). The majority of published work in this space over the last decade by scholars and commentators focuses on the difficulties local law enforcement agencies have in responding to various forms of cybercrime (Burns et al., 2004; Goodman, 1997; Holt et al., 2010; Senjo, 2004; Stambaugh et al., 2001). These studies have identified several factors that hinder the response capacity of local agencies, including:

- jurisdictional issues caused by geographic distance between victim and offender;
- lack of standard definitions for cybercrime across municipalities and states;
- minimal recognition of cybercrime among the general public;
- difficulty accessing and maintaining the equipment required to investigate these crimes;
- difficulty in training and retaining officers; and
- minimal managerial interest in or support for cybercrime investigation.

In light of these challenges, limited scholarship over the last decade has begun to explore the perceptions of local law enforcement toward cybercrimes (e.g. Bossler & Holt, 2012; Hinduja, 2004; Holt & Bossler, 2012; Holt et al., 2015; Marcum & Higgins, 2011; Marcum, Higgins, Freiburger, & Ricketts, 2010; Senjo, 2004; Stambaugh et al., 2001). These conditions all appear to affect local officers' opinions and attitudes toward cybercrime (Holt et al., 2015). Line officers in the US typically consider cybercrimes to be a low investigative priority, with the exception of child pornography and sexual exploitation (Hinduja, 2004; Holt & Bossler, 2012; Senjo, 2004; Stambaugh et al., 2001). In fact, local law enforcement does not feel they should have primary investigative responsibilities for cybercrime (Bossler & Holt, 2012; Burns et al., 2004; Holt et al., 2015). Instead they perceive that the best way to improve the nation's response to cybercrime is for individual citizens to be more responsible for their own safety while online. In addition, police feel that legislatures should develop laws pertaining to cybercrime that are clearer and punish offenders more harshly (Bossler & Holt, 2012). Finally, other scholars have examined the occupational experiences of digital forensic examiners, indicating that they face unique stressors as a result of the types of crimes they investigate (Holt & Blevins, 2012; Holt, Blevins, & Burruss,

2012). As a result, local law enforcement appears to have substantial limitations that hinder their ability to investigate cybercrime. Chapter 4 suggests there is a substantial amount of research required to improve our fundamental knowledge of the experiences of law enforcement with respect to cybercrime.

This book

As this chapter illustrated, the problem of cybercrime is both complex and diverse, and will continue to change as technology plays a more central role in our lives. Earlier we argued that it was necessary to illustrate the current criminological knowledge regarding cybercrime and how the field should move forward. Throughout the rest of this book, we present our roadmap of the state of cybercrime research and hope that invigorated debates follow this work in the future. The specific areas of cybercrime we have selected to focus on through our roadmap are: methodological issues in the study of cybercrime (Chapter 2); our empirical knowledge on the theoretical causes of cybercrime and the gaps that need to be addressed (Chapter 3); law enforcement's capabilities to respond to cybercrime and how this can be improved (Chapter 4); lessons learned from adopting a situational crime prevention framework to decrease cybercrime victimization (Chapter 5); and our projections of the future trends of cybercrime and technology.

Chapter 2 identifies the range of limitations currently present across the various academic and research studies of cybercrime. We discuss the relative lack of official statistics on cybercrime from law enforcement agencies across the globe and the limited data sources for victimization. The problem of the lack of juvenile population studies is also explored, identifying key examples of leading research using youth samples across the world. The preponderance of college populations and other convenient sample populations is also discussed, including their weaknesses and the inherent danger that may result from their over-reliance on our knowledge. The increasing use of online data sources for qualitative investigations of active cybercriminals is also examined, along with their ethical and empirical challenges. Finally, Chapter 2 covers the need to develop research methods and population samples to examine underestimated forms of cybercrime, such as malware infections, fraud, and hacking.

Chapter 3 examines the current research literature on the relevancy of traditional criminological theories to account for various forms of cybercrime. This chapter begins with a discussion of the prospective challenges that emerge when applying theories developed to account for traditional offenses in the real world to the virtual environment. The most commonly tested theories are covered in this chapter, particularly routine activities theory, rational choice theory, situational crime prevention, social learning, self-control, and subcultural theories. The common findings from each theory are explored, along with questions that emerge from this literature. In light of these findings, we present newer theories that have been designed specifically to account for cybercrimes, including digital drift, space/transition theory, and actor-network theory. We end the chapter discussing the limited tests of these theories and question the inherent value of these new theoretical frameworks relative to traditional theories.

Chapter 4 scrutinizes the literature involving the police response to cybercrime and illustrates new research agendas that would drastically help our understanding of this issue. First, we consider the research on the ability of local law enforcement officers to serve as first responders to cybercrime cases. Those with fewer technical skills may be unprepared to handle digital evidence or properly respond to cybercrime calls for service. Similarly, we contemplate the need for specialized roles in law enforcement agencies at the local level and how it might affect their ability to investigate these cases. Considering that the responsibility of many investigations falls on the shoulders of a select few, we highlight the stress that forensic examiners experience because of their exposure to child pornography and sensitive case loads and how this might increase officer burnout and retention. In addition, we report on the multitude of transnational issues that hinder cybercrime investigations, including the dilemmas posed by the lack of cooperative relationships between national police agencies and an absence of consistent legal statutes to prosecute offenses. Finally, we present the challenges posed by nation-state- and non-nation-state-sponsored attacks which blur the lines between cybercrime, terrorism, and acts of war.

Chapter 5 surveys the current literature regarding the prevention of cybercrime. It identifies the inherent challenges of preventing multiple forms of cybercrime through a lens of Situational Crime Prevention. First, we discuss the complexities of preventing cybercrimes as a result of the different factors affecting corporations and large organizations relative to individuals and end users. Then we consider the strengths and weaknesses of strategies designed to increase the effort that offenders must expend in order to successfully engage in cybercrimes. This includes the use of target hardening tools such as anti-virus programs and parental filtering software, as well as attempts to regulate access to various resources through passwords and other protective measures. Mechanisms designed to increase the risks of offending are also considered, including the use of intrusion detection systems that can automatically detect and block or mediate attacks. In addition, both the use of law enforcement investigations to infiltrate underground criminal communities and the use of informal reporting mechanisms to report unacceptable behaviors on social networking sites and other online spaces will be discussed as options to increase perceived risk. The mechanisms designed to reduce the perceived rewards of offending, such as the obfuscation of databases and sensitive information from online spaces, is also examined. Finally, we present various strategies employed to remove the capacity for offenders and victims to justify their behaviors. For instance, we detail the value of fair use policies for user behavior outlined by Internet service providers (ISPs) and corporations, as well as changes in legislation to ensure greater compliance and reporting in the case of data breaches.

Chapter 6, the final chapter, considers the ways that the landscape of cybercrime may change over the next decade and the ways that research agendas must shift in order to improve academic research and policy responses. After presenting possible trends on malware, identity theft, online harassment, and other forms of cybercrime and deviance, we identify how disruptive technologies may increase the ability of individuals to engage in cybercrimes and complicate the process of digital forensic evidence collection. For instance, Google Glass and other enhanced reality devices may make it easier for individuals to surreptitiously capture sensitive information or candid pictures at any point in time. Furthermore, the utility of social media to affect true social change in the real world will be contemplated. We further discuss the challenges posed by policies to regulate online spaces and affect real world behavior, such as cutting off Internet access in public spaces or entire nations in the case of the Arab Spring. Finally, we discuss potential techniques that might prove valuable in the enforcement of cybercrime at the transnational level, such as the emergence of an international criminal court to deal with cybercrime cases.

Key terms

Child pornography
Computer-assisted crimes
Computer crime
Computer-focused crimes
Computer-mediated communications (CMCs)
Cyberbullying
Cybercrime
Cyber-deception/theft
Cyber-deviance
Cyber-porn
Cyberterrorism
Cyber-trespass
Cyber-violence
Digital evidence
Digital immigrants
Digital natives
Folkways
Pornography
Technicways
Virtual communities of hate
Web defacements

Discussion questions:

1 How do digital natives view technology differently than digital immigrants? Is it possible that their policy preferences for addressing various forms of cybercrime would differ as well?
2 Does it matter which term (e.g. cybercrime, computer crime, hypercrime, computer-assisted crime, computer-focused crime) we use to describe offenses that occur in online environments? Why?
3 What are some current ways that technology can facilitate crime and deviance that were not possible in the past?
4 Do you think the effects of a cyber-attack could be similar to those of a physical terrorist attack?
5 Does Wall's (2001) cyber typology help you categorize different cyber-crimes and cyber-deviance acts in order to better understand similarities and differences? Provide an example.
6 What are different devices that contain digital evidence? Will newer forms of technology help offenders commit more crimes with less risk of being apprehended, or will these new forms provide more digital evidence for law enforcement to utilize to improve their investigations?
7 What level of government (local, state or national) do you think should have the primary responsibility for preventing and investigating cybercrime? Does the type of cybercrime matter?

References

Andress, J., & Winterfeld, S. (2013). *Cyber Warfare: Techniques, Tactics, and Tools for Security Practitioners*. Second edition. Waltham, MA: Syngress.

Ayers, J.M. (1999). From the streets to the Internet: The cyber-diffusion of contention. *The ANNALS of the American Academy of Political and Social Science*, 566, 132–143.

Bocij, P. (2004). *Cyberstalking: Harassment in the Internet Age and How to Protect your Family*. Westport, CT: Praeger.

Bossler, A.M., & Holt, T.J. (2012). Patrol officers' perceived role in responding to cybercrime. *Policing: An International Journal of Police Strategies & Management*, 35, 165–181.

Bowman-Grieve, L. (2009). Exploring "Stormfront": A virtual community of the radical right. *Studies in Conflict & Terrorism*, 32, 989–1007.

Brenner, S.W. (2008). *Cyberthreats: The Emerging Fault Lines of the Nation State*. New York: Oxford University Press.

Brenner, S.W. (2011). Defining Cybercrime: A review of federal and state law. In R.D. Clifford (Ed.), *Cybercrime: The Investigation, Prosecution, and Defense of a Computer-related Crime*. Third edition (pp. 15–104). Raleigh, NC: Carolina Academic Press.

Britz, M.T. (2010). Terrorism and technology: Operationalizing cyberterrorism and identifying concepts. In T.J. Holt (Ed.), *Crime On-line: Correlates, Causes, and Context* (pp. 193–220). Raleigh, NC: Carolina Academic Press.

Brodscky, J., & Radvanovsky, R. (2011). Control systems security. In T.J. Holt & B. Schell (Eds.), *Corporate Hacking and Technology-Driven Crime: Social Dynamics and Implications* (pp. 187–204). Hershey, PA: IGI-Global.

Buchanan, J., & Grant, A.J. (2001). Investigating and prosecuting Nigerian fraud. *United States Attorneys' Bulletin*, November, 29–47.

Burns, R.G., Whitworth, K.H., & Thompson, C.Y. (2004). Assessing law enforcement preparedness to address Internet fraud. *Journal of Criminal Justice*, 32, 477–493.

Business Software Alliance (2012). *Shadow Market: 2011 BSA Global Software Piracy Study*. globalstudy.bsa.org/2011/downloads/study_pdf/2011_BSA_Piracy_Study-Standard.pdf (accessed April 10, 2013).

Casey, E. (2011). *Digital Evidence and Computer Crime: Forensic Science, Computers, and the Internet*. Third edition. Waltham, MA: Academic Press.

Catalano, S. (2012). *Stalking Victims in the United States—Revised*. Washington, DC: US Department of Justice. www.bjs.gov/content/pub/pdf/svus_rev.pdf.

Chadwick, A. (2007). Digital network repertoires and organizational hybridity. *Political Communication*, 24, 283–301.

Chermak, S. (2003). Marketing fear: Representing terrorism after September 11. *Journal of Crime, Conflict and the Media*, 1, 5–22.

Chermak, S., Freilich, J., & Suttmoeller, M. (2013). The organizational dynamics of Far-Right hate groups in the United States: Comparing violent to non-violent organizations. *Studies in Conflict and Terrorism*, 36, 193–218.

Corb, A. (2011). *Into the Minds of Mayhem: White Supremacy, Recruitment and the Internet*. A report commissioned for Google Ideas.

Cunningham, S., & Kendall, T. (2010). Sex for sale: Online commerce in the world's oldest profession. In T.J. Holt (Ed.), *Crime On-line: Correlates, Causes, and Context* (pp. 40–75). Raleigh, NC: Carolina Academic Press.

Decary-Hetu, D., & Dupont, B. (2012). The social network of hackers. *Global Crime*, 13, 160–175.

Decary-Hetu D., Morselli C., and Leman-Langlois, S. (2012). Welcome to the scene: A study of social organization and recognition among warez hackers. *Journal of Research in Crime and Delinquency*, 49, 359–382.

Denning, D.E. (2011). Cyber-conflict as an emergent social problem. In T.J. Holt & B. Schell (Eds.), *Corporate Hacking and Technology-Driven Crime: Social Dynamics and Implications* (pp. 170–186). Hershey, PA: IGI-Global.

Durkin, K.F. (1997). Misuse of the Internet by pedophiles: Implications for law enforcement and probation practice. *Federal Probation*, 61, 14–18.

Durkin, K.F., & Bryant, C.D. (1999). Propagandizing pederasty: A thematic analysis of the online exculpatory accounts of unrepentant pedophiles. *Deviant Behavior*, 20, 103–127.

Earl, J., & Schussman, A. (2003). The new site of activism: On-line organizations, movement entrepreneurs and the changing location of social movement decision-making. In P.G. Coy (Ed.), *Consensus Decision Making, Northern Ireland and Indigenous Movements* (pp. 155–187). London: JAI Press.

Edward, S.S.M. (2000). The failure of British obscenity law in the regulation of pornography. *The Journal of Sexual Aggression*, 6, 111–127.

Ferraro, M., & Casey, E. (2005). *Investigating Child Exploitation and Pornography: The Internet, the Law, and Forensic Science*. New York, NY: Elsevier Academic Press.

Foltz, B.C. (2004). Cyberterrorism, computer crime, and reality. *Information Management & Computer Security*, 12, 154–166.

Franklin, J., Paxson, V., Perrig, A., & Savage, S. (2007). *An Inquiry into the Nature and Cause of the Wealth of Internet Miscreants.* Paper presented at CCS07, October 29–November 2, in Alexandria, VA.

Furnell, S. (2002). *Cybercrime: Vandalizing the Information Society.* London: Addison-Wesley.

Gonsalves, A. (2013). Islamic group promises to resume U.S. bank cyberattacks. *CSO Online.* February 28. www.csoonline.com/article/729598/islamic-group-promises-to-r esume-u.s.-bank-cyberattacks?source=ctwartcso.

Goodman, M.D. (1997). Why the police don't care about computer crime. *Harvard Journal of Law and Technology*, 10, 465–494.

Gopal, R., Sanders, G.L., Bhattacharjee, S., Agrawal, M.K., & Wagner, S.C. (2004). A behavioral model of digital music piracy. *Journal of Organizational Computing & Electronic Commerce*, 14, 89–105.

Grabosky, P.N. (2001). Virtual criminality: Old wine in new bottles? *Social and Legal Studies*, 10, 243–249.

Gruen, M. (2005). Innovative recruitment and indoctrination tactics by extremists: Video games, hip hop, and the World Wide Web. In J.J. Forest (Ed.) *The Making of a Terrorist* (pp. 11–22). Westport, CT: Praeger.

Higgins, K.J. (2014). Target, Neiman Marcus data breaches tip of the iceberg. *Dark Reading*, January 13, 2014. www.darkreading.com/attacks-breaches/target-neima n-marcus-data-breaches-tip-o/240165363.

Hinduja, S. (2004). Perceptions of local and state law enforcement concerning the role of computer crime investigative teams. *Policing: An International Journal of Police Strategies & Management*, 27, 341–357.

Hinduja, S. (2007). Computer crime investigations in the United States: Leveraging knowledge from the past to address the future. *International Journal of Cyber Criminology*, 1, 1–26.

Hinduja, S., & Patchin, J.W. (2009). *Bullying Beyond the Schoolyard: Preventing and Responding to Cyberbullying.* New York: Corwin Press.

Hoffman, B. (2006). *Inside Terrorism.* New York: Columbia University Press.

Hollinger, R.C., & Lanza-Kaduce, L. (1988). The process of criminalization: The case of computer crime laws. *Criminology*, 26, 101–126.

Holt, T.J., & Blevins, K.R. (2007). Examining sex work from the client's perspective: Assessing johns using online data. *Deviant Behavior*, 28, 333–354.

Holt, T.J., & Blevins, K.R. (2012). Examining job stress and satisfaction among digital forensic examiners. *Journal of Contemporary Criminal Justice*, 27, 230–250.

Holt, T.J., Blevins, K.R., & Burkert, N. (2010). Considering the pedophile subculture on-line. *Sexual Abuse: Journal of Research and Treatment*, 22, 3–24.

Holt, T.J., Blevins, K.R., & Burruss, G.W. (2012). Examining the stress, satisfaction, and experiences of computer crime examiners. *Journal of Crime and Justice*, 35, 35–52.

Holt, T.J., & Bossler, A.M. (2009). Examining the applicability of lifestyle-routine activities theory for cybercrime victimization. *Deviant Behavior*, 30, 1–25.

Holt, T.J., & Bossler, A.M. (2012). Police perceptions of computer crimes in two southeastern cities: An examination from the viewpoint of patrol officers. *American Journal of Criminal Justice*, 37, 396–412.

Holt, T.J., & Bossler, A.M. (2014). An assessment of the current state of cybercrime scholarship. *Deviant Behavior*, 35, 20–40.

Holt, T.J., Bossler, A.M., & Fitzgerald, S. (2010). Examining state and local law enforcement perceptions of computer crime. In T.J. Holt (Ed.), *Crime On-line: Correlates, Causes, and Context* (pp. 221–246). Raleigh: Carolina Academic.

Holt, T.J., Bossler, A.M., & Seigfried-Spellar, K. (2015). *Cybercrime and Digital Evidence: An Introduction.* London: Routledge.

Holt, T.J., Burruss, G.W., & Bossler, A.M. (2015). *Policing Cybercrime and Cyberterror.* Durham: Carolina Academic Press.

Holt, T.J., & Graves, D.C. (2007). A qualitative analysis of advanced fee fraud schemes. *The International Journal of Cyber-Criminology,* 1, 137–154.

Holt, T.J., & Kilger, M. (2012a). The social dynamics of hacking. Know Your Enemy Series. *The Honeynet Project.* honeynet.org/papers/socialdynamics.

Holt, T.J., & Kilger, M. (2012b). Examining willingness to attack critical infrastructure on and off-line. *Crime and Delinquency,* 58, 798–822.

Holt, T.J., & Lampke, E. (2010). Exploring stolen data markets on-line: Products and market forces. *Criminal Justice Studies,* 23, 33–50.

Holt, T.J., Strumsky, D., Smirnova, O., & Kilger, M. (2012). Examining the social networks of malware writers and hackers. *International Journal of Cyber Criminology,* 6, 891–903.

Internet Live Stats (2015). Internet users by country. www.internetlivestats.com/internet-users/.

James, L. (2005). *Phishing Exposed.* Rockland: Syngress

Jenkins, P. (2001). *Beyond Tolerance: Child Pornography on the Internet.* New York: New York University Press.

Jennings, K.M., & Zeitner, V. (2003). Internet use and civic engagement: A longitudinal analysis. *Public Opinion Quarterly,* 67, 311–334.

Jones, L.M., Mitchell, K.J., & Finkelhor, D. (2012). Trends in youth Internet victimization: Findings from three youth Internet safety surveys 2000–2010. *Journal of Adolescent Health,* 50, 179–186.

Jordan, T., & Taylor, P. (1998). A sociology of hackers. *The Sociological Review,* 46, 757–780.

Jordan, T., & Taylor, P. (2004). *Hacktivism and Cyber Wars.* London: Routledge.

Krone, T. (2004). A typology and online child pornography offending. *Trends & Issues in Crime and Criminal Justice,* 279, 2–6.

Lane, F.S. (2000). *Obscene Profits: The Entrepreneurs of Pornography in the Cyber Age.* New York: Routledge.

LEMAS (2010). *Law Enforcement Management and Administrative Statistics 2010.* Washington, DC: United States Department of Justice, Office of Justice Statistics.

Lenhart, A. (2010). *Is the Age at Which Teens Get Cell Phones Getting Younger.* Pew Internet and American Life Project. pewinternet.org/Commentary/2010/December/Is-the-age-at-which-kids-get-cell-phones-getting-younger.aspx.

Lenhart, A., & Madden, M. (2007). *Teens, Privacy, and Online Social Networks.* Pew Internet and American Life Project. www.pewinternet.org/Reports/2007/Teens-Privacy-and-Online-Social-Networks.aspx.

Lenhart, A., Madden, M., & Hitlin, P. (2005). *Teens and Technology.* Pew Internet and American Life Project. www.pewinternet.org/~/media/Files/Reports/2005/PIP_Teens_Tech_July2005web.pdf.pdf.

Lenhart, A., Purcell, K., Smith, A., & Zickuhr, K. (2010). *Social Media and Young Adults.* Pew Internet and American Life Project. www.pewinternet.org/Reports/2010/Social-Media-and-Young-Adults.aspx.

McGuire, M. (2007). *Hypercrime: The New Geometry of Harm.* London: Oxford.

McGuire, M., & Dowling, S. (2013). *Cyber Crime: A Review of the Evidence. Research Report 75, Summary of key findings and implications.* London: UK Home Office.

Marcum, C., & Higgins, G.E. (2011). Combating child exploitation online: Predictors of successful ICAC task forces. *Policing: A Journal of Policy and Practice*, 5, 310–316.

Marcum, C., Higgins, G.E., Freiburger, T.L., & Ricketts, M.L. (2010). Policing possession of child pornography online: Investigating the training and resources dedicated to the investigation of cyber crime. *International Journal of Police Science & Management*, 12, 516–525.

Martin, G. (2006). *Understanding Terrorism: Challenges, Perspectives, and Issues*. Second edition. Thousand Oaks, CA: Sage.

Milrod, C., & Monto, M.A. (2012). The hobbyist and the Girlfriend Experience: Behaviors and preferences of male customers of Internet sexual service providers. *Deviant Behaviors*, 33, 792–810.

Moore, K. (2011). *71% of Online Adults Now Use Video-sharing Sites*. Pew Internet and American Life Project. pewinternet.org/Reports/2011/Video-sharing-sites.aspx.

Motoyama, M., McCoy, D., Levchenko, K., Savage, S., & Voelker, G.M. (2011). An analysis of underground forums. *IMC'11*, 71–79.

Nazario, J. (2003). *Defense and Detection Strategies against Internet Worms*. Artech House.

Newman, G., & Clarke, R. (2003). *Superhighway Robbery: Preventing e-Commerce Crime*. Cullompton: Willan.

Nobles, M.R., Reyns, B.W., Fox, K.A., and Fisher, B.S. (2014). Protection against pursuit: A conceptual and empirical comparison of cyberstalking and stalking victimization among a national sample. *Justice Quarterly*, 31, 986–1014.

Odum, H. (1937). Notes on technicways in contemporary society. *American Sociological Review*, 2, 336–346.

Office for National Statistics. (2013). Internet access—Households and individuals, 2013. www.ons.gov.uk/ons/dcp171778_322713.pdf.

Parker, D.B. (1976). *Crime by Computer*. Charles Scribner's Sons.

Parker, F.B. (1972). Social control and the technicways. *Social Forces*, 22, 163–168.

Pauli, D. (2014). Oz privacy comish says breaches could be double this year. *The Register*, October 20. www.theregister.co.uk/2014/10/20/2014_a_bumper_year_for_a ussie_breaches/ (accessed November 1, 2014).

Peretti, K.K. (2009). Data breaches: What the underground world of "carding" reveals. *Santa Clara Computer and High Technology Law Journal*, 25, 375–413.

Pollitt, M.M. (1998). Cyberterrorism—Fact or fancy? *Computer Fraud & Security*, 2, 8–10.

Pool, J. (2005). *Technology and Security Discussions on the Jihadist Forums*. Jamestown Foundation, October 11.

Prensky, M. (2001). Digital natives, digital immigrants. *On the Horizon*, October, 9(5). Lincoln: NCB University Press. www.marcprensky.com/writing/prensky%20-% 20digital%20natives,%20digital%20immigrants%20-%20part1.pdf.

Quayle, E., & Taylor, M. (2002). Child pornography and the Internet: Perpetuating a cycle of abuse. *Deviant Behavior*, 23, 331–361.

Quinn, J.F., & Forsyth, C.J. (2013). Red light districts on blue screens: A typology for understanding the evolution of deviant communities on the Internet. *Deviant Behavior*, 34, 579–585.

Reyns, B.W., Henson, B., & Fisher, B.S. (2012). Stalking in the twilight zone: Extent of cyberstalking victimization and offending among college students. *Deviant Behavior*, 33, 1–25.

Rice-Hughes, D. (2005). Recent statistics on Internet dangers. www.protectkids.com/da ngers/stats.htm.

Roberts, J.W., & Hunt, S.A. (2012). Social control in a sexually deviant cybercommunity: A cappers' code of conduct. *Deviant Behavior, 33,* 757–773.

Rogers, M., & Seigfried-Spellar, K. (2013). Internet child pornography: Legal issues and investigative tactics. In T.J. Holt (Ed.), *Crime On-line: Correlates, Causes and Context* (113–132). Carolina Academic Press.

Schmid, A.P. (1988). *Political Terrorism.* Amsterdam: North Holland Press.

Schmid, A.P. (2004). Frameworks for conceptualising terrorism. *Terrorism and Political Violence, 16,* 197–221.

Schmid, A.P., & Jongman, A.J. (2005). *Political Terrorism: A New Guide to Actors, Authors, Concepts, Data Bases, Theories, & Literature.* New Brunswick, NJ: Transaction Publishers.

Seals, T. (2014). 2014 so far: The year of the data breach. *Infosecurity Magazine,* August 12. www.infosecurity-magazine.com/news/2014-the-year-of-the-data-breach/ (accessed August 19, 2014).

Senjo, S.R. (2004). An analysis of computer-related crime: Comparing police officer perceptions with empirical data. *Security Journal, 17,* 55–71.

Shoemaker, D., & Kennedy, D.B. (2009). Criminal profiling and cybercriminal investigations. In M. Pittaro and F. Schmalleger (Eds), *Crimes of the Internet* (pp. 456–476). Upper Saddle River, NJ: Prentice-Hall.

Simi, P., & Futrell, R. (2006). White power cyberculture: Building a movement. *The Public Eye Magazine, 52,* 69–72.

Siwek, S.E. (2007). The true cost of sound recording piracy to the U.S. economy. www.ipi.org/ipi%5CIPIPublications.nsf/PublicationLookupFullText/5C2EE3D2107 A4C228625733E0053A1F4.

Smith, A. (2011). *Smartphone Adoption and Useage.* Pew Internet and American Life Project. pewinternet.org/Reports/2011/Smartphones.aspx.

Socialbakers (2011). United States Facebook statistics. www.socialbakers.com/fa cebook-statistics/united-states.

Stambaugh, H., Beaupre, D.S., Icove, D.J., Baker, R., Cassady, W., & Williams, W.P. (2001). *Electronic Crime Needs Assessment for State and Local Law Enforcement.* Washington, DC: National Institute of Justice, US Department of Justice.

Stepanova, E. (2011). The role of information communications technology in the "Arab Spring": Implications beyond the region. *PONARS Eurasia Policy Memo* No. 159. www.gwu.edu/~ieresgwu/assets/docs/ponars/pepm_159.pdf.

Svokos, A. (2014). Yik Yak threats lead to charges for students. *Huffington Post,* November 25.

Symantec Corporation (2013). *Symantec Internet Security Threat Report, Volume 17.* www.symantec.com/threatreport/ (accessed June 23, 2014).

Taylor, P. (1999). *Hackers: Crime in the Digital Sublime.* London: Routledge.

US GAO (Government Accounting Office) (2007). *Cybercrime: Public and Private Entities Face Challenges in Addressing Cyber Threats.* United States Government Accountability Office Report to Congressional Requesters. www.gao.gov/new.items/ d07705.pdf.

Vance, R.B. (1972). Howard Odum's technicways: A neglected lead in American sociology. *Social Forces, 50,* 456–461.

Van Laer, J. (2010). Activists online and offline: The Internet as an information channel for protest demonstrations. *Mobilization: An International Journal, 15,* 347–366.

Wahba, P. (2014). Target finds rare tech edge: Its popular Cartwheel shopping app. *Fortune,* June 5. fortune.com/2014/06/05/target-cartwheel/.

Wall, D.S. (1998). Catching cybercriminals: Policing the Internet. *International Review of Law, Computers & Technology*, 12, 201–218.

Wall, D.S. (2001). Cybercrimes and the Internet. In D.S. Wall (Ed.), *Crime and the Internet* (pp. 1–17). New York: Routledge.

Wall, D.S. (2004). Digital realism and the governance of spam as cybercrime. *European Journal on Criminal Policy and Research*, 10, 309–335.

Wehinger, F. (2011). The Dark Net: Self-regulation dynamics of illegal online markets for identities and related services. *Intelligence and Security Informatics Conference*, 209–213.

Weimann, G. (2011). Cyber-fatwas and terrorism. *Studies in Conflict and Terrorism*, 34, 1–17.

Weitzer, R. (2005). New directions in research on prostitution. *Crime, Law and Social Change*, 43, 211–235.

Wolak, J., Finkelhor, D., & Mitchell, K. (2012). *Trends in Law Enforcement Responses to Technology-facilitated Child Sexual Exploitation Crimes: The Third National Juvenile Online Victimization Study (NJOV-3)*. Durham, NH: Crimes Against Children Research Center.

Wolak, J., Mitchell, K., & Finkelhor, D. (2006). *Online Victimization of Youth: Five Years Later*. Washington, DC: National Center for Missing & Exploited Children.

Woo, H., Kim, Y., & Dominick, J. (2004). Hackers: Militants or merry pranksters? A content analysis of defaced web pages. *Media Psychology*, 6, 63–82.

Wray, J. (2014). *Forrester Research World eReader Adoption Forecast, 2014 to 2019*. Cambridge, MA: Forrester Research.

Yar, M. (2013). *Cybercrime and Society*. Second edition. Thousand Oaks, CA: SAGE.

Zickuhr, K. (2011). *Generations Online in 2010*. Pew Internet and American Life Project. www.pewinternet.org/Reports/2010/Generations-2010/Overview.aspx.

2 Issues in empirical assessments of cybercrime

Chapter goals

- Describe the paucity of official statistics
- Discuss juvenile, college, and general population sampling issues
- Assess the use of online data sources in empirical research
- Explore strategies to study under-examined forms of cybercrime offending and victimization

As noted in Chapter 1, research on cybercrime has increased dramatically over the last decade. The majority of criminological research in the 1990s was largely expository in nature, arguing about the nature of cybercrime, the applicability of theory, or offender behavior as a whole (e.g. Goodman, 1997; Grabosky, 2001; Skinner & Fream, 1997; Wall, 1998). The transition to empirical research was not, however, immediately easy or achieved through large-scale survey data collection. Many researchers depended on either qualitative data with interviewees (e.g. Jordan & Taylor, 1998; Taylor, 1999), content analyses of media or court documents (Hollinger & Lanza-Kaduce, 1988; Smith, Grabosky, & Urbas, 2003), or online data from forums and various websites (e.g. Durkin & Bryant, 1999; Meyer, 1989; Quayle & Taylor, 2002). The initial quantitative studies utilized university student populations from single institutions (e.g. Hollinger, 1992; Skinner & Fream, 1997). This trend continues today, though sample populations are continually changing to include minors and adults, providing greater prospective insights (see Holt & Bossler, 2014).

The lack of generalizable population studies and data generated from official statistics from law enforcement are commonly acknowledged problems among cybercrime scholars (e.g. Holt, 2010; Holt, Burruss, & Bossler, 2015; Wall, 2001). There are, however, few critical assessments of the reasons for the state of the field, and the challenges evident in existing data sources. There are also few recommendations available as to how future research may benefit from novel data collection processes with various online data sources. Thus, this chapter considers the limits of existing data sources that can be used to examine cybercrime, as well as assess the findings of those studies using different data sets. The chapter concludes with an exploration of the use of new data sources collected from the web and from computer security tools to assess unique offenses.

The paucity of official statistics

Research on traditional forms of crime commonly utilizes data generated from official statistics, based on reports to law enforcement agencies, to estimate the prevalence or incidence of these offenses in the general population. In the US, individual calls for service made to a law enforcement agency that led to a report from an officer are likely to be logged and maintained as a statistic for crime (FBI, 2004). These incidents are then cataloged and aggregated as the Federal Bureau of Investigation's (FBI) **Uniform Crime Report (UCR)**, which provides statistics on both crimes reported to the police, and how many of those incidents were cleared, or solved by arrest, across the US. Currently, the UCR includes data from over 90 percent of all local law enforcement agencies and gives detailed information on both the number of incidents reported and the demographic characteristics of offenders.

To understand the value of the UCR, it is necessary to recognize how criminal incidents are reported. All serious felonies included in the UCR are segmented into Part I, or Index crimes, including homicides, aggravated assaults, robbery, forcible rape, burglary, larceny-theft, motor vehicle theft, and arson. Less serious felony offenses and misdemeanors are reported under the category of Part II crimes, which includes acts such as assault, fraud and prostitution. None of these categories, however, provides a way to identify cybercrimes that may have been reported to police, or at the very least determine if the offense was enabled by technology in some fashion (see also Tcherni, Davies, Lopes, & Lizotte, 2015). The rationale for this decision is that either the inclusion of a new offense category, or segmentation of existing reporting categories, would otherwise distort historical crime trends within the US (FBI, 2000).

The FBI has developed an alternative metric for cybercrime measurement through the creation of the **National Incident-Based Reporting System (NIBRS)**. This national reporting system enables a more nuanced understanding of crimes made known to police. Specifically, NIBRS allows agencies to enter information with respect to each criminal incident reported, including whether a computer was the target of the crime (FBI, 2000). This is invaluable information in order to understand certain forms of cybercrime, such as computer hacking. In addition, NIBRS data allow agencies to report if the offender was suspected of using a computer in the course of the offense. Such information enables law enforcement and researchers to understand computer-assisted crimes such as fraud and child pornography (FBI, 2000).

At the same time, cybercrime is not included as one of the 40 offense categories captured in NIBRS data. Instead, police agencies must determine where to classify cybercrimes within the existing reporting structure. The only way to subsequently disaggregate cybercrime is by segmenting reports on the basis of whether a computer was either involved in the offense or the target of the crime. In addition, the reporting rate for NIBRS is approximately 25 percent of all local law enforcement agencies in the US (FBI, 2004). Thus, there is a great degree of measurement error within the data with respect to cybercrime. This may account for the generally limited number of studies that utilize NIBRS data to assess cybercrime (e.g. Finkelhor & Ormrod, 2004).

The challenges noted in official data sources are also present in other primary data sources used to assess victimization. For instance, the US **National Crime Victimization Survey (NCVS)** collects data from a nationally representative sample of the US population to assess victimization and reporting, but has not added cybercrime victimization to its main survey instrument. The NCVS has developed small supplemental studies to capture data on cyberstalking (Nobles, Reyns, Fox, & Fisher, 2014; Catalano, 2012) and identity theft (Baum, 2004; Harrell & Langton, 2013). For instance, Nobles and colleagues (2014) analyzed the 2006 Supplemental Victimization Survey (SVS) to the NCVS regarding stalking and cyberstalking victimization. They found that 19 percent of stalking victims also reported cyberstalking victimization, suggesting there is overlap in this form of victimization. In addition, cyberstalking victims engaged in a higher number of protective behaviors, even though they experienced a shorter period of victimization compared with traditional stalking (Nobles et al., 2014). Furthermore, cyberstalking victims were more likely to consider what they experienced to be stalking relative to stalking victims.

Despite these advances, there are inherent errors in the measurement of cybercrime that make it difficult to discern the prevalence of certain forms of victimization. For instance, the NCVS-Supplemental Survey (Catalano, 2012), collected in 2008, used a population of 65,270 people to assess the rate of cyberstalking. The survey found that 26.1 percent of those who reported being stalked were sent email that made them fearful (Catalano, 2012). These measures are, however, prone to error. Analyses of the NCVS-SS were revised in 2012 to exclude incidents of repetitive and unsolicited communications which were actually spam messages incorrectly classified as either harassment or stalking. Although this correction did not substantially decrease the rate of cyberstalking, it demonstrates the inherent challenges in measuring cybercrimes generally (Catalano, 2012).

There are similar issues evident internationally, as in the UK with the British Crime Survey which later became the Crime Survey for England and Wales. This survey provides a nationally representative sample of the population of England and Wales and is structured in a similar fashion to the US NCVS (Office for National Statistics, 2015). This survey provided measures for fraud victimization and other cybercrimes until 2013, when they were removed in part owing to the emergence of the UK Action Fraud agency which acts as a single point of contact for victims of cybercrime. These historical data have been used to examine identity theft victimization (e.g. Reyns,

2013), though few have published from these data otherwise. Official publications indicate that cybercrime measures will be included in 2015 and 2016 (Cheeseman & Traynor, 2014), but it is unclear how it may be used by scholars moving forward.

Since local law enforcement agencies may not create an official report in cybercrime cases, or have the resources needed to investigate the complaint, specialized agencies have emerged over the last 15 years to serve as a reporting mechanism. In the US, the Internet Crime Complaint Center (IC3) serves as a vital reporting mechanism for cybercrime victims. The center was established in 2000 as a joint operation of three federal agencies: the FBI, the National White Collar Crime Center (NWC3), and the Bureau of Justice Assistance. The IC3 serves as a coordination point for all three of these agencies to respond to cybercrime complaints, based on the presence of FBI agents and analysts in the center, along with technical support staff and specialists from the NWC3.

One of the primary roles of the IC3 is to receive complaints from respective cybercrime victims through an online complaint form which asks the respondent multiple questions regarding the incident, the offenders (if known), and the behaviors of the victim. This information is then analyzed by the IC3 staff, and forwarded to the appropriate law enforcement agency when deemed necessary (NWC3, 2014). In addition, the IC3 provides information on all incidents reported to their center in an aggregated yearly report on cybercrime. Their report provides details on the range of incidents reported, the age and sex of the victim and offender, the location of the victim, and the suspected or known location of the offender.

The reports provided by the IC3 are inherently valuable as there are few other dedicated resources to understand cybercrime trends. The number of complaints to the center has increased steadily from 16,838 in 2000 when the IC3 began operations to 262,831 in 2013. These data are helpful, though it is possible that the rates are not a true reflection of the number of cybercrime incidents occurring. The fact that victims must seek out and complete the IC3 form online underestimates the total number of cybercrimes taking place. In addition, an increase in reporting may also demonstrate increased recognition of the center. Thus, the data must be carefully contextualized before being used as a barometer for cybercrime victimization.

Despite the limitations of their reporting mechanisms, the IC3 provides useful information on various forms of cybercrime. Their data have not been used with much frequency, however, by those in the academic community. At present, there are only two studies that appear to use IC3 data as a means to understand victimization (Dolan, 2004; Heinonen, Holt, & Wilson, 2013). Each of these studies focused on a unique offense captured in the IC3 data, specifically online auction fraud and non-delivery of goods. These are some of the more commonly reported victimization experiences over time according to these data, and may reflect the general level of risk associated with transactions in online markets such as eBay.

Dolan (2004) explored the correlates of reported auction fraud in 2002. The most common types of fraud reported were non-delivery of an item the victim paid for in full, followed by receipt of a counterfeit good. The demographic composition of victims was commonly a male between the ages of 30 and 40 years of age, with a bachelor's degree and an annual salary between US$50,000 and $60,000. The average victim of fraud participated in auctions at least once per month, increasing their potential for risk of loss. The majority of victims (77 percent) did not stop participating in auctions after their victimization experience, suggesting they were willing to accept a degree of risk in online environments. Dolan (2004) also found that respondents were not satisfied with either law enforcement or auction houses as both groups did little to resolve their complaint. Though Dolan's (2004) research was largely descriptive, Heinonen and colleagues (2013) used IC3 complaint data from 2009 and 2010 and examined whether the victim reported their experience to any law enforcement or consumer protection entity, as well as to the suspect who sold them the item. They found that older females were more likely to report their experiences, as were those who lost greater dollar amounts, and who had prior contact with the seller.

Juvenile, college, and general population sampling issues

Existing cross-sectional and longitudinal data sets that are used to examine real world deviance, delinquency, and crime are only marginally better than official statistics and have limited value to assess cybercrime. Measures related to technology use are increasingly included in survey instruments, but may not include questions associated with cybercrime victimization or offending. For instance, the US National Longitudinal Study of Adolescent to Adult Health, or Add Health, dataset has been used by a range of researchers to understand issues related to the social, behavioral, and physical health of young people (Add Health, 2015). There are over 5,000 works associated with Add Health data, including a number of publications by criminologists to identify correlates of both crime and victimization (Add Health, 2015).

There are now four waves of data available for analysis, based on a nationally representative sample of youth in grades 7 to 12 who were surveyed in 1994 and 1995. A battery of questions was presented to these youth, with following waves using similar question sets. Only the fourth wave of data, collected in 2008 and 2009, includes several measures for technology use (Add Health, 2015). The questions are relatively simple assessments of individual behavior, including whether the respondent owns a computer, how much time they spend using the Internet, and the amount of time spent playing games or using a computer generally. There are, however, no specific questions associated with cybercrime offending and victimization. In addition, the inclusion of these questions at Wave 4 makes it difficult to track individuals' technology use over time.

The inherent limitations of official data sources and extant secondary data sets with cybercrime measures led many cybercrime researchers to develop self-report survey data sets from college and juvenile population samples over the last decade (see Holt & Bossler, 2014 for review). The absence of pertinent behavioral and attitudinal measures to assess traditional criminological theories simply required in many cases unique data sets with measures that are not otherwise present in official statistics. In most cases, scholars turned to the development of general cybercrime surveys with single university samples (e.g. Higgins, 2005; Holt & Bossler, 2009; Reyns et al., 2013; Skinner & Fream, 1997; for exception see Morris & Higgins, 2009). College samples in general are generated through either email-based solicitations to proportional samples of enrolled students (e.g. Holt & Kilger, 2012), or paper-based surveys distributed in large, general enrollment courses to capture as large a population as possible (e.g. Holt & Bossler, 2009).

In general, college samples are quite common in the criminological literature and have been used for a range of exploratory tests of theory with traditional offenses (e.g. Payne & Chappell, 2008). Cybercrime scholars have successfully employed college samples for tests of self-control and social learning theories for over a decade (Bossler & Burruss, 2011; Buzzell et al., 2006; Higgins, 2005; Higgins, Wolfe & Marcum, 2008; Holt et al., 2010; Skinner & Fream, 1997). University students appear appropriate for the examination of cybercrime as they commit a disproportionately higher amount of cybercrime, including software piracy (Higgins, 2005; Higgins et al., 2008; Ingram & Hinduja, 2008). In fact, college samples are ideal for studying these behaviors as college students are constantly introduced to others who may pirate software and encourage these behaviors in support of learning or acquiring software needed to complete various courses during matriculation (Holt & Copes, 2010).

Though this type of data is inherently valuable, there is an underlying limitation that may bias the current findings of the literature with respect to rates and predictors of cybercrime. Self-report samples, especially from university populations, are geographically and temporally bound and are not generalizable to wider populations. Though authors typically recognize this point in their studies, the sheer quantity of studies being published from university samples, particularly the number of studies published from a single data set that simply exchange the dependent variable in the model, may bias later research. Replication of ideas from the same data set does not often strike new ground, and may arbitrarily increase the perception of relationships between variables that may not be present in other data sources (e.g. Burruss, Bossler, & Holt, 2013). In other words, the findings may be limited to that specific sample. Thus, researchers must take care not to overuse a singular data set in order to enhance and expand our knowledge of cybercrime.

Juvenile samples comprise a much smaller proportion of the cybercrime literature, though they are an essential group to survey (e.g. Hay, Meldrum, & Mann, 2010). As youth gain access to technology at increasingly earlier ages, it is critical that we understand how the devices are being used and what impact this may have on the onset and escalation of participation in various forms of cybercrime. Sampling techniques are varied, and driven primarily by the institutional regulations regarding ethical approval and survey administration. For instance, recent research using juvenile samples employed electronic surveys managed by the institutions' IT staff so as to provide efficient data collection and managed security for the data (e.g. Bossler et al., 2011; Hinduja & Patchin, 2012). By contrast, Marcum, Higgins, and Ricketts (2014) surveyed students at four rural high schools in North Carolina using paper survey instruments to understand rates of cybercrime offending and victimization. Both forms of data collection are valid, though there is some evidence that paper survey instruments may have greater response rates relative to online surveys (Bickart & Schmittlein, 1999; Dey, 1997; Sheehan, 2001).

Due to the difficulty that researchers may have in gaining access to juvenile populations, some have employed an alternative strategy to capture youth experiences. Specifically, a small number of studies have begun to sample incoming college freshmen to retrospectively understand their experiences during their senior year of high school (e.g. Marcum, 2009; Marcum, Ricketts, & Higgins, 2010). This practice is helpful to understand the behaviors of youth, though these populations may have more in common with general college samples rather than those of high school students. In addition, the generally small size of sample populations, whether comprising college students or juveniles, greatly diminishes their statistical power or generalizability to larger populations (see Holt & Bossler, 2014, for review).

The development of unique college and juvenile samples has been invaluable to our understanding of cybercrime offending and victimization. At the same time, the cross-sectional nature of these data sets does not allow for a robust understanding of the tactics or perceptions of offenders over time. There are few longitudinal data sets that can be used to assess cybercrime at this time. A rare exception to this is a short-term longitudinal sample of college student piracy published by Higgins, Wolfe, and Marcum (2008). The data were collected over a four-week period to identify changes in neutralizing behaviors related to digital piracy. The results indicated that individuals who engaged in high levels of piracy during the first week of the study reported lower levels of piracy during week four. Similarly, youth with more neutralizing beliefs during week one reported fewer neutralizations at week four.

The declines observed in the study are interesting, though the authors indicated that this was likely a function of the fact that respondents were being reminded throughout the surveys that piracy was an illegal act. The exposure to criminalizing messages may have affected behavior over the short term, but there is no way to know how long such an effect may have lasted. The general timeframe covered by a four-week design may not demonstrate truly longitudinal behavior patterns. There was also a great deal of attrition in the sample population, as 292 students completed the first survey while only 185 (67%) completed the fourth survey. The loss of approximately 33 percent of the sample may account for the decline in piracy. Greater research is needed with longer periods of observation and larger sample sizes to confirm or refute these findings.

There are, however, several multi-wave samples of youth that can be used to understand cyberbullying. For example, The Health Behavior in School-Aged Children Survey is an internationally representative project capturing data from youth aged 11, 13, and 15 in 44 countries across Europe and North America. The data are collected every four years, and are not a true panel design. At the same time, the survey involves questions related to youth physical health, diet, exercise, recreational activities, technology use, and experiences with bullying on and off-line. The value of these data has led to a massive number of published studies utilizing them to understand technology use patterns among youth internationally (e.g. Boniel-Nissim, et al., 2015), as well as correlates of bullying victimization (Archimi & Kuntsche, 2014; Chester et al., 2015; García-Moya, Suominen, & Moreno, 2014; see www.hbsc. org/publications/journal/ for more details).

Longitudinal data sources on cybercrime are developing internationally, as evidenced by the Longitudinal Internet Studies for the Social Sciences (LISS) data. These data capture identity theft, hacking, stalking, harassment, and malicious software infection victimization incidents in addition to traditional forms of crime in a probability sample of Dutch households (see Van Wilsem, 2013b). Though there have been several published studies using data from one wave which have examined the overlap between physical and online routines as well as the causes of hacking and harassment (Van Wilsem, 2011, 2013a, 2013b), there had been, as of time of writing, few attempts to analyze the data longitudinally across multiple waves. It is hoped that this will change over the next decade as few longitudinal data sets exist that contain cybercrime measures.

The use of online data sources

The inherent limitations of the existing corpus of quantitative data, whether from official statistics or self-report data, have led some researchers to seek alternative data sources to understand cybercrimes. The virtual, faceless, and anonymous nature of the Internet creates a unique milieu where individuals are willing to discuss deviant and criminal activities in the open through various online communications platforms, including Internet Relay Chat (IRC), forums, blogs, and social media (e.g. Holt, 2010; Maratea, 2011; Quinn & Forsyth, 2005). The information that can be derived from analyzing these data sources can be invaluable to understand cybercrime from the perspective of the offender. We will consider the qualitative and quantitative research derived from the unique and most common communications platforms online.

Forums, bulletin boards, and newsgroups

There are myriad forms of computer-mediated communication (CMC) that may be mined for criminological inquiry, each with their own strengths and weaknesses. Some of the most common resources for Internet-based research are **forums** (see Blevins & Holt, 2009; Holt, 2007, 2009; Holt & Blevins, 2007; Holt et al., 2008, 2009; Holt & Lampke, 2010; Hutchings & Holt, 2015; Motoyama et al., 2011; Mann & Sutton, 1998; Malesky & Ennis, 2004; Taylor, 1999; Williams & Copes, 2005; Yip, Webber, & Shadbolt, 2013), **Bulletin Board Systems (BBS)** (Jenkins, 2001; Landreth, 1985; Meyer, 1989), and **newsgroups** (Durkin & Bryant, 1999; Gauthier & Forsythe, 1999; Loper, 2000; Wilson & Atkinson, 2005). All of these forms of CMC allow individuals to interact in near real time to discuss various issues. These platforms also maintain archives of older content which individuals can read, and post in, making these sites asynchronous as well.

The structure of forums, BBS, and newsgroups are topic-based, with multiple sub-sections centered on a given issue of interest to a particular audience. For instance, in a single hacker forum there may be sub-forums related to hardware hacking, software, programming/coding, and mobile platforms, to name a few. The forum is then populated by threads, or strings, which begin when an individual creates a post asking a question or giving an opinion. Other people respond to the remarks with posts of their own which are connected together to create strings or threads of a discussion. A thread or string may be active for years, depending on the interests of the forum and its general longevity within the community (e.g. Holt, 2010, 2013b).

The longevity of discussions coupled with the relatively natural flow of conversation between the participants led Mann and Sutton (1998) to argue that forums constitute "a kind of marathon focused discussion group" (p. 210). In this respect, researchers can use the social interactions between participants to understand social organization practices (e.g. Decary-Hetu & Dupont, 2012), subcultural norms of deviant communities (Holt, 2007; Jenkins, 2001; Roberts & Hunt, 2012), the practices of offenders involved in various forms of cybercrime (e.g. Cooper & Harrison, 2001), and online markets for various illicit services (e.g. Holt, 2013; Hutchings & Holt, 2015; Milrod & Monto, 2012).

Though much of this research is qualitative in nature, quantitative scholars have used these data to operationalize and measure offender behavior and test various hypotheses related to criminality on and off-line. For instance, Cunningham and Kendall (2010) used posts from online prostitution review sites to analyze changes in sex work, including prices, activities, and the demographic composition of providers, from 1999 to 2008. Similarly, Motoyama and colleagues (2011) examined changes in the social connectivity of vendors in stolen data markets to assess how their relationships develop relative to the legitimacy of their products. They found that seller connectivity increases as seller reputations grow, such that approximately 10 percent of sellers accounted for almost 50 percent of all products sold in their sample of forums (Motoyama et al., 2011).

Though there is overwhelming value in the findings developed through forum and BBS data, researchers must recognize the limitations of their data based on the open or closed structure of the community where their data were collected. Forums and BBS are usually either open or access-controlled, which affects the ability of the researcher to observe exchanges between participants. Open forums enable anyone to view the contents of the threads without having to register a username and password with the site (e.g. Holt, 2010). The content of open forums is also likely to be indexed by Google or other search engines which minimizes the privacy and security of the users. In fact, researchers typically treat these data as naturally occurring conversation, as what might be observed on a public street. As a result, open forums provide access to large amounts of data without the need to interact with anyone in the forum (Mann & Sutton, 1998).

Data from open forums have been used to study a range of cybercrimes, including digital pirates (see Cooper & Harrison, 2001; Holt & Copes, 2010), hacker communities (Holt, 2007, 2009; Mann & Sutton, 1998; Taylor, 1999), identity thieves (Franklin, Paxson, Perrig, & Savage, 2007; Holt & Lampke, 2010; Motoyama et al., 2011; Yip et al., 2013), malicious software creators (Chu, Holt, & Ahn, 2010; Holt, 2013a, 2013b), pedophiles (Durkin & Bryant, 1999; Holt, Blevins, & Burkert, 2010; O'Halloran & Quayle, 2010), self-injurers (Adler & Adler, 2007), and the customers of sex workers (Blevins & Holt, 2009; Holt & Blevins, 2007; Holt, Blevins, & Kuhns, 2008, 2014; Milrod & Monto, 2012; Pruitt & Krull, 2011). These data, however, are limited and potentially biased, as the participants may realize the open nature of the site, and minimize their discussion of serious criminality (Holt, 2007). In fact, Herley and Florencio (2010) argue that studies of the market for stolen data derived from open forums actually underestimates the economic harm these cybercrimes cause and may be populated by actors with little actual experience buying and selling data (see also Wehinger, 2011).

The alternative for researchers is to attempt to gain access to closed forums which restrict access of any content to only individuals who register with the site (thus creating a username and password-protected account) (Jenkins, 2001; Landreth, 1985). Closed forums may also limit the amount of time that an individual may spend in a single sub-forum, or throttle the number of times that a person may post per day or week for a period of time. A very small proportion of closed sites may also only allow individuals to create an account after they have been vetted and vouched for by one or two existing members (see Hutchings & Holt, 2015). This practice is generally uncommon in online communities, but may be a clear signifier that the group is engaged in serious criminal activity and is attempting to decrease their risk of penetration from outsiders.

An immediate ethical dilemma is present for researchers attempting to gain access to closed forum communities—the use of deception. A site that requires an individual either to create an account or post in order to maintain their registration begs the question as to whether the researcher must disclose their identity to the community (see Hine, 2005; Rutter & Smith, 2005). Covert observations may be preferable for criminological inquiry as indicating that an individual is present on the site for research may contaminate the conversation and change the behavior of participants (Holt, 2015; Loper, 2000; Mann & Sutton, 1998). Alternatively, some communities may actively shutter themselves or ban the researcher's username and IP address to minimize the likelihood of future access (Holt, 2015). As a result, the majority of criminological research with forum or BBS data has been collected surreptitiously, with no posting on the part of the researcher or acknowledgement that they are there to observe the exchanges for the purposes of scholarship (see Holt, 2015 for discussion; Taylor, 1999 for exception).

The ethical implications of covert research have been questioned, especially by sociologists, arguing that user populations may feel that they have been treated unfairly or spied on because of covert data collection techniques (see Bell, 2001; Kendall, 2004; Miller & Slater, 2000; Sveningsson, 2004). Instead, some argue active participant observations within online communities with implicit acknowledgement of the researcher's presence are preferable in order to truly observe the group dynamics at play within any online community (Bell, 2001; Kendall, 2004; Miller & Slater, 2000; Sveningsson, 2004). Engaging an online community directly may also create trust between the researcher and the community, allowing them to ask users pointed questions and observe interactions between participants with respect to contentious topics. Furthermore, follow-up questions can be posed to probe a specific issue of interest to the researcher. Finally, researchers may use the long-standing nature of a site as a means to understand its progression over time (see Miller & Slater, 2000; Rutter & Smith, 2005).

True online ethnographic criminological research, however, is noticeably absent from the literature at this time. A number of studies have combined online data with off-line interviews and participant observations (e.g. Holt, 2007, 2009; Steinmetz, 2015), but few have developed an understanding of a phenomenon through lived experiences in an online environment alone. One of the only studies to attempt a fully virtual ethnography was conducted by Williams (2006). This work examines the social control mechanisms employed in response to deviance in a single online community called Cyberworlds, a sort of massive multiplayer online world where individuals interact via a graphical environment and text-based chat. The study demonstrates that online communities regulate themselves through user norms and informal social controls. At the same time, there were few instances of serious criminality that would otherwise draw the attention of law enforcement and intelligence agencies. Regardless, this study is a good example of how researchers may operate in an online space.

As an alternative to active data collection, some researchers have begun to employ archival data from abandoned or closed forums to understand the behavior of cybercriminals engaged in the market for stolen data (Franklin et al., 2007; Motoyama et al., 2011; Yip et al., 2013). This strategy is useful as archives may contain the private messages exchanged between participants within the site, which are otherwise unavailable to active researchers. This information can demonstrate social relationships between buyers and sellers, as well as the negotiation processes of market actors. At the same time, such data may not reflect the current processes of participants within these markets, thus limiting our understanding of the market generally. In fact, the use of these data may be similar to interview data of incarcerated offenders. There is substantive debate as to whether prisoners' perspectives on offending are valid, as they were unsuccessful in the real world (see Copes, Jacques, Hochstettler, & Dickinson, 2015 for review). In much the same way, these markets have been shut down, either due to law enforcement intervention or internal strife which led to the site's collapse (e.g. Yip et al., 2013). As a result, data regarding the participants and practices of actors in shuttered markets may not be a direct analogue to the practices of active players in current markets.

Websites, blogs, and texts

In addition to forums and BBS, researchers have begun to use the information available in various websites as a means to understand cybercrime and deviance using both qualitative and quantitative techniques. Websites include a range of content, such as social media feeds like Facebook and Twitter, as well as blogs and simple text-based pages. The content of these sites provides direct information on the thoughts of an individual in their own words through text, images, and video, as well as links to other groups and entities that share their interests (Hine, 2005). In turn, this information can be used to understand perceptions of or attitudes toward offending from a different perspective from the social exchanges observed in forums.

Criminological researchers have increasingly used content from web pages to understand aspects of cybercrime and offender behavior. For instance, Lee-Gonyea, Castle, and Gonyea (2009) performed a content analysis of a sample of websites used by male escorts to advertise their services. The escorts appeared to use the Internet to share information about themselves, their services, and the process of solicitation online. A study by D'Ovidio and colleagues examined a sample of pedophile support websites and the content posted there to understand the ways these sites facilitate a social learning process of pedophilia (D'Ovidio, Mitman, El-Burki, & Shuman, 2009). Finally, a number of sociological and criminological studies of deviance have examined the ways that individuals utilize dating sites and personal advertisements online to solicit various partners (Frederick & Perrone, 2014; Grov, 2004; Tewksbury, 2003). For instance, a number of studies using data from dating and personal ad websites have examined bugchasing, where HIV negative individuals actively seek out sex with HIV positive partners for the purposes of becoming infected (Grov, 2004; Tewksbury, 2003, 2006). This research suggests that there are differences in the ads of individuals actively pursuing HIV infection, and may vary from the larger population of users on these sites.

A small number of studies have used data from blogs and social networking sites to understand self-disclosure of criminality and behavior. Web logs, or **blogs**, also provide an important, though underutilized data source in criminological research generally (Hookway, 2008). Blogs serve as a sort of electronic diary that documents individual experiences through user-generated text, video, and images, which are typically listed in reverse chronological order that can be tracked over time. Many blog sites operate to allow users to form their blog as a single web page, though increasingly social networking websites, like Facebook, serve the same purpose as a blog by documenting an individual's thoughts and feelings (Hookway, 2008).

Similar to forums and BBS, blogs may be openly accessible and historically archived, though some individuals are beginning to require registration in order to access their contents. Social networking profiles may also be publicly accessible and indexed via search engines, or set to private in order to limit outsider access. As a consequence, researchers attempting to access blog or social network content must carefully consider the ethical implications of their work. Since these sites typically provide personally identifiable information, or can be aggregated to document an individual's real world identity, there is some degree of risk for researchers to use quotes or provide information in research articles as it may cause an individual personal harm. Some individuals have begun to post disclaimers on their blogs or profiles to dissuade third parties from using their information without their expressed consent.

The extent to which these messages actually affect the ethical decision-making process of researchers remains to be seen. Since much of this content can be reviewed with minimal difficulty on the part of the researcher, deceptive or surreptitious data collection may be readily employed to capture information. A key example of such a study was conducted by Denney and Tewksbury (2013), who utilized a social networking site designed to facilitate contacts between members of the BDSM community. The authors sought to understand how the amount of information and degree of sexual content individuals provide in their user profile affected the likelihood of successful contacts from other members of the site. Interestingly, user profiles on this site are not publicly accessible; the only way individuals can view content is to register a user account with the site. Thus, the authors covertly created four different profiles, all of whom were male and in the same geographic area. They varied the remainder of the profiles on the basis of height, weight, sexual interests, and the use of a picture ranging from a face to nude genitals to a fully erect penis (Denney & Tewksbury, 2013).

The authors then analyzed the content of the profiles which contacted and viewed any one of the four experiment profiles. The majority of individuals who made contact had no photo associated with their profile, though they made more frequent contact with the fictitious profiles that featured nudity. Those who viewed profiles also tended to have usernames with sexual undertones, or an association with their specific fetish preferences. This descriptive research is novel, in that it utilizes the structure of the site to surreptitiously observe user behaviors.

At the same time, it raises questions as to the ethical nature of their study. It is plausible that the authors took all appropriate steps to protect the research participants and had their study approved by their university's institutional review board. This information may have been excluded in the published study for the sake of brevity, though it demonstrates the need for researchers to elaborate on the ethical principles guiding methodological decisions.

For example, the profiles created for the study were fictitious, and the authors did not publish the name of the site where they collected data. Such a measure is to be applauded as it helps shield the participants of the site (see Holt, 2015). Several researchers have chosen to publish the names of communities from which they sampled (e.g. D'Ovidio et al., 2009), which may be particularly damaging as a deviant community may realize that they are being used as a research resource and go underground due to fear of detection (see Holt, 2015). At the same time, the researchers presented the usernames of those who contacted or viewed their profiles in the body of their research (Denney & Tewksbury, 2013). There is no indication given as to whether these names have been falsified or revised in any way to protect the user identities. If the usernames were provided verbatim, then it is possible that others may find their online identities via search engine queries.

The authors also give no indication as to whether they revealed their deception to the wider online community they involved in this study. Since they were working with a website where individuals have a clear reason for participating, it is possible that Denney and Tewksbury chose to end the project without disclosing the study for the sake of anonymity. This is sensible, but the publication of usernames and quotes from profiles may again compromise the privacy and confidentiality of the participants and lead them to feel betrayed (see Silverman, 2013 for discussion).

These points are not trivial, and are often subjects of some discussion in the course of research design in traditional criminological field work in the real world. The same issues are real and present with online research, and must not be ignored because of the ability to access large quantities of data via simple web searches. It is vital that ethical issues in online research be given greater consideration as the field moves forward to ensure that researchers fully understand the implications of their work, from design to data collection to publication (see also Holt, 2010b; Silverman, 2013). Otherwise, we run the risk of alienating online populations and forcing user behaviors to change as a result of fear of being included in research or being monitored without their consent.

The rich nature of blog and social network data has only begun to be explored by criminologists. For instance, Holt, Strumsky, Smirnova, and Kilger (2012) mined a series of 336 blogs associated with eight hacker groups in a large social networking website to understand their online communication patterns, self-disclosure of personal information, and larger network structures. They found that there was a small proportion of highly skilled hackers relative to a larger population of semi-skilled actors who were housed within a larger network of user profiles generally (Holt et al., 2012). The highly skilled hackers were centrally located within the network, indicating that they were influential members of these communities (Holt et al., 2012).

Gang researchers have also begun to explore the ways that various street gangs are utilizing social networking sites, whether for recruitment, communication, or simple bragging and conversation (Decary-Hetu & Morselli, 2011; Morselli & Decary-Hetu, 2010; Womer & Bunker, 2010).[1] For instance, Decary-Hetu and Morselli (2011) searched Facebook and Twitter profiles using known gang names within geographic regions of Canada to identify their presence in these sites. They found that there was a substantive increase in the number of fans of many gang pages or group profiles from 2010 to 2011, though the majority of individuals followed the Bloods, Hells Angels, and Latin Kings, Crips, and MS-13 groups on both Twitter and Facebook. A separate analysis of the content of these groups suggested that the group page content was managed by individuals rather than a group and promoted their street activities and cultural symbols of membership (Morselli & Decary-Hetu, 2010). Womer and Bunker (2010), however, found that these pages play less of a role in recruitment and were more simply a vehicle for bragging and expressions of violent sentiment. Thus, research using social networking platforms may prove invaluable to understand the practices of both cybercriminals and traditional street crime groups.

Email as a data source

A small number of researchers have used one of the most common and plentiful forms of CMC as a source of both quantitative and qualitative scholarship: email. The sheer quantity of email accounts maintained and the number of messages sent every day around the world means that there are potentially billions of accounts and messages, if not trillions, that could be utilized for research purposes. For instance, individuals may post their email address in public places so as to enable individuals to contact them for goods, services, or information. Some researchers have capitalized on this information to develop research samples and test hypotheses related to online behavior. One of the most novel applications of email to assess respondent behavior was developed by Pruitt (2008). He collected email addresses provided by male escorts on a national advertising website and contacted them from two email addresses: one a university email address and the other from a generic webmail service provider. The response rate was substantially higher for messages sent from a regular account, relative to his university email address.

Beyond sampling frameworks, cybercrime researchers have begun to use the content of email messages as a data source to understand offender practices online (e.g. Holt & Graves, 2007; King & Thomas, 2009; Nhan, Kinkade, & Burns, 2009; Rege, 2009; Wall, 2004). Email and instant messaging chats can be used as a platform to contact individuals with fraudulent schemes and draw in prospective victims. The majority of email-based fraud schemes are facilitated by unsolicited emails sent in bulk quantities, or **spam**, to victims around the world (Wall, 2004). Since email is ubiquitous and has virtually no cost, individuals can send messages to millions of individuals at a time, and include images, text, links and attachments to make their message appear more legitimate. Additionally, a sender may include malicious software as an attachment so as to harm the recipient without the need for them to actually make contact.

There are now small bodies of research growing around unique forms of spam-based fraud, each typically employing the content or quantity of messages sent to victims as the basis for analyses. The largest proportion of studies has examined **advance fee fraud messages**, or so called Nigerian email scams (see Edelson, 2003; Holt & Graves, 2007; King & Thomas, 2009; Nhan et al., 2009). Most use convenience samples of emails received by the researcher, or their institution, though a small proportion also use messages posted on 419 reporting and baiting websites (e.g. Nhan et al., 2009). These studies demonstrate that the senders use various schemes to draw in victims, ranging from posing as a public official who has skimmed funds from business contracts to being a wealthy heir who needs help moving funds out of their country (see Edelson, 2003; Holt & Graves, 2007). The senders use different linguistic techniques in order to entice the victim to respond, ranging from religious messages to misspellings to emotional pleas for aid (Holt & Graves, 2007; King & Thomas, 2009; Nhan et al., 2009). Recipients are also asked to provide the sender with their contact information, home address, phone numbers, and in some cases, banking details (see Holt & Graves, 2007). In turn, the sender can then contact the recipient in order to solicit funds from the victim over time.

Similarly, a small number of computer scientists have published on the phenomenon of **pump and dump emails**, wherein scammers advertise and push individuals to buy stocks with generally low values (Bohme & Holz, 2006; Frieder & Zittrain, 2007; Hanke & Hauser, 2006). The spam senders purchase these stocks in advance of their advertising campaign and wait for recipients to begin buying the stocks. As the value of the stocks begins to increase due to buyer interest, the spammers will then sell in order to make a substantial profit over and above their initial investment. These so-called pump and dump schemes are thought to generate a good profit for the sender, though it is difficult to discern the frequency with which these frauds take place. Estimates from studies using spam archives suggest that as much as 15% of all spam in a given year is associated with stock sales (Bohme & Holz, 2006; Hanke & Hauser, 2006). As a result, this may be a very lucrative and hidden form of cybercrime which can only be understood by examining the content and quantity of spam email sent.

A final example of the use of email as a data point is a study published by Kigerl (2012) examining the macro-level correlates of the rate of spam emails sent from a country. The spam messages were gathered from the 2008 spam archives of Untroubled Software, and coded through the use of a software script. Kigerl (2012) then extracted the originating IP address of the email and traced it to its country of origin. This information was then used to build a one-year rate of spam delivery for 132 countries based on the total number of messages received in this archive. The rate of spam was found to be associated with a nation's gross domestic product (GDP) and the number of Internet users per capita. Those nations with higher unemployment rates also had higher rates of spam distribution.

The techniques employed by Kigerl (2012) are novel, and demonstrate that data can be derived from a range of sources. The spam rate was, however, limited by the ability to determine a country of origin for the message. Since the IP address of an email can be faked, or spoofed, it is possible that the location measure may misrepresent the actual rate of spam sent from a nation. Furthermore, the analyses excluded a number of countries because the spam archive had no messages received from a specific place. Thus, this study demonstrates that there are limitations with email as a data source that must be considered, no matter how large a sample can be developed.

Developing metrics for hidden forms of victimization

There are a number of industry sources that may also be used to assess the scope of cybercrime, though they tend to have substantial limitations. For instance, anti-virus vendors collect data on malicious software infections and provide reports on a quarterly and yearly basis (e.g. Symantec Corporation, 2013). These estimates are particularly useful to document the presence of malware in the wild at any point in time and identify trends in common attack methods. At the same time, the corporations that provide these statistics do not give much information on the way the data are collected or how representative the results may be. Typically, data are generated from machines that use their software to provide an estimate for attacks (Symantec Corporation, 2013). This makes it difficult to extrapolate findings to larger populations as they may use different products, or no security tools whatsoever.

As a consequence, there is a need to identify alternative data sets and strategies to better understand rates of offending and offender behavior of cybercrime in general, but also more complex and underestimated forms specifically. In this section, we discuss some of these recently used data sets and methodologies. We do not mean this coverage to be exhaustive, but rather to discuss some promising strategies which may further the field.

The noted qualitative criminologist Richard Wright opined on more than one occasion that the field of criminology spent so much effort on trying to explain the causes of crime and its prevention but spent so little time studying crime itself—what it looks like and how it was committed. Much of his work clearly reflected this view (e.g. Jacques & Wright, 2014; Topalli, Jacques, & Wright, 2015; Wright & Decker, 1994, 1997). This observation applies equally well to most forms of cybercrime. Earlier scholars examining cybercrime discussed the novelties of cyberspace and cybercrime itself, focusing on how similar and different it was to traditional crimes (e.g. Furnell, 2002; Grabosky, 2001; Wall, 1998).

Over time, scholars mostly gravitated toward studying the correlates of various forms of cybercrime, utilizing concepts from traditional criminological theories (e.g. Higgins, 2005; Hinduja, 2001; Hollinger, 1992; Holt & Bossler, 2009; Skinner & Fream, 1997). There was less emphasis placed on studying how specific cybercrimes occurred, with the exception of the detailed work on Nigerian scams (Holt & Graves, 2007; King & Thomas, 2009; Nhan et al., 2009). A reason for this could be the strong research focus on forms of online harassment and cyberstalking, which may have unique individual etiologies but require minimal technical sophistication and are channeled through email, text, and social media.

A more salient explanation may be the lack of technical expertise among most scholars in computer-related matters. Computer science research has placed substantive emphasis on the ways that cybercriminals create and disseminate malware, control botnets, and steal and sell identities (see Chapter 5 for a discussion of some of these studies). These matters are often given minimal emphasis by all but a select few criminologists. It is unclear if this is just a function of the social nature of the field, or a direct avoidance due to a lack of technical proficiency. Regardless, criminologists must expand and improve their technical knowledge in order to better contribute to the understanding of how and not just why cybercrimes are committed.

One key way that criminologists can contribute to our general understanding of how cybercrimes occur is through crime script analysis. **Crime scripts** examine criminality from the offender's perspective in order to identify the process of a given act from start to finish in sequential order (see Chapters 3 and 5 for elaboration). This process enables researchers to understand the decision-making process of an offender, including identifying criminal opportunities, determining the logistics of an act, and ways to exit from the crime scene with minimal risk. Crime script analyses have unique value for situational crime prevention (SCP) models, as they provide a framework to apply interventions at all phases of crime to harden targets, reduce rewards of crime, and affect provocations to offend. Researchers have used this framework to examine various real world crimes (Brayley et al., 2011; Cornish, 1994; Hancock & Laycock, 2010), though there is generally little research regarding cybercrime.

Hutchings and Holt (2015) recently published a crime script analysis of the process of selling stolen data in online markets. They conducted an analysis of 13 English- and Russian-speaking stolen data forums in order to identify the ways that various actors interacted with each other and the processes and actions that they took, from setting up the initial software to finalizing transactions to exiting the marketplace. These specific insights serve as potential intervention points where techniques and strategies can be used to deter the offender or stop the process of sales (see Chapter 5 for discussion). Since script analyses are unique to each offense type, additional research is needed with other specific cybercrime types and settings in order to better understand both the offense and unique prevention strategies to affect the actors.

Another understudied form of cybercrime in the literature is the creation, dissemination, and use of malicious software. Few criminological studies have examined the process or activities of malware writers and users, such as Holt's (2013) examination of the processes of malicious software markets. This study used a sample of Russian-language web forums and found that most individuals offering cybercrime services were supported by botnet malware and offered competitive pricing for products and services. Otherwise, the majority of criminological scholarship has examined the causes and correlates of malware infection victimization at the individual level using routine activities theory or low self-control (Bossler & Holt, 2009; Holt & Bossler, 2013; Ngo & Paternoster, 2011).

Given that malware infections are a global problem, it may be more valuable to study patterns of the creation and distribution of malicious software at the aggregate level to understand the scope of these attacks. To that end, Burruss, Holt, and Bossler (2013) utilized an open source malware repository to examine the macro-correlates of malware creation. Their data were generated from an existing **open source repository**, where individuals from around the world could report information on a piece of malware, including its author, their country of origin, and any other details about the code itself.

Using the total amount of malware that originated from a specific country, Burruss and colleagues (2013) found that malware production was not dependent on a nation's economy unless it affected the development of their technological infrastructure (e.g. Internet connectivity) as well. They also found that more repressive governments created environments supportive of malware creation.

This sort of analysis may not have been possible without access to such a unique data source. Malware information is often presented in aggregate statistics from anti-virus vendors, and rarely provides the country of origin for a piece of code. The data repository used in this analysis also contained information on malware dating back to 2001, suggesting it was a well-known resource within the computer underground. The value of such a data source is limited by the fact that it undercounted both the total amount of malware created, and had a number of missing data points regarding the country of origin. The authors attempted to control for missing data through the use of zero-inflated negative binomial regression analyses (Burruss, Holt, & Bossler, 2013), but it does not change the general weaknesses of the data. At the same time, open source repositories may serve as a valuable source for the future study of more hidden forms of cybercrime, such as the creation of malware.

Another resourceful use of an online index was that of Decary-Hctu, Morselli, and Leman-Langlois's (2012) examination of the warez scene, or the online community where hackers distribute illegally obtained intellectual property. The index they examined had detailed information on cracked files, including the hacker group that claimed responsibility for its release, its release date, the type of file (e.g. movie, television show), size of the file, number of downloads, and a direct download link to the NFO file, which is a file extension commonly used by individuals in the piracy scene to advertise new files.

Data were collected for this study between 2003 and 2009, and found a total of 3,164 active hacker groups sharing cracked files. Indices similar to this are excellent sources to study group dynamics as well as the productivity and longevity of hacker groups. In fact, they may provide better insight on these specific issues than the interviewing of individual hackers and pirates. This index of data also captures the practices of hacker groups from around the world, providing a more international view of the hacker community. As with any index, a limitation is that it will only include information about hacker groups that utilize that index as a clearinghouse. As a result, there are likely patterns regarding region, language, skill, and other variables that influence what groups are more likely to use any specific index. In addition, it provides no information on the individual hackers in order to better understand their motivations and life course trajectories.

Another increasingly common form of cybercrime with hidden dynamics is data breaches where sensitive information is lost through various means by internal and external attackers. A group of scholars used an existing repository of information compiled by the Privacy Rights Clearinghouse on data breaches that were publicly disclosed between 2005 and 2012 (Collins et al., 2011; Khey & Sainato, 2013). The **Privacy Rights Clearinghouse** website provides detailed information on the date of breach, location, type of organization (e.g. health, education, non-profit, etc.), type of breach (e.g. malware, insider, etc.), and the total number of records lost that included sensitive financial data or social security identifiers (see Khey & Sainato, 2013 for detailed discussion).

Research using these data by Collins and associates (2011) found that the existence of reporting legislation led to an increase of incidents reported in the healthcare sector, while breaches reported by educational institutions declined. Khey and Sainato (2013) found that although data breaches occurred in geographically distinct clusters, there was no discernible pattern by industry type within specific areas or timeframes. An interesting note of this study was that breaches were concentrated in New York and California, where more stringent legal consequences exist. The authors conclude that increasing punishments will not affect the occurrence of data breaches and that strategies to reduce victimization possibly will need to occur through non-legal means, including increased security protocols and industry compliance.

The work of these scholars (Collins et al., 2011; Khey & Sainato, 2013) further validates that the use of publicly available data is useful to improve our understanding of the correlates of data breaches and other forms of cybercrime. These data will be useful in continuing to examine data breach trends, such as their frequency and whether they are increasing, the sectors that are more vulnerable than others, and the parts of the country that are more susceptible. These data are, however, limited to general examinations because data are not available on the entities' security protocols, network specifications, and actions taken by security personnel before, during, and after an incident. The data also give minimal detail on the victims who had their data stolen, and how they may have been impacted. Considering that this type of information is frequently proprietary to a corporation, financial institution, or victim, it would be extremely difficult to expand a data set in a meaningful way at this time.

A final source of data that has been used by criminologists over the last few years includes data from honeypots and Intrusion Prevention Systems (IPS) (see Chapter 5 for more detail). These technologies are installed on computer networks in order to monitor network traffic, send alerts to a management server when a threat is detected, and collect information on attacks and anomalous traffic, such as its source (IP address) and level of severity (see Maimon et al., 2013 for discussion). These data are commonly used by computer science researchers to analyze attacks and attacker behavior, though there may be benefits to their use for criminological inquiry.

For example, Maimon and colleagues (2013) analyzed data collected from an IPS at a major American university to examine the origin of computer-focused incidents, including computer exploits, port scans, and denial of service attacks. The authors hypothesized that the pattern of computer incidents would be related to the daily activity patterns of its users. They found that these three forms of computer attack were more likely to occur during university official business hours and that an increase in the number of foreign network users increased computer incidents originating from IP addresses from those users' countries of origin (see Chapter 3 for discussion of how this relates to routine activities theory and previous criticisms of the theory being applied to cyberspace).

Since the IPS provides the IP addresses of the origin of the attack, these scholars were able to collect information about those countries from other sources, such as GDP, technological infrastructure, etc., and run further analyses. At the same time, the IP information may not actually represent the original source of the attacker. Hackers frequently utilize other computer systems as a platform for attacks, as with botnets which can use hundreds of victim machines to send spam and engage in denial of service attacks (e.g. Bacher et al., 2005). Such data must be interpreted with extreme caution due to their potential for measurement error.

Similarly, honeypot data have begun to be employed by criminologists to understand the behavior of attacks in computer networks. Honeypots are computers that are created for the purpose of being attacked in order for security professionals to collect information to better protect their systems and have a better understanding of who is behind the attacks (Spitzner, 2002). Specifically, production honeypots are used by information technology managers to detect attacks and intrusions of their networks, while research honeypots are more typically used by cybersecurity experts to study who is attacking their systems and with what techniques and tools (Spitzner, 2002). Since either type of honeypot is not assigned any production value, any network activity that is either sent their way or initiated by these computers is an indication that they have been infiltrated and are being utilized by outsiders for unauthorized purposes.

For over a decade, honeypots have been viewed as a cost-effective strategy to increase the security of an organization by collecting the above described information in order to conduct network forensics (Jang et al., 2013; Nasir & Al-Mousa, 2013). Over this time, network security specialists have had to continue to improve the design of honeypots in order to address limitations and increase their effectiveness at collecting the behavior of attackers. Attackers have become particularly adept at identifying honeypots, enabling them to avoid interacting with these systems (Nasir & Al-Mousa, 2013). Thus, honeypots are not a perfect mechanism for analysis but rather a unique point of data collection regarding hacker activity.

Although honeypots are nothing new for security specialists, their use in criminology is novel. Data collected from honeypots have begun to allow researchers to examine patterns of computer intrusions and identify potential prevention measures. For example, Maimon, Alper, Sobesto, and Cukier (2014) used data from research honeypots at one major American university to test the effectiveness of warning banners in reducing the frequency and length of computer intrusions, thus testing an element of its deterrent value (see Chapter 3 for information on deterrence theory). They deployed 80 honeypots on the university network, and assigned an attacker to either a control group or treatment group which received a warning banner message. The warning indicated that unauthorized access was prohibited and subject to criminal and civil penalties under US laws, and that the system was being monitored and may lead to law enforcement contact.

The authors then analyzed and compared the behaviors of the treatment and control group and found that 40 percent of the incidents receiving a warning terminated immediately in comparison with only 25 percent of the incidents not receiving a warning. This difference, however, was not significant. In addition, the warning banner did not reduce the frequency of repeat trespassing incidents, but did reduce the duration of the act. This type of work may not only expand our knowledge of computer intrusions and deterrence in the virtual world, but our knowledge of restrictive deterrence and sanction threats in the real world as well.

In a subsequent study by Maimon, Wilson, Ren, and Berenblum (2015), the authors utilized honeypot data from academic institutions in Israel and China to examine the spatial and temporal dimensions of system trespassing incidents. An interesting result was that their findings differed by whether they were examining the Israeli or Chinese honeypots. The majority of brute-force attacks against Chinese target computers came from Asia and almost 43 percent of the attacks against Israeli computers also came from Asia. For system trespassing incidents, the majority of incidents against Chinese computers originated in Asia, while for Israel, half of the incidents originated in Europe once Chinese IP addresses were excluded from the analyses. These results partially support the conclusion that attacks against academic institution networks are more likely to originate from physically proximate IP addresses.

The findings of these studies are interesting and demonstrate the potential value of honeypots for criminological inquiry. They also have limitations which create questions for scholars that must be addressed. First, the behavior of attackers within each honeypot are unique to that environment. The findings may be limited to each system and may not always be comparable to other networks. This is evident in that the Israeli and Chinese honeypots led to substantially different conclusions (Maimon et al., 2015), and differed from that of the American university (Maimon et al., 2013).

It may also be impossible to replicate the findings from any given study across different types of institutions (governments, industry, and academia) and locations due to regional and network differences in the systems. The practices of hackers change over time, and there are substantive variations in the skill levels of hackers who may attack one sort of system over another. In order to address these issues, researchers must identify ways to effectively collaborate with partners in industry and business in order to capture data from a distributed series of honeypots. In turn, we may be able to compare differences in the practices of attackers in meaningful ways based on the type of institution targeted and its geographic location.

An even more critical issue lies in the fact that the automated nature of many attacks today may mean that a honeypot is not actually capturing the practices of a live attacker, but rather the behavior of a botnet inside a network. Such a difference is important as a botnet operator may set the parameters for an attack and allow the attack script to run until it fails or is successful. In this case, botnets would obviate the value of a warning banner as the operator may not see such a message at any time.

Similarly, Maimon et al. (2015) recognize that it is not possible to know if system trespassers ever determined they were attacking honeypots rather than more valuable systems within the institution. Hayatle, Youssef, and Otrok (2012) demonstrated that the architecture and operation limitations of honeypots allow hackers essentially to fingerprint whether a system is a honeypot with a high degree of certainty. For instance, a hacker may attempt to use a target computer to try to send out spam in order to determine if it is a honeypot. If the computer does not follow the command since it is programmed to limit outbound messages and web traffic for liability purposes, the hacker may conclude that he is not dealing with a legitimate computer.

This finding is not only problematic for security professionals in protecting their systems, but for researchers as well. If hackers are aware that they are dealing with honeypots, they may choose to cease any further attempt at system access. Instead, the data may simply reflect the practices of automated attacks and individuals who do not have the expertise to identify these systems. This does not negate the utility of honeypot data, but limits its value in understanding the rational decision-making process of offenders. In addition, the findings cannot be extended to all sorts of attackers, but rather very specific groups. Thus, researchers who choose to work with honeypot data must carefully design and implement their network structures to minimize the likelihood of identification. Researchers may also benefit from examinations of hackers to determine the proportion of actors who can differentiate honeypots from production systems and their general attitudes toward honeypots if they were found on a network they were attempting to access.

Finally, it should be noted that honeypot data do not provide any information on the individuals responsible for the trespassing or intrusion. Information on their technical skill, motivations, demographics, and a host of other criminology-related concepts, such as peer support, values, or impulsivity, are not available. Attempts have been made to infer such data through profiling techniques (see Kilger, 2011), though the actual value of these techniques for research has yet to be proven. Thus, the lack of individual-level data may limit their use for the testing of many individual-level criminological theories. We encourage researchers to recognize these limits and make every effort to expand our knowledge of system intrusions.

Summary and conclusions

Taken as a whole, this chapter demonstrated the range of data sources available to assess cybercrime, as well as the inherent limitations and challenges they pose for researchers. Criminological scholarship has employed various official and self-report data sources, though there are perhaps the most substantial limitations present in official data such as the UCR and NCVS. The absence of clear measures for cybercrime in official data limits their general value for research. It is unlikely that the UCR will ever be revised to include cybercrimes, thus it is essential that this information be improved upon in NIBRS data collection. As more agencies provide data to NIBRS reporting, this may become an essential source for cybercrimes made known to the police and the demographic correlates associated with offenders.

The NCVS can also be improved upon through the continued inclusion of measures related to cybercrime victimization. Since this study provides vital information on victimization incidents, whether or not they are reported to law enforcement, it could be the best resource to identify the dark figure of cybercrime. In fact, conducting an SVS related to computer hacking and electronic identity theft may be an excellent model to use to obtain greater detail on the correlates of victimization. The SVS data available on stalking and cyberstalking have demonstrated their utility to understand person-based cybercrimes. Thus, extending this model to include property-based offenses would be an excellent addition to improve our knowledge of cybercrime.

Researchers need not limit cybercrime data collection from official data to only aggregated police data. The larger universe of criminal justice agencies all have data that may be useful to examine cybercrime from different perspectives. There have been generally few studies using this type of data, though several recent examples demonstrate the utility of official data sources. For instance, Hutchings (2014) used both court documents and interviews with police officers and active hackers to triangulate data sources associated with the organizational practices of hackers. Similarly, Decary-Hetu and Dupont (2012) developed data from police records to understand the social networks of botnet operators arrested in a major raid in Canada. Finally, Marcum, Higgins, and Tewksbury (2012) used prison data from three US states to explore the sentences given to cybercrime offenders. All of these studies demonstrate that cybercrime scholarship can use criminal justice data, so long as the researchers creatively identify ways to access data sources that can address key research questions.

This chapter also demonstrated that criminologists depend heavily on college samples to measure cybercrime offending and victimization. Though the convenience of these data cannot be understated, it is clear that additional data sources are needed from broader populations. Juvenile data sources are increasingly available, particularly for researchers interested in understanding cyberbullying and harassment. Data examining hacking, malicious software generation, and other more sophisticated forms of cybercrime among these populations would be of tremendous value, as evidence suggests hackers become interested in technology at early ages (e.g. Bachmann, 2010; Holt, 2007; Schell & Dodge, 2002). There is also minimal data available in the US on the prevalence of cybercrime offending and property-based victimization among the general population. Gathering data in a similar fashion to the Dutch LISS panel data would provide valuable insights on correlates for cybercrime victimization and offending across various age groups. Such data would be especially practical to understand variations in technological expertise, social and technical guardianship, and their association to offending and victimization in diverse populations.

Researchers must also continue to develop data sets from diverse online sources to understand offender behavior in various contexts. Studies leveraging the rich potential sources of social media, email, and web forum data all demonstrate the depth and breadth of information that can be generated through qualitative and quantitative investigations. Not only can these data inform our knowledge of computer-focused offenses like hacking and malware, but also our knowledge of computer-assisted offenses, including prostitution, fraud, and child sexual exploitation. In addition, forum and blog data can be invaluable to develop meaningful crime script analyses of the practices of offenders in their own words. The ethical dilemmas posed by these data sources must also be examined in greater depth, as online data collection methods are still a relatively new practice. There are few published best practices for inquiry, but this information is sorely needed to ensure researchers neither alienate unwitting subjects who were covertly sampled nor risk loss of access to underground criminal networks (see Holt, 2015).

The same is true for online repositories of various data, whether from communally managed resources to not-for-profit group databases. Their value to understand emergent forms of cybercrime from different perspectives may greatly expand our comprehension of offenses. The ingenuity and creativity required to develop data may invigorate the larger field. At the same time, there may be resistance to publishing data from these sources in certain criminological outlets due to the perception that these data are neither of sufficient rigor nor of enough value for the larger body of scholarship. Researchers must recognize and communicate these limitations upfront, but demonstrate their utility in examining cybercrime in ways that may otherwise be impossible.

There is also a need for criminologists to more fully avail themselves of research and data collection techniques from computer science and information security. Research integrating honeypots is an excellent example of this sort of synthesis, and is in keeping with the interdisciplinary nature of criminological scholarship overall. Such attempts can help expand cybercrime scholarship beyond simple survey measures for basic forms of hacking and digital piracy to more sophisticated and serious offenses including cyberterrorism and fraud. In turn, this will help push cybercrime research from the margins of the field and ensure the social sciences can inform computer science research as much as it may inform our scholarship.

Key terms

Advance fee fraud messages
Blogs
Bulletin Board Systems (BBS)
Crime scripts
Forums
National Crime Victimization Survey (NCVS)
National Incident-Based Reporting System (NIBRS)
Newsgroups
Open source repository

Privacy Rights Clearinghouse
Pump and dump emails
Spam
Uniform Crime Report (UCR)

Discussion questions

1   What data set provides the best snapshot of the amount of cybercrime that occurs in the US? Does it vary by cybercrime type?
2   Why have governments been slow to add cybercrime measures to their data collection methods?
3   How generalizable are the results from studies that use college samples to study cybercrime? Does it vary by cybercrime type?
4   What are the strengths and weaknesses of using websites, blogs, forums, and emails to study cybercriminals?
5   How else can scholars utilize honeypot data to better understand computer trespassing and intrusions?
6   What other methods should scientists explore to study cybercrime?
7   What methods do you consider to be the best in studying active cybercriminals?

Note

1   The various studies discussed in this section all focus on the practices of gang members using actual Internet data. Other researchers have used surveys with gang members to understand the extent to which they use technology, though they do not actually vet the responses against Internet sources to determine the legitimacy of respondent claims (Moule et al., 2014). Thus, we avoid discussing these studies here as they do not explicitly use online data in the course of their research.

References

Add Health (2015). *Add Health: The Longitudinal Study of Adolescent to Adult Health*. www.cpc.unc.edu/projects/addhealth.

Adler, P.A., & Adler, P. (2007). The demedicalization of self-injury: From psychopathology to sociological deviance. *Journal of Contemporary Ethnography*, 36, 537–570.

Archimi, A., & Kuntsche E. (2014). Do offenders and victims drink for different reasons? Testing mediation of drinking motives in the link between bullying subgroups and alcohol use in adolescence. *Addictive Behaviors*, 39, 713–716.

Bacher, P., Holz, T., Kotter, M., & Wicherski, G. (2005). *Tracking Botnets: Using Honeynets to Learn More About Bots*. The Honeynet Project and Research Alliance. www.honeynet.org/papers/bots/.

Bachmann, M. (2010). The risk propensity and rationality of computer hackers. *International Journal of Cyber Criminology*, 4, 643–656.

Baum, K. (2004). *First Estimates from the National Crime Victimization Survey: Identity Theft, 2004*. Washington, DC: US Department of Justice, Office of Justice Statistics. www.ojp.usdoj.gov/bjs/pub/pdf/it04.pdf.

Bell, D. (2001) *An Introduction to Cyberculture*, New York: Routledge.

Bickart, B., & Schmittlein, D. (1999). The distribution of survey contact and participation in the United States: Constructing a survey-based estimate. *Journal of Marketing Research*, 36, 286–294.

Blevins, K., & Holt, T.J. (2009). Examining the virtual subculture of johns. *Journal of Contemporary Ethnography*, 38, 619–648.

Bohme, R., & Holz, T. (2006). The effect of stock spam on financial markets. www.ssrn.com/abstract=897431 or dx.doi.org/10.2139/ssrn.897431.

Boniel-Nissim, M., Lenzi, M., Zsiros, E., de Matos, M.G., Gommans, R., Harel-Fisch, Y., & van der Sluijs, W. (2015). International trends in electronic media communication among 11-to 15-year-olds in 30 countries from 2002 to 2010: Association with ease of communication with friends of the opposite sex. *The European Journal of Public Health*, 25, 41–45

Bossler, A.M. & Burruss, G.W. (2011). The general theory of crime and computer hacking: Low self-control hackers? In T.J. Holt & B.H. Schell (Eds.), *Corporate Hacking and Technology-Driven Crime: Social Dynamics and Implications* (pp. 38–67). Hershey, PA: ISI Global.

Bossler, A.M., & Holt, T.J. (2009). On-line activities, guardianship, and malware infection: An examination of routine activities theory. *International Journal of Cyber Criminology*, 3, 400–420.

Bossler, A.M., Holt, T.J., & May, D.C. (2012). Predicting online harassment victimization among a juvenile population. *Youth and Society*, 44, 500–523.

Brayley, H., Cockbain, E., & Laycock, G. (2011). The value of crime scripting: deconstructing internal child sex trafficking. *Policing*, 5, 132–143.

Burruss, G.W., Bossler, A.M., & Holt, T.J. (2013). Assessing the mediation of a fuller social learning model on low self-control's influence on software piracy. *Crime & Delinquency*, 59, 1157–1184.

Burruss, G.W., Holt, T.J., & Bossler, A.M. (2013). Exploring the utility of open source data to prediction malicious software creation. In T. Saadawi, L.H. Jordan, and V. Boudreau (Eds.), *Cyber Infrastructure Protection: Volume II* (pp. 183–218). New York: US Army War College, Strategic Studies Institute.

Buzzell, T., Foss, D., & Middleton, Z. (2006). Explaining use of online pornography: A test of self-control theory and opportunities for deviance. *Journal of Criminal Justice and Popular Culture*, 13, 96–116.

Catalano, S. (2012). *Stalking Victims in the United States-Revised*. Washington, DC: US Department of Justice. www.bjs.gov/content/pub/pdf/svus_rev.pdf.

Cheeseman, R., & Traynor, J. (2014) CSEW: Re-weighting, re-classification, and 2015/16 survey developments. Crime Surveys User Conference. ukdataservice.ac.uk/media/455329/crimeconference8dec2014cheesemantraynor.pdf.

Chester, K.L., Callaghan, M., Cosma, A., Donnelly, P., Craig, W., Walsh, S., & Molcho, M. (2015). Cross-national time trends in bullying victimization in 33 countries among children aged 11, 13 and 15 from 2002 to 2010. *The European Journal of Public Health*, 25, 61–64.

Chu, B., Holt, T.J., & Ahn, G.J. (2010). *Examining the Creation, Distribution, and Function of Malware On-line*. Washington, DC: National Institute of Justice.

Collins, J.D., Sainato, V.A., & Khey, D.N. (2011). Organizational data breaches 2005–2010: Applying SCP to the Healthcare and Education Sectors. *International Journal of Cyber Criminology*, 5, 794–810.

Cooper, J., & Harrison, D.M. (2001). The social organization of audio piracy on the Internet. *Media, Culture, and Society*, 23, 71–89.

Copes, H., Jacques, S., Hochstetler, A., & Dickinson, T. (2015). Interviewing offenders: The active versus inmate debate. In J.M. Miller & H. Copes (Eds.), *The Routledge Handbook of Qualitative Criminology* (pp. 157–172). London: Routledge.

Cornish, D.B. (1994). Crimes as scripts. Proceedings of the International Seminar on Environmental Criminology and Crime Analysis, 30–45: Florida Statistical Analysis Center, Florida Criminal Justice Executive Institute.

Cunningham, S., & Kendall, T. (2010). Sex for sale: Online commerce in the world's oldest profession. In T.J. Holt (Ed.), *Crime On-line: Correlates, Causes, and Context* (pp. 40–75). Raleigh, NC: Carolina Academic Press.

Decary-Hetu, D., & Dupont, B. (2012). The social network of hackers. *Global Crime*, 13, 160–175.

Decary-Hetu, D., & Morselli, C. (2011). Gang presence in social networking sites. *International Journal of CyberCriminology*, 5, 878–890.

Decary-Hetu, D., Morselli, C., & Leman-Langlois, S. (2012). Welcome to the scene: A study of social organization and recognition among warez hackers. *Journal of Research in Crime and Delinquency*, 49, 359–382.

Denney, A.S., & Tewksbury, R. (2013). Characteristics of successful personal ads in a BDSM on-line community. *Deviant Behavior*, 34, 153–168.

Dey, E.L. (1997). Working with low survey response rates: The efficacy of weighting adjustments. *Research in Higher Education*, 38, 97–114.

Dolan, K.M. (2004). Internet auction fraud: The silent victims. *Journal of Economic Crime Management*, 2, 1–22.

D'Ovidio, R., Mitman, T., El-Burki, I.J., & Shuman, W. (2009). Adult-child sex advocacy websites as social learning environments: A content analysis. *International Journal of Cyber Criminology*, 3, 421–440.

Durkin, K.F., & Bryant, C.D. (1999). Propagandizing pederasty: A thematic analysis of the online exculpatory accounts of unrepentant pedophiles. *Deviant Behavior*, 20, 103–127.

Edelson, E. (2003). The 419 scam: Information warfare on the spam front and a proposal for local filtering. *Computers and Security*, 22, 392–401.

FBI (Federal Bureau of Investigation) (2000). *National Incident-Based Reporting System: Volume 1: Data Collection Guidelines*. www2.fbi.gov/ucr/nibrs/manuals/v1all.pdf.

FBI (Federal Bureau of Investigation) (2004). *Uniform Crime Reporting Handbook*. Washington, DC: US Department of Justice. www.fbi.gov/about us/cjis/ucr/addi tional-ucr-publications/ucr_handbook.pdf.

Finkelhor, D., & Ormrod, R. (2004). Child pornography: Patterns from NIBRS. *OJJDP Juvenile Justice Bulletin*. www.ncjrs.gov/pdffiles1/ojjdp/204911.pdf?q=p ornography.

Franklin, J., Paxson, V., Perrig, A., & Savage, S. (2007). An Inquiry into the nature and cause of the wealth of internet miscreants. Paper presented at CCS07, October 29–November 2, in Alexandria, VA.

Frederick, B.J., & Perrone, D. (2014). "Party N Play" on the Internet: Subcultural formation, Craigslist, and escaping from stigma. *Deviant Behavior*, 35, 859–884.

Frieder, L., & Zittrain, J. (2007). Spam works: Evidence from stock touts and corresponding market activity. Berkman Center Research Publication No. 2006–2011. *Harvard Public Law Working Paper No. 135*; Oxford Legal Studies Research Paper No. 43/2006. ssrn.com/abstract=920553 or dx.doi.org/10.2139/ssrn.920553.

Furnell, S. (2002). *Cybercrime: Vandalizing the Information Society*. London: Addison-Wesley.

García-Moya, I., Suominen, S. & Moreno, C. (2014). Bullying victimization prevalence and its effects on psychosomatic complaints: Can sense of coherence make a difference? *Journal of School Health*, 84, 646–653.

Gauthier, D.K., & Forsyth, C.J. (1999). Bareback sex, bug chasers, and the gift of death. *Deviant Behavior*, 20, 85–100.

Goodman, M.D. (1997). Why the police don't care about computer crime. *Harvard Journal of Law and Technology*, 10, 465–494.

Grabosky, P.N. (2001). Virtual criminality: Old wine in new bottles? *Social & Legal Studies*, 10, 243–249.

Grov, C. (2004). Make me your death slave: Men who have sex with men and use the Internet to intentionally spread HIV. *Deviant Behavior*, 25, 329–349.

Hancock, G. & Laycock, G. (2010). Organised crime and crime scripts: Prospects for disruption. In K. Bullcock, R.V. Clarke & N. Tilley (Eds.) *Situational Prevention of Organised Crimes* (pp. 172–192). New York: Taylor & Francis.

Hanke, M., & Hauser, F. (2006). On the effects of stock spam emails. *Journal of Financial Markets*, 11, 57–83.

Harrell, F., & Langton, L. (2013). Victims of identity theft, 2012. *US Department of Justice Bulletin NCJ243779*. www.bjs.gov/content/pub/pdf/vit12.pdf.

Hay, C., Meldrum, R., & Mann, K. (2010). Traditional bullying, cyber bullying, and deviance: A general strain theory approach. *Journal of Contemporary Criminal Justice*, 26, 130–147.

Hayatle, O., Youssef, A., & Otrok, H. (2012). Dempster-Shafer evidence combining for (anti-) honeypot technologies. *Information Security Journal: A Global Perspective*, 21, 306–316.

Heinonen, J., Holt, T.J., & Wilson, J. (2013). Product counterfeits in the on-line environment: An empirical assessment of victimization and reporting characteristics. *International Criminal Justice Review*, 22, 353–371.

Herley, C., & Florencio, D. (2010). Nobody sells gold for the price of silver: Dishonesty, uncertainty and the underground economy. In T. Moor, D.J. Pym, & C. Ioannidis (Eds.), *Economics of Information Security and Privacy* (pp. 35–53). New York: Springer.

Higgins, G.E. (2005). Can low self-control help with the understanding of the software piracy problem? *Deviant Behavior*, 26, 1–24.

Higgins, G.E., Wilson, A.L., & Fell, B.D. (2005). An application of deterrence theory to software piracy. *Journal of Criminal Justice and Popular Culture*, 12, 166–184.

Higgins, G.E., Wolfe, S.E., & Marcum, C.D. (2008). Music piracy and neutralization: A preliminary trajectory analysis from short-term longitudinal data. *International Journal of Cyber Criminology*, 2, 324–336.

Hinduja, S. (2001). Correlates of Internet software piracy. *Journal of Contemporary Criminal Justice*, 17, 369–382.

Hinduja, S., & Patchin, J.W. (2012). *Cyberbullying Prevention and Response: Expert Perspectives.* New York: Routledge.

Hine, C. (Ed.) (2005). *Virtual Methods: Issues in Social Research on the Internet.* Oxford: Berg.

Hollinger, R.C. (1992). Crime by computer: Correlates of software piracy and unauthorized account access. *Security Journal* 2, 2–12.

Hollinger, R.C., & Lanza-Kaduce, L. (1988). The process of criminalization: The case of computer crime laws. *Criminology*, 26, 101–126.

Holt, T.J. (2007). Subcultural evolution? Examining the influence of on- and off-line experiences on deviant subcultures. *Deviant Behavior*, 28, 171–198.

Holt, T.J. (2009). Lone hacks or group cracks: Examining the social organization of computer hackers. In F. Smalleger and M. Pittaro (Eds.), *Crimes of the Internet* (pp. 336–355). Upper Saddle River, NJ: Pearson Prentice Hall.

Holt, T.J. (2010a). Examining the role of technology in the formation of deviant subcultures. *Social Science Computer Review*, 28, 466–481.

Holt, T.J. (2010b). Exploring strategies for qualitative criminological and criminal justice inquiry using on-line data. *Journal of Criminal Justice Education*, 21, 300–321.

Holt, T.J. (2013a). Examining the forces shaping cybercrime markets online. *Social Science Computer Review*, 31, 165–177.

Holt, T.J. (2013b). Exploring the social organization and structure of stolen data markets. *Global Crime*, 14, 155–174.

Holt, T.J. (2015). Qualitative criminology in online spaces. In J.M. Miller & H. Copes (Eds.) *The Routledge Handbook of Qualitative Criminology* (pp. 173–188). London: Routledge.

Holt, T.J., & Blevins, K.R. (2007). Examining sex work from the client's perspective: Assessing johns using online data. *Deviant Behavior*, 28, 333–354.

Holt, T.J., Blevins, K.R., & Burkert, N. (2010). Considering the pedophile subculture on-line. *Sexual Abuse: Journal of Research and Treatment*, 22, 3–24.

Holt, T.J., Blevins, K.R., & Kuhns, J.B. (2008). Examining the displacement practices of johns with on-line data. *Journal of Criminal Justice*, 36, 522–528.

Holt, T.J., Blevins, K.R., & Kuhns, J.B. (2014). Examining diffusion and arrest avoidance practices among johns. *Crime and Delinquency*, 60, 261–283

Holt, T.J., & Bossler, A.M. (2009). Examining the applicability of lifestyle-routine activities theory for cybercrime victimization. *Deviant Behavior*, 30, 1–25.

Holt, T.J., & Bossler, A.M. (2013). Examining the relationship between routine activities and malware infection indicators. *Journal of Contemporary Criminal Justice*, 29, 420–436.

Holt, T.J., & Bossler, A.M. (2014). An assessment of the current state of cybercrime scholarship. *Deviant Behavior*, 35, 20–40.

Holt, T.J., Burruss, G.W., & Bossler, A.M. (2010). Social learning and cyber deviance: Examining the importance of a full social learning model in the virtual world. *Journal of Crime and Justice*, 33, 15–30.

Holt, T.J., Burruss, G.W. and Bossler, A.M. (2015) *Policing Cybercrime and Cyberterror*. Chapel Hill, NC: Carolina Academic Press.

Holt, T.J., & Copes, H. (2010). Transferring subcultural knowledge on-line: Practices and beliefs of persistent digital pirates. *Deviant Behavior*, 31, 625–654.

Holt, T.J., & Graves, C. (2007). A qualitative analysis of advanced feed fraud schemes. *The International Journal of Cyber Criminology*, 1, 137–154.

Holt, T.J., & Kilger, M. (2012). Examining willingness to attack critical infrastructure online and offline. *Crime & Delinquency*, 58, 798–822.

Holt, T.J., & Lampke, E. (2010). Exploring stolen data markets on-line: Products and market forces. *Criminal Justice Studies*, 23, 33–50.

Holt, T.J., Strumsky, D., Smirnova, O., & Kilger, M. (2012). Examining the social networks of malware writers and hackers. *International Journal of Cyber Criminology*, 6, 891–903.

Hookway, N. (2008). Entering the blogosphere: Some strategies for using blogs in social research. *Qualitative Research*, 8, 91–113.

Hutchings, A. (2014). Crime from the keyboard: Organized cybercrime, co-offending, initiation, and knowledge transmission. *Crime, Law & Social Change*, 62, 1–20.

Hutchings, A., & Holt, T.J. (2015). Crime script analysis and online black markets. *British Journal of Criminology*, 55, 596–614.

Ingram, J.R., & Hinduja, S. (2008). Neutralizing music piracy: An empirical examination. *Deviant Behavior*, 29, 334–365.

Jacques, S., & Wright, R. (2014). A sociological theory of drug sales, gifts, and frauds. *Crime and Delinquency*, 60, 1057–1082.

Jang, H., Kim, M., Song, J., & Park, H. (2013). A proactive honeynet based on feedback from a Darknet. *Journal of Next Generation Information Technology*, 4, 69–76.

Jenkins, P. (2001). *Beyond Tolerance: Child Pornography on the Internet*. New York: New York University Press.

Jordan, T., & Taylor, P. (1998). A sociology of hackers. *The Sociological Review*, 46, 757–780.

Kendall, L. (2004). Participants and observers in online ethnography: Five stories about identity. In M.D. Johns, S.L. Chen, & G.J. Hall (Eds.), *Online Social Research: Methods, Issues, and Ethics* (pp. 125–140). New York: Peter Lang.

Khey, D.N., & Sainato, V.A. (2013). Examining the correlates and spatial distribution of organizational data breaches in the United States. *Security Journal*, 26, 367–382.

Kigerl, A. (2012). Routine activity theory and the determinants of high cybercrime countries. *Social Science Computer Review*, 30, 470–486.

Kilger, M. (2011). Social dynamics and the future of technology-driven crime. In T.J. Holt & B. Schell (Eds.), *Corporate Hacking and Technology Driven Crime: Social Dynamics and Implications* (pp. 205–227). Hershey, PA: IGI-Global.

King, A., & Thomas, J. (2009). You can't cheat an honest man: Making ($$$s and) sense of the Nigerian email scams. In F. Schmalleger & M. Pittaro (Eds.) *Crime of the Internet* (pp. 206–224). Saddle River, NJ: Prentice Hall.

Landreth, B. (1985). *Out of the Inner Circle*. Washington: Microsoft Press.

Lee-Gonyea, J.A., Castle, T., & Gonyea, N.E. (2009). Laid to order: Male escorts advertising on the Internet. *Deviant Behavior*, 30, 321–348.

Loper, D.K. (2000). The criminology of computer hackers: A qualitative and quantitative analysis. Doctoral dissertation, Michigan State University. *Dissertation Abstracts International*. Volume: 61-08, Section: A, Page: 3362.

Maimon, D., Alper, M., Sobesto, B., & Cukier, M. (2014). Restrictive deterrent effects of a warning banner in an attacked computer system. *Criminology*, 52, 33–59.

Maimon, D., Kamerdze, A., Cukier, M., & Sobesto, B. (2013). Daily trends and origin of computer-focused crimes against a large university computer network. *British Journal of Criminology*, 53, 319–343.

Maimon, D., Wilson, T., Ren, W., & Berenblum, T. (2015). On the relevance of spatial and temporal dimensions in assessing computer susceptibility to system trespassing incidents. *British Journal of Criminology*, 55, 615–634.

Malesky Jr., L.A., & Ennis, L. (2004). Supportive distortions: An analysis of posts on a pedophile Internet message board. *Journal of Addictions and Offender Counseling*, 24, 92–100.

Mann, D., & Sutton, M. (1998). Netcrime: More changes in the organisation of thieving. *British Journal of Criminology*, 38, 201–229.

Maratea, R. (2011). Screwing the pooch: Legitimizing accounts in a zoophilia on-line community. *Deviant Behavior*, 32, 918–943.

Marcum, C.D. (2009). Identifying potential factors of adolescent online victimization in high school seniors. *International Journal of Cyber Criminology*, 2, 346–367.

Marcum, C., Higgins, G., & Ricketts, M. (2010). Potential factors of online victimization of youth: An examination of adolescent online behaviors utilizing Routine Activities Theory. *Deviant Behavior*, 31, 1–31.

Marcum, C.D., Higgins, G.E., & Ricketts, M.L. (2014). Juveniles and cyber stalking in the United States: An analysis of theoretical predictors of patterns of online perpetration. *International Journal of Cyber Criminology*, 8, 47–56.

Marcum, C.D., Higgins, G.E., Ricketts, M.L., & Wolfe, S.E. (2014). Hacking in high school: Cybercrime perpetration by juveniles. *Deviant Behavior*, 35, 581–591.

Marcum, C.D., Higgins, G.E., and Tewksbury, R. (2012). Incarceration or community placement: Examining the sentences of cybercriminals. *Criminal Justice Studies*, 25, 33–40.

Marcum, C.D., Ricketts, M.L., & Higgins, G.E. (2010). Assessing sex experiences of online victimization: An examination of adolescent online behaviors utilizing Routine Activity Theory. *Criminal Justice Review*, 35, 412–437.

Martin, J. (2014). Lost on the Silk Road: Online drug distribution and the "cryptomarket." *Criminology & Criminal Justice*, 14, 351–367.

Meyer, G.R. (1989). *The Social Organization of the Computer Underground*. Masters thesis, Northern Illinois University. csrc.nist.gov/secpubs/hacker.txt.

Miller, D., & Slater, D. (2000). *The Internet: An Ethnographic Approach*. New York: Berg.

Milrod, C., & Monto, M.A. (2012). The hobbyist and the Girlfriend Experience: Behaviors and preferences of male customers of Internet sexual service providers. *Deviant Behaviors*, 33, 792–810.

Morris, R.G., & Higgins, G.E. (2009). Neutralizing potential and self-reported digital piracy: A multitheoretical exploration among college graduates. *Criminal Justice Review*, 34, 173–195.

Morselli, C., & Decary-Hetu, D. (2010). Crime facilitation purposes of social networking sites: A review and analysis of the "cyberbanging" phenomenon. *Small Wars & Insurgencies*, 23, 39–50.

Motoyama, M., McCoy, D., Levchenko, K., Savage, S., & Voelker, G.M. (2011). An analysis of underground forums. *IMC'11*, 71–79.

Moule, R.K., Pyrooz, D.C., & Decker, S.H. (2014). Internet adoption and online behaviour among American street gangs: Integrating gangs and organizational theory. *British Journal of Criminology*, 54, 1186–1206.

Nasir, Q., & Al-Mousa, Z. (2013). Honeypots aiding network forensics: Challenges and notions. *Journal of Communications*, 8, 700–707.

Navarro, J.N., & Jasinski, J.L. (2013). Why girls? Using routine activities theory to predict cyberbullying experiences between girls and boys. *Women & Criminal Justice*, 23, 286–303.

Ngo, F.T., & Paternoster, R. (2011). Cybercrime victimization: An examination of individual and situational level factors. *International Journal of Cyber Criminology*, 5, 773–793.

Nhan, J., Kinkade, P., & Burns, R. (2009). Finding a pot of gold at the end of an Internet rainbow. *International Journal of Cyber Criminology*, 3, 452–475.

Nobles, M.R., Reyns, B.W., Fox, K.A., & Fisher, B.S. (2014). Protection against pursuit: A conceptual and empirical comparison of cyberstalking and stalking victimization among a national sample. *Justice Quarterly*, 31, 986–1014.

NWC3 (National White Collar Crime Center) (2014). *State-of-the-Art Training*. www. nw3c.org/training.

Office for National Statistics (2015). *Collection: Crime Statistics*. www.gov.uk/governm ent/collections/crime-statistics.

O'Halloran, E., & Quayle, E. (2010). A content analysis of a "boy love" support forum: Revisiting Durkin and Bryant. *Journal of Sexual Aggression*, 16, 71–85.

Payne, B.K., & Chappell, A. (2008). Using student samples in criminological research. *Journal of Criminal Justice Education*, 19, 175–192.

Pruitt, M.V. (2008). Deviant research: Deception, male Internet escorts, and response rates. *Deviant Behavior*, 29, 70–82.

Pruitt, M.V., & Krull, A.C. (2011). Escort advertisements and male patronage of prostitutes. *Deviant Behavior*, 32, 38–63.

Pyrooz, D.C., Decker, S.H., & Moule, R.K. (2015). Criminal and routine activities in online settings: Gangs, offenders, and the Internet. *Justice Quarterly*, 32, 471–499.

Quayle, E., & Taylor, M. (2002). Child pornography and the Internet: Perpetuating a cycle of abuse. *Deviant Behavior*, 23, 331–361.

Quinn, J.F., & Forsyth, C.J. (2005). Describing sexual behavior in the era of the Internet: A typology for empirical research. *Deviant Behavior*, 26, 191–207.

Rege, A. (2009). What's love got to do with it? Exploring online dating scams and identity fraud. *International Journal of Cyber Criminology*, 3, 494–512.

Reyns, B.W. (2013). Online routines and identity theft victimization: Further expand-ing routine activity theory beyond direct-contact offenses. *Journal of Research in Crime and Delinquency*, 50, 216–238.

Reyns, B.W., Burek, M.W., Henson, B., Fisher, B.S. (2013). The unintended con-sequences of digital technology: Exploring the relationship between sexting and cybervictimization. *Journal of Crime & Justice*, 36, 1–17.

Reyns, B.W., Henson, B., & Fisher, B.S. (2011). Being pursued online: Applying cyberlifestyle-routine activities theory to cyberstalking victimization. *Criminal Justice & Behavior*, 38, 1149–1169.

Roberts, J.W., & Hunt, S.A. (2012). Social control in a sexually deviant cybercommunity: A capper's code of conduct. *Deviant Behavior*, 33, 757–773.

Rutter, J., & G.W.H. Smith. (2005). Ethnographic presence in a nebulous setting. In C. Hine (Ed.). *Virtual Methods: Issues in Social Research on the Internet* (pp. 87–99). Oxford: Berg.

Schell, B.H., & Dodge, J.L. (2002). *The Hacking of America: Who's Doing it, Why, and How*. Westport, CT: Quorum Books.

Sheehan, K.B. (2001). E-mail survey response rates: A review. *Journal of Computer Mediated Communication*, 6. www.ascusc.org/jcmc/vol6/issue2/sheehan.html.

Silverman, D. (2013). *Interpreting Qualitative Data: Methods for Analyzing Talk, Text, and Interaction*. Fourth edition. Thousand Oaks, CA: SAGE Publications.

Skinner, W.F., & Fream, A.M. (1997). A social learning theory analysis of computer crime among college students. *Journal of Research in Crime and Delinquency*, 34, 495–518.

Smith, R., Grabosky, P., & Urbas, G. (2003). *Cyber Criminals on Trial*. Cambridge: Port Melbourne.

Spitzner, L. (2002). *Honeypots: Tracking Hackers*. Boston: MA: Addison-Wesley Longman.

Steinmetz, K.F. (2015). Craft(y)ness: An ethnographic study of hacking. *British Journal of Criminology*, 55, 125–145.

Sveningsson, M. (2004). Ethics in Internet ethnography. In E.A. Buchanan (Ed.). *Virtual Research Ethics: Issues and Controversies* (pp. 45–61). Hershey, PA: Information Science Publishing.

Symantec Corporation (2014). *Symantec Internet Security Threat Report, Volume 18.* www.symantec.com/threatreport/.

Taylor, P. (1999). *Hackers: Crime in the Digital Sublime.* London: Routledge.

Tcherni, M., Davies, A., Lopes, G., & Lizotte, A. (2015). The dark figure of online property crime: Is cyberspace hiding a crime wave? *Justice Quarterly.* DOI: 10.1080/07418825.2014.994658.

Tewksbury, R. (2003). Bareback sex and the quest for HIV: Assessing the relationship in Internet personal advertisements of men who have sex with men. *Deviant Behavior,* 24, 467–482.

Tewksbury, R. (2006). "Click here for HIV" An analysis of internet-based bug chasers and bug givers. *Deviant Behavior,* 27, 379–395.

Topalli, V., Jacques, S., & Wright, R. (2015). It takes skills to take a car: Perceptual and procedural expertise in carjacking. *Aggression and Violent Behavior,* 20, 19–25.

Van Wilsem, J. (2011). Worlds tied together? Online and non-domestic routine activities and their impact on digital and traditional threat victimization. *European Journal of Criminology,* 8, 115–127.

Van Wilsem, J. (2013a). Hacking and harassment—Do they have something in common? Comparing risk factors for online victimization. *Journal of Contemporary Criminal Justice,* 29, 437–453.

Van Wilsem, J. (2013b). Bought it, but never got it: Assessing risk factors for online consumer fraud victimization. *European Sociology Review,* 29, 168–178.

Wall, D.S. (1998). Catching cybercriminals: Policing the Internet. *International Review of Law, Computers, & Technology,* 12, 201–218.

Wall, D.S. (2001). Cybercrimes and the Internet. In D.S. Wall (Ed.), *Crime and the Internet* (pp. 1–17). New York: Routledge.

Wall, D. (2004). Digital realism and the governance of spam as cybercrime. *European Journal on Criminal Policy and Research,* 10, 309–335.

Wehinger, F. (2011). The Dark Net: Self-regulation dynamics of illegal online markets for identities and related services. *Intelligence and Security Informatics Conference,* 209–213.

Williams, M. (2006). *Virtually Criminal.* London: Taylor & Francis.

Williams, P., & Copes, H. (2005). "How edge are you?" Constructing authentic identities and subcultural boundaries in a Straightedge Internet forum. *Symbolic Interaction,* 28, 67–89.

Wilson, B., & Atkinson, M. (2005). Rave and Straightedge, the virtual and the real: Exploring online and offline experiences in Canadian youth subcultures. *Youth and Society,* 36, 276–311.

Womer, S., & Bunker, R.J. (2010). Sureños gangs and Mexican cartel use of social networking sites. *Small Wars and Insurgencies,* 21, 81–94.

Wright, R., & Decker, S.G. (1994). *Burglars on the Job: Street Life and Residential Break-ins.* Boston, MA: Northeastern University Press.

Wright, R., & Decker, S. (1997). *Armed Robbers in Action.* Boston, MA: Northeastern University Press.

Yip, M., Webber, C., & Shadbolt, N. (2013). Trust among cybercriminals? Carding forums, uncertainty, and implications for policing. *Policing and Society,* 23, 1–24.

3 Applications of criminological theory to cybercrimes

Chapter goals

- Assess the ability of routine activities theory to be applied to crimes in the virtual world
- Explore the commission of cybercrime through a rational choice framework with a focus on deterrence theory
- Compare and contrast the contributions of social learning theory and the general theory of crime to various forms of cybercrime
- Examine how subcultural frameworks have been used in the literature
- Explore the underutilization of strain theory in explaining cybercrime
- Debate the need for new or revised theoretical paradigms to explain crime committed in the virtual world

Around the turn of the last century, researchers began to discuss the ways that cybercrime differed from traditional crime (Grabosky, 2001; Wall, 1998). These initial debates were largely informed by both the novel nature of the Internet at that time and the increasingly ubiquitous presence of technology in daily life. David Wall (1998) argued that some forms of cybercrime have direct analogues to real world crimes like fraud. In these cases, cybercrimes may be considered "old wine in new bottles," meaning that the offense is consistent but the medium in which offenders operate is new.

The development of crimes like computer hacking and computer intrusion via malicious software, however, are totally dependent on the advent of computer technology and the Internet. These offenses may constitute "new wine in new bottles," meaning that both the offense and the space where they operate are unique (Wall, 1998). At the same time, it was observed that the access afforded by computers and the Internet to virtually any population of victims around the world, coupled with the anonymity provided by virtual spaces, radically altered the process of offending. This led Wall to suggest that cyberspace may be considered as neither old nor new bottles, but instead "its characteristics are so novel that the expression 'new wine, but no bottles!' becomes a more fitting description" (Wall, 1998: 202).

Peter Grabosky (2001) countered this argument by focusing on the motivations of offenders, regardless of the crime type. He suggested that cybercrimes are "old wine in a new bottle," as actors are:

> driven by time-honoured motivations, the most obvious of which are greed, lust, power, revenge, adventure, and the desire to take "forbidden fruit." None of the above motivations is new. The element of novelty resides in the unprecedented capacity of technology to facilitate acting on these motivations.
>
> (Grabosky, 2001: 243–244)

Based on this observation, Grabosky (2001) suggested that the larger body of traditional criminological theories should have utility to account for cybercrimes. He specifically identified Cohen and Felson's (1979) routine activities theory as a framework that may work to explain cybercrime because of the interactions of victims, offenders, and guardians in virtual environments. The empirical assessment of criminological theories during this period was scant and exploratory in nature (e.g. Hinduja, 2003; Skinner & Fream, 1997), leading to conjecture about the utility of criminological theories for cybercrime. Instead, researchers discussed the potential operational dynamics of a theory in cyberspace without any empirical analysis either to support or refute their claims (e.g. Grabosky & Smith, 2001; Yar, 2005).

The literature began to expand rapidly in the mid-2000s with the publication of various empirical tests of criminological theories to both cybercrime offending (e.g. Hinduja, 2003; Higgins & Makin, 2004) and cyber victimization (e.g. Holt & Bossler, 2009). These studies greatly increased our knowledge of the correlates of a wide variety of different forms of cybercrime victimization and offending using various juvenile, college, and nationally representative samples (see Holt & Bossler, 2014).

As will be discussed in this chapter, the majority of these studies utilized some of criminology's most dominant theories—routine activities, deterrence, self-control, social learning, and subcultural theories. All of these theories were developed before the Internet became a fixture of modern life. As a result, there is minimal direction from the original theorists as to how concepts may apply virtually, how specific variables may be operationalized (particularly peer networks), or the extent to which virtual and real behaviors intersect. The current literature is rife with multiple ways to measure a single construct, some of which are based on original exploratory operationalizations of cybercrime from the 1990s and early 2000s (e.g. Skinner & Fream, 1997). In addition, with the rapid evolvement of technological trends, researchers may not be aware of the popularity of a given form of social media or communication and exclude it from a survey. These factors shape the state of the literature today, though there are some consistent trends that have emerged across various tests of criminological theories.

In this chapter, we provide a systematic review of the primary criminological theories that have been tested to account for cybercrime: routine activities theory, deterrence theory, social learning theory, the general theory of crime, and subcultural theories. We consider their findings and the ways they improve our understanding of the impact of technology on the practices of offenders, why cyber offenders and deviants commit various forms of cyber offenses and deviance, and the risk factors that increase some individuals' odds of being victimized in the cyber world. We conclude the chapter by discussing three recent attempts by scholars to either modify traditional criminological theories or create new cybercrime-specific theories which address the unique characteristics that cyberspace and technology contribute to the offending equation.

Routine activities theory

Cohen and Felson's (1979) **routine activities theory** is the most popular and empirically supported theory to explain various forms of victimization. Their framework was initially designed to account for macro-level crime trends as a result of social and technological changes (e.g. women joining the labor force; electronic goods becoming more transportable) that affected both residential behavior and property. They observed that direct-contact predatory victimization occurred when a **motivated offender, suitable target**, and the **absence of a capable guardian** converged in time and space. Although all three elements must be present in order for crime to occur, changes in daily routine activities that influence any of the three components can impact crime rates.

Cohen and Felson (1979) primarily focused on the components of suitable targets and guardianship, as they assumed that motivated offenders (i.e. individuals who have both the inclination and ability to commit crime) would always be present and driven by various desires, whether financial, emotional, or sexual. Targets can be persons, property, or money, and may be suitable for an attacker on the basis of how attractive it is on a range of conditions. Guardians serve to protect the target from harm, and can take multiple forms including physical and/or technological strategies (e.g. security cameras, motion lights, alarm systems, locks, and other mechanisms; e.g. Coupe & Blake, 2006; Cromwell & Olson, 2004), social guardians (peers or individuals sharing the same physical space who may act on the victim's behalf; Fisher, Cullen, & Turner, 2000; Zhang, Welte, & Wiecxorek, 2001), and personal factors (actions taken to protect oneself, such as carrying pepper spray; e.g. Fisher et al., 2000).

Scholars have historically utilized routine activities theory to primarily focus on the relationships between individual behaviors that increase proximity to motivated offenders and the ability of guardians to minimize the potential for offenders to access the prospective victim. Tests of this theory have been shown to be successful in predicting a wide variety of both property crime, such as burglary (e.g. Cohen & Felson, 1979; Coupe & Blake, 2006) and larceny (e.g. Mustaine & Tewksbury, 1998), and violent victimization, such as physical assault (Stewart et al., 2004) and robbery (Spano & Nagy, 2005).

Critiques of routine activities in virtual environments

Early cybercrime scholars recognized that routine activities theory had great potential to account for cybercrime victimization (Grabosky & Smith, 2001; Newman & Clarke, 2003). Each component of the theory logically connects to individuals, entities, or behaviors in online environments. Motivated offenders are plentiful online, and are fueled by various motives including economic gain (Hutchings & Holt, 2015), personal desires (Holt & Bossler, 2009) or sexual proclivities (Holt, Blevins, & Burkert, 2010; Jenkins, 2001). Suitable targets in cyberspace may be individuals, computers, data, or various other items depending on the type of crime being examined. Their suitability or attractiveness may vary based on the interests, motivations, and preferences of the offender. Various guardians are also present online, and can be conceptualized as physical (e.g. antivirus software and password protection), social (e.g. peers), and personal (e.g. computer skills) (see Holt & Bossler, 2014 for review).

Substantial initial criticisms of this theory were raised by Majid Yar (2005), who argued that routine activities cannot be transferred wholesale to online environments. He argued that the spatial dimension of cyberspace is different from that of physical space in that the average lifespan of virtual places is short and not stable. Yar (2005) also expressed concern regarding the temporal dimensions of cyberspace as he believed that there would be no specific time in which actors were present or absent. This view would predict that online behaviors of victims, offenders, and organizations lack pattern, and that change to these patterns would not increase possible interactions between offenders and victims.

Finally, Yar (2005) argued that offenders and victims in cyberspace do not interact in real time and in the same physical proximity as they do with traditional offenses. The Internet enables asynchronous interactions, such as sending an email which may not be read or reviewed until hours after it is received. In addition, offenders may be in any part of the world, yet have the ability to access victims globally and instantaneously (Yar, 2005). These issues led Yar to suggest that the Internet is spatio-temporally disorganized which limits the utility of routine activities theory to cybercrime.

Researchers have addressed these criticisms by recognizing that all three components (motivated offender, suitable target, and lack of capable guardian) can be conceptually understood in a virtual world and that a victim's interaction with specific content (whether malware or hurtful text) is similar to a physical interaction in the real world (e.g. Bossler & Holt, 2009; Holt & Bossler, 2009). Other scholars have argued that Yar's (2005) criticisms may have relevance for certain offenses, but are not valid for offenses like network intrusions (Maimon et al., 2015). For example, Maimon et al. (2015) state that Yar's comments on the spatial distribution of cyberspace may be true for certain websites, but computer networks of universities, government agencies, and corporations are fairly stable presences in cyberspace as they are extremely important for the efficient functioning of those entities.

Reyns, Henson, and Fisher (2011) noted that previous scholars had not theoretically addressed the lack of physical convergence of the offender and target. They developed a cyberlifestyle-routine activities theory by building upon the work of Eck and Clarke (2003) who examined crimes in which no face-to-face contact occurred between victims and offenders. Reyns et al. (2011) conceptualize the convergence of the victim and offender as one that occurs through the system of networked devices that constitute the Internet. This network allows for a conduit to exist which eventually leads to victim-offender convergence in time. Although Reyns et al. (2011) successfully addressed Yar's (2005) theoretical critiques, it is important to note that current empirical tests of cyberlifestyle-routine activities theory use similar measurements to previous routine activity tests and have not led to improved evaluations of the theory.

Empirical assessment of routine activities theory to cybercrime

A diverse range of scholarship has emerged testing routine activities theory's capability to account for person- and economic-based cybercrimes. The majority of studies focus on online harassment and cyberstalking victimization and have mixed results. Many of these studies find that time spent in specific online behaviors, including chatrooms, social networking sites, and email, may differentially increase exposure to motivated offenders (e.g. Bossler et al., 2012; Hinduja & Patchin, 2009; Holt & Bossler, 2009; Moore et al., 2010; Ngo & Paternoster, 2011; Reyns et al., 2011; Ybarra et al., 2007; see Hinduja & Patchin, 2008 for exception). Reyns et al.'s (2011) analysis of college students found that the number of photos posted on an online social network increased online harassment victimization, while the number of daily social network updates increased unwanted online sexual advances. Similarly, the number of social networking accounts one opens as well as their use of instant messaging (IM) was related to cyberstalking victimization. Finally, allowing strangers to access personal online information via social networking feeds and other sources was related to unwanted contact, harassment, sexual advances, and cyberstalking (Reyns et al., 2011).

In recent studies using data from a national sample of Dutch citizens, Van Wilsem (2011, 2013a) found that online harassment victimization was related to using webcams, social networking sites, forums, and "intensive online purchasing." Van Wilsem (2011) demonstrated that routine activities in one setting (i.e. physical or virtual worlds) influenced the risks of threat victimization in the other. He therefore argued that previous scholars had unnecessarily focused only on the connection between online activities and online victimization, underestimating the role that technology has played in intermingling our physical and virtual lives.

In addition to daily online routines, scholars have consistently found that committing cybercrime or cyber-deviance is one of the strongest risk factors for being harassed or stalked in the virtual world. Researchers have found that engaging in bullying, harassment, computer hacking, digital piracy, sexting, and other forms of cybercrime and deviance can increase the risk of being harassed or bullied online (Bossler et al., 2012; Holt & Bossler, 2009; Holt et al., 2012; Hinduja & Patchin, 2009; Ngo & Paternoster, 2011; Reyns et al., 2011; Reyns et al., 2013; Van Wilsem, 2013a; Ybarra et al., 2007). The behavior of one's peers, particularly whether they commit acts of cyber-deviance, also increases online victimization as this presumably increases exposure to motivated offenders while also decreasing social guardianship (Bossler et al., 2012; Hinduja & Patchin, 2008; Holt & Bossler, 2009; Reyns et al., 2011). In many cases, it is simply the respondents' "friends" who are harassing them; thus measures of friends' online harassment and respondent online harassment victimization will be highly correlated (Bossler et al., 2012).

Physical or technological guardianship in online environments, such as parental filtering software and antivirus programs, do little to reduce the risk of online harassment victimization (Holt & Bossler, 2009; Marcum, 2010; Ngo & Paternoster, 2011; Van Wilsem, 2013a). Antivirus software programs are not intended to minimize the risk of harassment and stalking. Bossler et al. (2012), however, found that protective software was correlated with online harassment victimization in their juvenile sample. Similarly, Reyns et al. (2011) found that the use of online profile trackers was related to increased risks of unwanted contact, threats, and cyberstalking. Because both of these studies used cross-sectional data, in line with almost all other studies on the topic, researchers are unable to determine whether the respondents installed this software before or after experiencing victimization. As a result, it is possible that the adoption of protective software was a result of the victimization.

Levels of computer skills, serving as a proxy for personal guardianship, have generally shown no significant relationship to online harassment victimization in college or adult samples (Holt & Bossler, 2009; Van Wilsem, 2013a). Bossler et al. (2012) found that increased skill levels decreased private forms of online harassment victimization but were not significant for public forms. The authors interpret this finding as evidence that juveniles with higher skill levels cannot prevent motivated offenders from using public chatrooms or social media to harass them, but can use their technical skills to reduce private forms (e.g. email, IM) by blocking those individuals.

The importance of specific online routine behaviors in understanding online economic crime is also dependent on the type of victimization examined (e.g. phishing scams, online fraud, etc.). Ngo and Paternoster's (2011) examination of phishing victimization in a college sample found little evidence that measures derived from the three components of routine activities theory, other than whether the respondent committed cyber deviance, were related to phishing victimization rates. As a result, it may be that phishing victimization is driven by factors beyond individual risks. This finding was reinforced by Kigerl's (2012) recent macro-level analysis of phishing domains hosted internationally which found that those nations with a higher gross domestic product (GDP) and more Internet users per capita had more phishing sites hosted within that nation. This is likely a function of the fact that these nations have greater technological resources at their disposal, creating greater opportunities for criminal activity (Kigerl, 2012). Two studies do not provide a robust sample with which to assess the capability of a theory to explain a form of victimization. Thus, greater research is needed to assess the utility of routine activities theory with phishing victimization.

There is also a limited body of research examining the applicability of routine activities theory to online fraud and theft victimization. For instance, Van Wilsem (2013b) used a national sample of citizens in the Netherlands to assess the relationship between various behavioral measures and online fraud. He found that buying products online and participating in web forums increased victim visibility online, making them more accessible to motivated offenders and increasing their likelihood of becoming a victim. Reyns (2013) found similar results using the British Crime Survey. Individuals who banked online or spent more time emailing were 50 percent more likely to be victims of identity theft; online shopping and downloading items from the Internet led to a 30 percent increase.

Holt and Turner (2012) found that certain protective factors decreased the risk of someone electronically obtaining an individual's financial information without their knowledge or permission. In a sample of students, faculty, and staff at a large university, they found that almost 15 percent of individuals who reported engaging in various forms of cyber-deviance or experienced some form of cybercrime victimization were likely to have their identity stolen electronically. Within this group, those respondents who updated protective software programs, such as anti-virus, spybot, and ad-aware, were less likely to be victimized. Individual computer skills, however, had no impact on the risk of victimization.

Research considering this framework with respect to malware infections is also mixed. There are few consistent behavioral factors affecting the risk of victimization (Bossler & Holt, 2009, 2010; Holt & Bossler, 2013), and mixed support for the presence and use of protective software programs to reduce the likelihood of infection (Bossler & Holt, 2009; Choi, 2008; Holt & Bossler, 2013; Holt & Turner, 2012; Ngo & Paternoster, 2011). There is some evidence that pirating media or viewing pornography can increase an individual's proximity to malware because individuals are continuously downloading and opening suspect files (Bossler & Holt, 2009; Choi, 2008; Holt & Bossler, 2013; Holt & Copes, 2010; Szor, 2005; Wolfe, Higgins, & Marcum, 2008). Similarly, engaging in hacking behaviors can increase the risk of malware victimization through exposure to motivated attackers (e.g. Chu et al., 2010; Holt, 2007). There is also limited support for the relationship between peer involvement in cyber-deviance and the risk of infections generally (Bossler & Holt, 2009, 2010).

Finally, recent routine activities research has examined computer/network intrusions using honeypots at research universities in the US (see Chapter 2 for more detail; Maimon et al., 2013), Israel, and China (Maimon et al., 2015). Maimon et al. (2013) used data recorded by an Intrusion Prevention System to examine trends associated with computer exploits, port scans, and denial of service attacks against a major university's computer network to test two hypotheses they derived from routine activities theory. They found that computer intrusion patterns were related to the daily activity patterns of network users (i.e. more computer attacks occurring during the university's official business hours). In addition, an increase in foreign-born network users was linked to additional computer attacks originating from those users' countries of origin (Maimon et al., 2013).

Using a sample of honeypots housed in independent academic institutions in China and Israel, Maimon and colleagues (2015) found mixed evidence that a computer network's geographic location influenced the physical origin of successful brute-force attacks and system trespassing incidents. Some 68 percent of the brute-force attacks against Chinese computers originated from IP addresses in Asia. At the same time, 43 percent of the brute-force attacks against the Israeli computers also came from Asia, which the authors argue illustrates the threats posed by Chinese hackers rather than any insights regarding the geographical proximity of attacks. In addition, their attempts at replicating the authors' previous work (Maimon et al., 2013) was also only partially supported as only the Israeli honeypots were more likely to be attacked during official business hours. Taken together, the findings from the work of Maimon and colleagues do not support Yar's (2005) concerns regarding the spatio-temporal disconnect of cyberspace. Instead, their research supports both the applicability of routine activities theory to cyber-space and demonstrates some utility in honeypot data to assess routine activities hypotheses.

In summary, scholars have theoretically and empirically demonstrated that Cohen and Felson's (1979) routine activities theory can be as productive in explaining crime online as it has in the physical world. The theory has been most successful in examining person-oriented cybercrimes, such as online harassment and cyberstalking. The work of Maimon and colleagues has also demonstrated that applying routine activities theory to computer network intrusions may be productive as well. Applications of the theory to economic-oriented cybercrimes and malware infection have seen less success, although some significant correlates have been found.

Of the three components of routine activities theory, measures of online behavior tapping into victim proximity to offenders has shown the most pro-mise in predicting cybercrime victimization. Measures related to online activities are not consistent from one study to the next. It is not clear whether these incongruent findings are owing to: different populations being examined (e.g. adults, college students, or juveniles); different offense types (e.g. online harassment, cyberstalking, fraud, etc.); measurement issues (multiple operationalizations of dependent and independent variables); the use of cross-sectional data; or other factors. This has led to a laundry list of possible risky behaviors that affect the risk of victimization which may not be supported across the larger literature. The most consistent behavior that predicts cyber-crime victimization is the respondents' own participation in cyber-deviance (Bossler et al., 2012; Holt & Bossler, 2009; Holt et al., 2012; Hinduja & Patchin, 2009; Ngo & Paternoster, 2011; Reyns et al., 2011; Reyns et al., 2013; Van Wilsem, 2013a; Ybarra et al., 2007). Studies that do not include measures of respondent deviance are excluding an important predictor and creating model misspecification.

To date, the evidence regarding the impact of guardianship measures is mixed. Again, it is not clear whether the findings are due to measurement and data issues rather than a reflection of the general role of guardianship in cyberspace. One of the only consistent factors associated with victimization is peer deviance, which partially taps into social guardianship, as well as proximity to offenders (Bossler et al., 2012; Hinduja & Patchin, 2008; Holt & Bossler, 2009; Reyns et al., 2011). Scholars need to continue to examine its relationship with victimization. Scholars must also spend effort in improving measurements of guardianship and develop longitudinal data sets to better understand this relationship.

Finally, it should be noted that although the body of literature regarding online routine activities is growing, some scholars may feel that researchers have exhausted this issue with respect to cybercrime victimization. This section demonstrates that more research is needed to refine the theoretical relationships and measurement issues evident across these studies. Only then can we begin to better understand the value of this theory to account for cybercrime victimization.

Rational choice and deterrence theories

The **Classical School**, dating back to the mid-eighteenth century, was the intellectual product of the Enlightenment Era which viewed humans as hedonistic, rational, and calculating (Bernard, Snipes, & Gerould, 2010). Crime was therefore viewed as the result of individuals exercising free will and rational thought, not the result of supernatural forces. The Classical School viewed human action as a result of individuals weighing the benefits and costs of a behavior and choosing the path that increased pleasure and minimized pain. As a result, the state's role should be to create structure in society and to convince individuals that crime was neither profitable nor pleasurable and would lead to punishment (e.g. Beccaria, 1963; Newman & Marongiu, 1990). Governments that want to reduce crime must clearly codify behavior to inform citizens on what was not allowed, set the pain of punishments to be equal to the pleasure associated with specific crimes, apprehend criminals when laws were broken, and swiftly punish them (Paternoster, 1987).

Rational choice theory

Rational choice theory is predicated upon the classical model of human decision making, whereby individuals actively choose to participate in crime based on their assessments of perceived risks and potential rewards for their actions (Becker, 1968; Clarke, 1983; Cornish & Clarke, 1987; Mischel, 1968). The decision-making calculus of an individual is informed and influenced by a variety of situational factors including environmental cues and vicarious and personal experiences (Clarke, 1997). The process is also limited, or bound, by the actors' knowledge of an area or an activity, as well as drugs and alcohol which hinder the decision-making process (e.g. Cherbonneau & Copes, 2006). The rational choice perspective has stimulated significant study into the offending processes of various real world criminals, including armed robbers (Wright & Decker, 1997), auto thieves (Cherbonneau & Copes, 2006), burglars (Cromwell & Olson, 2004; Wright & Decker, 1994), and drug dealers (Jacobs, 1996, 2000). These studies provide important insight into the rewards and enticements of crime, as well as the ways offenders perceive and respond to preventative policing activities (Cherbonneau & Copes, 2006; Cromwell & Olson, 2004; Jacobs, 1996, 2000; Wright & Decker, 1994, 1997).

Research applying rational choice frameworks to cybercrime is limited and sorely needed. A handful of speculative studies has been published arguing that hackers and malware writers are rational actors driven by money or other interests (Gordon & Ma, 2003). Similarly, email scammers are argued to rationally structure messages in an attempt to draw in unsuspecting victims (e.g. Holt & Graves, 2007; King & Thomas, 2009; Whitty, 2013). One of the few studies attempting to empirically assess the rational decision-making practices of cybercriminals was published by Bachmann (2010). He surveyed a sample of participants at a major US hacker conference and found that hackers reported a greater preference for rational thinking styles. Hackers' risk propensities were also inversely correlated with their rationality, suggesting that rational thoughts minimize an individual's willingness to engage in risky behaviors. Both of these factors were significantly associated with the success of a hacking incident, with greater rationality and reduced risk propensity increasing the likelihood of a hack (Bachmann, 2010).

Similarly, Higgins (2007) assessed the relationships between rational decision making and two other theoretical frameworks in order to account for intentions to engage in digital piracy. Using a college sample, he included measures for situational factors that could impact an individual's willingness to pirate, such as the likelihood of being caught, perceived shame if caught, the risk of external sanctions, how morally wrong it would be to use pirated material, and the value of pirated materials generally. His findings demonstrated that as individuals placed greater value on pirated material, their perception of shame decreased, though an increase in their perceptions of external sanctions decreased the value of digital piracy and their willingness to pirate (Higgins, 2007). Thus, he suggests that there is some value in examining the application of rational choice for some forms of cybercrime.

A small number of qualitative studies have also considered the ways that individuals utilize technology in order to minimize their risk of detection or arrest. From a rational choice framework, offenders perceive and manage the risks of offending based upon their observations and assessments of environmental and situational cues (Gibbs, 1975; Langlais, 2008; Sanchirico, 2006). Criminals can change their offending patterns or tactics in response to policing strategies in order to address the risks they face, or minimize the potential to be harmed by other offenders (Gibbs, 1975; Jacobs, 1996). These studies demonstrate that access to technology has a substantial benefit for offenders by enabling the direct transmission of arrest avoidance techniques through forums and other forms of computer-mediated communication (e.g. Holt, Blevins, & Kuhns, 2008, 2014). Two studies on the online communications of the customers of prostitutes found that they provided direct information on techniques to minimize the risk of arrest (Holt et al., 2014). Additionally, they gave details on law enforcement practices in the field in order to facilitate displacement to other communities or forms of prostitution (Holt et al., 2008). In particular, they gave detailed information on techniques to solicit prostitutes and methods to meet with sex workers in order to minimize personal harm or arrest (Holt et al., 2014). Thus, the Internet may serve as a conduit for more informed decision making in the real world on the part of some offenders because of their participation in online communities.

Deterrence theory

Cesare Beccaria (1963) laid out the essential principles of **deterrence theory** in the 1700s in his treatise on the justice system, which directly reflect principles of the Classical School. Essentially, this perspective argues that humans will be deterred from crime if the justice system response is certain, swift, and proportionately severe. In this respect, the **certainty** of the punishment relates to the likelihood that an individual who commits a crime will be detected and caught by justice system actors in order to be punished. The swiftness, or **celerity**, of punishment recognizes that individuals must be sanctioned quickly following their actions. The **severity** of punishments must also be proportionate to the offense performed. Punishments that are disproportionately severe or too lenient will have minimal impact on the decision-making process of offenders. Thus, a criminal must experience a punishment that is equivalent to the harm they caused to others (Paternoster, 1987). These tenets underlie most Western criminal justice systems, and serve as the basis for modern forms of punitive sanctions to offenders.

Criminal justice research has examined the value or utility of deterrence to various offenses for the last half-century (e.g. Becker, 1968; Tittle, 1969). Research with respect to traditional crime has found modest support for deterrence theory using various forms of data, including retrospective accounts, perceptual surveys, and longitudinal assessments (Nagin, 1998; Paternoster, 1987; Pratt et al., 2006; Yu & Liska, 1993). In general, perceptual studies show that certainty of punishment, not severity, is more important (e.g. Nagin, 1998). Increasing the likelihood that an individual will be caught should decrease an individual's willingness to offend relative to the severity of the punishments, such as longer prison sentences or fines. There does appear to be a small population of deterrable offenders who are more likely to respond to punishments and be kept from acting out (Pogarsky, 2002).

Almost every nation has criminalized some form of hacking, malware dissemination, data theft, online fraud, and child sexual exploitation (e.g. Brenner, 2011). Based on basic deterrence principles, the passage and enforcement of these laws should provide a deterrent structure in which cybercriminals are made aware of these restrictions, perceive there to be high levels of certainty of being caught, and receive appropriately severe punishments that fit the crime.

Despite the proliferation and harmonization of cybercrime laws, there has been generally little research on the deterrence of cybercrime. Evidence across multiple samples suggests that rates of piracy are quite high (e.g. Business Software Alliance, 2014; Higgins, 2005; Burruss, Bossler, & Holt, 2013), which may be an indication that punishments have little impact on behavior. To examine this issue, Bachmann (2007) utilized survey data in the US to consider the impact of an anti-piracy campaign enforced by the Recording Industry Association of America. The results demonstrated a temporary reduction in proxy measures for piracy rates, though trends began to reverse after several months.

Several studies have also attempted to identify the conditions that generally deter pirating behaviors (Higgins, Wilson, & Fell, 2005; Wolfe et al., 2008). In general, studies have suggested that certainty of punishment, not severity, reduced the likelihood of piracy in keeping with prior traditional deterrence research (Nagin, 1998). In addition, informal levels of social control, such as guilt and embarrassment, may be more influential in decreasing digital piracy than various forms of legal actions. For example, Wolfe, Higgins, and Marcum (2008) found that guilt had a more substantial role in preventing individuals from downloading music illegally relative to other factors (e.g. perception of whether family and friends might find out about the piracy; fear of getting a virus).

A similarly small number of studies have examined the potential for computer hackers to be deterred through formal or informal mechanisms (Maimon et al., 2014; Skinner & Fream, 1997). Skinner and Fream (1997) found that decreases in computer intrusions were related to the severity of punishments associated with the intrusions, not the certainty of detection by either administrators or fellow students. Recent research by Maimon and associates (2014) applied an experimental research design to assess the influence of warning banners on the progression, frequency, and duration of active computer intrusions within a simulated computing environment. The use of different warnings, ranging from no message to an indication that the attacker is being monitored, made no difference on the termination of the hack (Maimon et al., 2014). Individuals remained inside the system regardless of exposure to a warning message, though it shortened the length of time spent in the system during an incident. Since warnings had no impact on the overall volume of repeated trespassing incidents, Maimon et al. (2014) argue that there may be no way to deter hackers from engaging in acts of cyber-trespass through common sanction threats. This result is sensible given the persistence with which hacks continue against various government, industry, and civilian targets.

Finally, a recent study by Kigerl (2009) attempted to analyze the impact of the federal CAN SPAM Act on the total quantity of spam sent within the US. While the problem of email spam is often viewed as a nuisance by the general public, it is instrumental in facilitating a range of fraud schemes and distributing malicious software (e.g. Wall, 2004). Attempts to regulate the distribution of spam emails should be welcomed as they may potentially deter some actors from attempting to use email as a first point of contact with victims. Using time series analyses of a sample of millions of emails received between 1998 and 2008, the author found that the law had no impact on either the amount of spam sent or from which location it was sent (Kigerl, 2009). Additionally, the content of spam messages did not change to comply with the Act's guidelines in significant ways. As a result, this analysis provides further evidence that some forms of cybercrime may be difficult to deter through traditional criminal justice system mechanisms.

The relative lack of success in deterrence frameworks has been noted in research on cyberwarfare as well. The Internet enables hackers to harm government and critical infrastructure targets, leading researchers and policy-makers to find ways to prevent or deter nation-states from engaging in cyber attacks (e.g. Blank, 2001; Brenner, 2007; Geers, 2012). It is extremely difficult to affect actor decision making online because actors can anonymize their location and identity (Guitton, 2012; Rid, 2013). As a result, nations can deny their responsibility in any incident or attribute a specific hack to citizens rather than military or state-sponsored actors (Rid, 2013). There may also be no way to deter or affect the thought process of hackers who are acting on behalf of a terrorist or extremist group, as they may neither fear punishment nor attempt to minimize their identity in order to be properly associated with an attack (Denning, 2011). If attacks by cyberterrorism groups cannot be deterred because they are neither rational nor affected by punitive sanctions, then changes to the law will have no impact on behavior.

In summary, the rational choice and deterrence literature regarding cybercrime is limited. Additional qualitative research on hackers and other cyber-criminals would be beneficial to better understand the decision-making process in the initiation, habituation (or persistence), and desistance stages of the criminal career. This research should specifically examine how various cybercriminals weigh the benefits of offending (whether financial, social, or personal) in comparison to that of the consequences, particularly formal legal sanctions. In addition, experimental research in real computing environments would also benefit this understanding of the decision-making process and determine the extent to which hacking and other forms of cybercrime realistically fit into a deterrence framework. In addition, it is not difficult to imagine various modifications of Maimon and colleagues' (2014) work with banners to examine other aspects of deterrence (e.g., whether the punishment for the offense is provided in the banner; altering the levels of punishment). Finally, it is also essential for scholars to continue to assess the deterrent capabilities of nations to prevent serious cyber-attacks against critical infrastructure. With only two basic strategies possible—target hardening and deterrence—research must enhance our understanding of these phenomena and improve the measures and samples used.

Situational crime prevention

The rational choice and routine activities theory frameworks have been expanded upon over the last few decades to produce a series of principles to prevent crimes (Clarke, 1983; Cornish & Clarke, 2003; Newman & Clarke, 2003). The perspective that crime is a consequence of opportunity and rational decision making provides a basis to understand how crime may be deterred through strategies that either remove benefits from offending and/or increase risks of detection or arrest. Combining these insights with research on crime pattern theories (Spelman & Eck, 1989), which argue that crimes occur around certain places or times (i.e. hot spots) and affect certain individuals more frequently than others, increases the power of deterrent strategies by developing techniques to manage places and products more effectively (Cornish & Clarke, 2003).

The general model of **situational crime prevention (SCP)** is a rational choice framework, arguing that offenders make decisions to offend based on their assessment of the perceived risks and potential rewards of crime, as well as situational factors such as environmental cues and social pressures (Cornish & Clarke, 2003). Situational crime prevention focuses on five categories that influence decision making: (1) making it more challenging to engage in crime; (2) increasing the risk of detection through formal and informal means; (3) reducing the rewards that may result from crime; (4) reducing provocations to offend; and (5) removing any excuses for committing the crime (Clarke, 1983, 1997, 1999; Cornish & Clarke, 2003). Within each category, there are five techniques that can be applied to affect the likelihood of crime (see Table 3.1 for a detailed breakdown).

There is generally little empirical research applying situational crime prevention to different forms of cybercrime. Most of these studies utilized aspects

Table 3.1 Twenty-five techniques of situational crime prevention

Increase the effort	Increase risks	Reduce rewards	Reduce provocations	Remove excuses
1 Target harden	6 Extend guardianship	11 Conceal targets	16 Reduce frustrations and stress	21 Set rules
2 Control access to facilities	7 Assist natural surveillance	12 Remove targets	17 Avoid disputes	22 Post instructions
3 Screen exits	8 Reduce anonymity	13 Identify property	18 Reduce emotional arousal	23 Alert conscience
4 Deflect offenders	9 Utilize place managers	14 Disrupt markets	19 Neutralize peer pressure	24 Assist compliance
5 Control tools/ weapons	10 Strengthen formal surveillance	15 Deny benefits	20 Discourage imitation	25 Control drugs and alcohol

Source: Adapted from Cornish & Clarke, 2003

of SCP to examine a specific crime type (Collins, Sainato, & Khey, 2011; Hutchings & Holt, 2015; Khey & Sainato, 2013) or provide summary overviews of existing knowledge regarding a form of cybercrime within an SCP framework (e.g. Hinduja & Kooi, 2013; Rege, 2013). Studies using empirical data tend to focus on data breaches and the misuse of personal data. For instance, Collins, Sainato, and Khey (2011) applied an SCP framework to account for the likelihood that a healthcare or educational institution would report a data breach between 2005 and 2010.

Using inferential statistics, the authors found that changes in legislation related to healthcare breach notifications increased the probability that a healthcare organization would report a breach. There was generally little variation in breach reporting by region, and the majority of incidents appeared to stem from malicious insiders or losses of physical records rather than external breaches (Collins et al., 2011). The number of incidents reported by educational institutions declined during the same period, which the authors suggest could be a function of improved security and differences in the interests of attackers obtaining data during this period.

Using similar data, Khey and Sainato (2013) examined the spatial distribution of data breaches to consider how situational crime prevention techniques may account for variations in incidents. Using a geospatial analysis, the authors found that there was no particular pattern of hotspots or clusters for breaches over time, across the type of victim organization, or by punitive legislation to sanction offenders. Khey and Sainato (2013) concluded that the absence of pattern means that organizations must be held accountable for minimizing the likelihood of data breaches and finding ways to harden resources from compromise. The authors argued that there is a need to develop techniques based on an SCP model that minimize the likelihood of breaches by external attackers like hackers, internal employees who maliciously acquire data for profit, and from accidental loss via careless employees.

Finally, crime script analyses (see Chapter 2) allow scholars to understand both the decision-making process of an offender and prevention strategies that can be taken at various intervention points of the criminal offending process, making it useful for SCP. Hutchings and Holt (2015) applied a crime script analysis to 13 web forums used to buy and sell stolen data. They determined that there were various roles played by actors within each forum. Individuals could buy, sell, and supply data, while others served as place managers by acting as a moderator. A small proportion of users also acted as teachers by writing detailed tutorials on the process of buying, selling, and using data (Hutchings & Holt, 2015). Individual roles were acquired only after they prepared an account on a forum, acquired an electronic currency account to send or receive payments, and gained an understanding of the specialized language used by market actors. For instance, individuals seeking to buy stolen credit or debit cards would need to search for the word "dump" as that is the phrase used by actors to refer to this information (Hutchings & Holt, 2015). Individuals selling stolen data had to create a thread in the forum to post an advertisement for their data, and negotiate with buyers outside the forum, typically through ICQ messaging, an instant messaging protocol. After paying for a product and receiving it, then buyers would have to take additional steps in order to obtain cash from the data they purchased, whether through money laundering services or other means (Hutchings & Holt, 2015). As a result, the authors demonstrated the scope of the economy and identified weaknesses in the supply chain of data that could be exploited by law enforcement.

Taken as a whole, the descriptive nature of these studies demonstrates the value of SCP research for our understanding of cybercrime. The findings provide some indication of how victims and targets can be insulated from compromise, though trends of cybercrime victimization would suggest that there is no necessary way to stem the flow of malware and hacking incidents. Thus, there is a need for continued research in this area, particularly if we are to better link criminological theory to potential computer security practices to decrease the incidence of cybercrime (see Chapter 5 for greater detail).

Social learning and low self-control

The other dominant theoretical paradigm that has shaped criminological research is the **positivist perspective**, which argues that behavior is shaped by various forces internal and external to the individual which are beyond their control. Positivist theories recognize that human behavior is not a decision, but rather a consequence of social, psychological, and biological factors (Bernard et al., 2010). This perspective undergirds the majority of theoretical frameworks within the field of criminology and has led to the identification of various correlates of criminal behavior. The two most prominent individual-level positivist theories used to explain both traditional and virtual forms of crime are Akers's (1998) social learning theory and Gottfredson and Hirschi's (1990) general theory of crime.

Social learning theory

The primary theory applied by criminologists to a wide variety of criminal and deviant behaviors over the last 50 years is Akers's (1998) **social learning theory**. This theory was proposed in the 1960s as an expansion of Sutherland's (1947) differential association theory which argued that criminal behavior was learned through interactions and communication with others, with the most important influences derived from time spent with intimate personal groups. Through social engagement with others, some individuals were exposed to beliefs and attitudes that supported rule-breaking behavior as well as techniques of offending. The more frequently an individual was exposed to definitions supporting the violation of law, defined as rationalizations and attitudes supporting criminality, relative to definitions that did not support law violation, the more likely that individual would engage in crime.

Akers initially expanded this theory to include aspects of operant conditioning and reinforcements for behavior, though it has subsequently been reformulated into a processual theory of offending. Akers's (1998) social learning theory argues that the learning process of any behavior, including crime, includes at least four principal components: (1) **differential association**; (2) **definitions**; (3) **differential reinforcement**; and (4) **imitation**. The process begins with differential associations with deviant others which expose individuals to models of offending as well as definitions supportive of criminal or deviant behavior and justifications that neutralize the possible negative consequences of deviance. Social learning theory argues that the more beliefs and attitudes an individual has that are supportive of deviant behavior, the more likely they will be to engage in those activities. Exposure to delinquent peers and definitions supporting criminality are critical sources of imitation for first-time offenders. Future offending behavior is dependent, however, on the ways that individuals experience reinforcements for their actions. The experience of reinforcements through economic gain, emotional fulfillment, or social acceptance as well as experiences with punishments are all critical in influencing whether behaviors persist or desist over time.

Social learning theory has been one of the most commonly tested criminological theories to date, with substantial empirical support across a wide range of deviant and criminal activities (Akers & Jensen, 2006; Gau, 2009; Lee, Akers, & Borg, 2004; Pratt et al., 2009). This is one of several reasons why social learning theory was applied by early scholars who wanted to understand the causes of cybercrime. In the 1980s and 1990s, technologies were less user friendly and required a degree of knowledge that individuals had to develop in order to effectively use the devices. Skinner and Fream (1997) recognized this dynamic in one of the first published studies examining social learning and cybercrime, stating that individuals must "learn not only how to operate a highly technical piece of equipment but also specific procedures, programming, and techniques for using the computer illegally" (Skinner & Fream, 1997: 498). While technologies have become ever-more simple to use, a learning process is still evident in the adoption of various applications, understanding etiquette in social media, and knowing which platforms are more appropriate for specific forms of cybercrime, such as digital piracy and computer hacking.

Social learning theory has been used extensively to assess digital piracy. Scholars have found that individuals who associated with peers who engaged in piracy were more likely to engage in piracy themselves (Higgins & Marcum, 2011; Hinduja & Ingram, 2008; Holt, Bossler, & May, 2012). Friends and intimate relationships serve as a source of information for the process of identifying and acquiring pirated materials and serve as potential sources of imitation for piracy (Hinduja, 2003; Holt & Copes, 2010; Holt et al., 2010; Ingram & Hinduja, 2008; Skinner & Fream, 1997). These associations may decrease in importance as the pirating becomes easier for the individual as their experience and skill increase.

In addition, pirates hold definitions that favor the violation of intellectual property laws and techniques that limit their personal responsibility for their actions (Higgins & Marcum, 2011; Ingram & Hinduja, 2008; Skinner & Fream, 1997). For example, pirates often rationalize their behavior by believing that there is minimal economic injury to corporations and artists, corporations charge too much for their products, and everyone is doing it (e.g. Higgins & Marcum, 2011; Holt & Copes, 2010). The continuation of piracy is influenced by holding these beliefs, but also by the actual or perceived positive reinforcement, such as financial (e.g. free music) and social (e.g. praise, recognition) rewards (Decary-Hetu et al., 2012; Hinduja, 2003; Holt & Copes, 2010).

Social learning theory has also demonstrated particular salience for computer hacking as hackers appear to operate in a global subculture that communicates motives and techniques of offending (e.g. Holt, 2007, 2009; Jordan & Taylor, 1998; Meyer, 1989). Peer associations are a key factor in predicting hacking behaviors in both quantitative (Bossler & Burruss, 2011; Holt, Bossler, & May, 2012; Marcum et al., 2014; Morris & Blackburn, 2009; Skinner & Fream, 1997) and qualitative studies (e.g. Holt, 2007; Jordan & Taylor, 1998). Hackers consistently report maintaining peer relationships with other hackers, whether on or off-line (Decary-Hetu et al., 2012; Holt, 2009; Holt & Kilger, 2008; Schell & Dodge, 2002).

It is unclear whether virtual or real peer relationships have a greater impact on real world behavior, as most studies do not assess variations in the quantity and value individuals place on peers across the digital divide. Limited research using online data sources and social network analysis techniques demonstrate that skilled hackers are central to larger social networks of less skilled actors (Decary-Hetu et al., 2012). Qualitative research suggests that virtual peer groups may be more significant because hackers may be unable to identify others in the real world who share their interests (Holt, 2009; Holt & Kilger, 2008; Schell & Dodge, 2002). Regardless, peer relationships are correlated with involvement in hacking activities (Bossler & Burruss, 2011; Holt, 2009; Holt et al., 2010; Skinner & Fream, 1997).

Consistent with social learning theory, these deviant associations provide models for peers to imitate hacking (e.g. Morris & Blackburn, 2009) and are pivotal in the introduction and acceptance of techniques of neutralization to excuse or justify malicious or unethical behaviors (Bossler & Burruss, 2011; Holt et al., 2010; Skinner & Fream, 1997). Hackers often argue that their actions do not necessarily cause harm (Gordon & Ma, 2003; Morris, 2011), and may blame victims for having poor skill or security to prevent victimization (Jordan & Taylor, 1998; Taylor, 1999). In addition, research on the hacker subculture (e.g. Decary-Hetu et al., 2012; Holt, 2007) convincingly demonstrates that the subculture provides positive reinforcement for individuals who portray knowledge and mastery of technology. This applies as well to the warez scene in which hackers who distribute intellectual property and are more productive than other groups receive additional recognition from their peer groups (Decary-Hetu et al., 2012).

In summary, social learning theory is the most empirically supported theory to explain both traditional and virtual crimes. Most of the social learning research conducted examining cybercrime has focused on different forms of piracy, though recent studies have begun to include computer hacking. Additional social learning theory testing is needed to examine its applicability to other forms of cybercrime, such as cyberbullying and financially motivated cybercrimes like fraud.

An additional issue within the cybercrime literature, particularly for studies of piracy, is the exclusion of imitation and reinforcement measures from models. The lack of measures for both imitation and reinforcement has plagued the traditional literature (Akers & Jensen, 2006) and has continued into the cybercrime literature. Research therefore needs to consider using fuller measures of the entire social learning process rather than only focusing on peers and definitions (Burruss et al., 2013). Finally, a focus needs to be placed on collecting and analyzing longitudinal data in order to better understand the interplay between the components of the social learning process and their effects on the initiation, continuation, and desistance of cybercrime.

General theory of crime

Gottfredson and Hirschi's (1990) **general theory of crime**, which came to prominence over the last 30 years, challenges the basic assumptions of learning theory. The development of what Gottfredson and Hirschi call the general theory of crime stems from the tradition of control theories which suggest that motivations to engage in crime are generally invariant among all individuals. Instead, the level of control placed on individuals from internal or external sources varies, enabling them to feel more or less free from social conventions and restrictions on behavior. Those who experience the least control are more likely to engage in crime and deviance.

Gottfredson and Hirschi (1990) use this rationale as a basis to develop a theory that can account for virtually all crime due to commonalities across offenders and offense types. They argue that crime is simple and requires minimal skill or ability on the part of the offender to gain instant gratification. Offenders share specific behavioral and attitudinal characteristics, including impulsivity, short-sightedness, insensitivity, and a willingness to engage in risk-taking behaviors. Criminal behavior is therefore a consequence of one's level of **self-control**, or the ability to constrain behavior through internal regulation (Gottfredson & Hirschi, 1990). Low self-control is argued to also be the cause of failure in school, poor relationships with others, and various risky behaviors, including smoking, drinking, drug use, and unprotected sex. Decades of research has demonstrated that low self-control is one of the strongest correlates of crime and is consistently linked to a wide variety of crime and deviance (e.g. Pratt & Cullen, 2000).

Similar to research on social learning theory, the general theory of crime has also been frequently applied to various forms of cybercrime. Following the logic of the theory, the general theory of crime would hold that most forms of cybercrime are rather simple in nature, require little to no skills, and lead to consequences which are greater than the benefits for the offender. Sending a mean or hurtful message via email, text, or social media post requires no real skill, only a dislike for the recipient (e.g. Holt, Bossler, & May, 2012). The same is true for digital piracy as there are multiple avenues to access and acquire pirated media. Empirical research has found that individuals with low self-control are more likely to engage in online harassment (Holt et al., 2012), download online pornography (Buzzell et al., 2006), commit digital piracy (Higgins & Marcum, 2011), and perpetrate online economic crimes (Moon, McCluskey, & McCluskey, 2010). These relationships are consistent across college (Higgins & Marcum, 2011) and juvenile populations (Holt, Bossler, & May, 2012; Marcum et al., 2014).

While this relationship makes sense for simpler forms of cybercrime, the effect of low self-control on more complex crimes such as computer hacking may not be immediately clear. The creation, implementation, and management of active malicious software infections require specialized knowledge in computer programming and may require days or weeks of time to lead to specific data outcomes (e.g. Bachmann, 2010; Holt, 2007; Schell & Dodge, 2002). Hackers report greater cognitive and verbal skills (Schell & Dodge, 2002). Many hackers are also high school and college graduates with stable employment, all indicating some interest in long-term goals (Bachmann, 2010; Holt, 2007; Holt, Strumsky, Smirnova, & Kilger, 2012; Schell & Dodge, 2002). As a result, more advanced forms of computer hacking may require a much greater amount of technical proficiency, which is incongruent with low self-control (Bossler & Burruss, 2011; Holt & Kilger, 2012).

There is generally limited research on low self-control and computer hacking. For instance, scholars have found that low self-control is related to minor forms of hacking (e.g. accessing another's computer account or files without knowledge or permission; guessing passwords for social media accounts) in youth samples (Holt, Bossler, & May, 2012; Marcum et al., 2014). Bossler and Burruss (2011) also found that individuals in a college sample who engaged in three forms of hacking (guessing another person's password into his/her computer account or files; accessing another's computer account or files without his/her knowledge or permission to look at information; and adding, deleting, changing, or printing any information in another's files without permission) were more likely to have low self-control.

Controlling for an individual's involvement in a social learning process demonstrated a key relationship between self-control and hacking (Bossler & Burruss, 2011). Individuals who did not have delinquent peers, definitions supporting offending, or reinforcements for hacking needed *higher* levels of self-control to hack. At the same time, individuals with lower levels of self-control were more likely to participate in a social learning process which linked them with delinquent peers who served as models and provided definitions that supports offending (Bossler & Burruss, 2011). The authors interpreted this as an indication that social learning theory is pivotal to understand hacking. Individuals with low self-control require social relationships in order to gain the skills needed to hack, while those with higher self-control will be able to engage in more complex hacks on their own.

The general lack of empirical research on computer hacking demonstrates a need for additional research in order to expand our understanding of this theory. There is, however, no denying the importance of low self-control in understanding the commission of cybercrime. Research consistently indicates that self-control may predict crime in the cyberworld as well as it does in the terrestrial world. At this time, it is doubtful that further testing examining the basic relationship between low self-control and various forms of simple cybercrime, deviance, or risky online behaviors will provide any further insights than what is currently known. Instead, studies using longitudinal data to examine the unique interplay between low self-control and the social learning process in explaining more complex forms of cybercrime, such as skilled computer intrusions, would provide additional benefit to both the general criminological literature as well as to our knowledge of more complex forms of cybercrime.

Subcultural theories of crime

Although social learning theory and other criminological theories identify peer associations and individual perceptions of crime as pertinent factors in predicting individual offending, these theories do not focus on the meaning that offending has for some individuals. Researchers utilizing a **subcultural perspective** have been able to improve our knowledge of the ways that individuals account for their involvement in crimes, from gang membership (Miller, 1958; Short, 1968) to digital piracy (e.g. Cooper & Harrison, 2001). Subcultures in a criminological and sociological context are any group with values, norms, traditions, and rituals which set them apart from the dominant culture (Kornblum, 1997; Brake, 1980). Deviant subcultures form as a response to either a rejection of the dominant culture (see Miller, 1958), or around a distinct phenomenon that may not be valued by the larger society (Quinn & Forsythe, 2005; Wolfgang & Ferracuti, 1967). Members of a deviant subculture place substantive value on various activities, engaging in certain behaviors, or cultivating skills that may aid them in life (Maurer, 1981). As a result, the members of a subculture develop codes of conduct and rules that structure how they view the world and interact with others in and out of their subculture (Foster, 1990).

Different types of subcultural frameworks have been developed and vary based on assumptions about the members' adherence to conventional norms and values. For example, Cohen (1955) argued that a gang subculture operates in direct opposition to the middle class values espoused by the dominant society. This perspective on subculture assumes an outright rejection of conventional norms and values. Other frameworks do not require members of a subculture to perfectly adhere to its specific values. Anderson's (1999) code of the streets and Wolfgang and Ferracuti's (1967) subculture of violence theories argue that individuals in urban areas and the South respectively are exposed to norms and values encouraging the use of violence to threats. Each person must decide whether or not to respond to encounters with violence, leading to variations in rates of assault and homicide at the individual level.

Considering that these differing perspectives have not been resolved in the current literature on traditional offenses, it is not surprising that they have not been clearly addressed in subcultural studies of cybercrime and deviance either. The majority of research utilizing the Internet as a venue to understand offending behaviors does not attempt to present a unified theory of why criminal activities persist online. Instead, the majority of studies focus on subcultural norms and values unique to subgroups of offenders, including computer hackers (Holt, 2007; Jordan & Taylor, 1998; Meyer, 1989; Steinmetz, 2015; Taylor, 1999;), digital pirates (Cooper & Harrison, 2001; Holt & Copes, 2010; Steinmetz & Tunnell, 2013), pedophiles (Durkin & Bryant, 1999; Holt, Blevins, & Burkert, 2010; Jenkins, 2001; Quayle & Taylor, 2002), and a range of sexual deviance (Denney & Tewksbury, 2013; Grov, 2004; Maratea, 2011; Roberts & Hunt, 2012; Tewksbury, 2006).

Many of these studies reflect generally acknowledged concepts about the Internet and its role as a facilitator for deviance (Quinn & Forsyth, 2005; Rosenmann & Safir, 2006). The distributed nature of the Internet and the anonymity that it provides to the user, enables individuals to connect to others who share similar interests, values, opinions, and behaviors regardless of whether the individual participates in similar groups in the physical world (Quinn & Forsyth, 2005). Due to fear of legal ramifications or social rejection, some individuals may not feel able to discuss their interests or activities in the real world. Technology allows individuals to connect to others without these fears, and even enables individuals to explore their curiosities in an online environment without fear of detection (Blevins & Holt, 2009; Holt, 2007; Quinn & Forsyth, 2005).

With the constant evolution of technology, along with its continual impact on our social lives, scholars must continue qualitative studies of online subcultural groups in order to better understand how technology creates enclaves for individuals to engage in crime and deviance. Over time, new subcultures will emerge as either newer forms of technology are created or newer legislation is passed. In addition, it is important to assess how specific subcultures, such as hackers, evolve over time because of changes to either technology or world events.

General strain theory

Another positivist theory that has grown to prominence over the last 30 years is Agnew's (1992) **general strain theory**. This theory is an individual-level expansion of Merton's (1938) classic strain theory, which argues that individuals may engage in crime as a result of exposure to strain. Agnew (1992) conceives of strain as a failure to achieve positively valued goals, the removal of positive stimuli, or the presentation of noxious stimuli. Experiencing strain may produce negative emotions, such as anger and frustration, and crime or deviance may result if the individual lacks appropriate coping mechanisms to deal with the stressful situation or negative emotions. Although this theory has not been tested as extensively as that of social learning theory and self-control, the basic arguments of the theory have received empirical support. Various life strains increase participation in delinquency (Agnew & White, 1992; Broidy, 2001) and may be mediated by increased levels of negative emotions, particularly anger (Brezina, 1998; Mazerolle & Piquero, 1997).

Recent scholarship demonstrates that the cyberworld provides an environment in which individuals can easily vent their frustration and anger at others without having to make direct contact, thus decreasing risk of injury (Hay, Meldrum, & Mann, 2010; Moon, Hwang, & McCluskey, 2011; Patchin & Hinduja, 2011). In fact, limited tests of general strain theory in the virtual world have primarily focused on cyberbullying (Hay et al., 2010; Moon et al., 2011; Patchin & Hinduja, 2011). Agnew (2001) previously identified bullying as a particularly relevant strain that increases the risk of delinquent behavior based on four conditions: (1) bullying is perceived as unjust by the victim; (2) the importance of peer relationships between victim and offender will place a high level of significance on the bullying; (3) bullying typically occurs away from traditional forms of social control, such as parents; and (4) bullying provides a model for the victim to express his or her own aggressive behavior.

Research on bullying on and off-line supports these propositions, as youth who experience higher levels of strain, including doing poorly in school, perceiving unfair treatment from individuals in authority, and experiencing negative life events, are more likely to bully others both in the physical and virtual worlds (Moon et al., 2011; Patchin & Hinduja, 2011). In addition, several scholars have studied the effects of experiencing stress from cyberbullying. Hay et al. (2010) found in a sample of middle and high school students that both traditional and cyberbullying victimization increased future offending, self-harm behaviors, and suicidal ideation. In fact, the effect of cyberbullying on future offending was greater than that of physical bullying. Wright and Li (2013) found that cyberbullying victimization and peer rejection led to increased online aggression even when controlling for past cyber-aggressive behavior. Future tests examining longitudinal data would benefit our knowledge of how negative life events impact the commission of cyberbullying as well as the relationship between cyberbullying victimization and offending.

Although scholars have demonstrated general strain theory's utility in addressing cyberbullying offending and victimization, it has received little examination for other types of cyber-offending. Online predatory crimes, such as certain forms of computer hacking, may logically be explained by stress and negative emotions. General strain theorists may argue that experiencing negative life events, such as breaking up with a long-time boyfriend or girlfriend, losing a job, doing poorly in school, or having issues with authority, may lead individuals to experience negative emotions. In turn, an individual may attempt to guess an individual's social media profile via password guessing or gain access to another's computer in order to cause damage to those who they feel have wronged them. In addition, scholars could study the relationship between involvement in political or ideologically driven hacks, such as those of Anonymous, and exposure to strains or frustrations regarding either an incident in the real world or their perception of governmental policies (Olsen, 2012). Thus, scholars need to both theoretically and empirically address the ways that general strain theory can be applied to various forms of cybercrime.

Debate over the need for new theoretical paradigms

The current body of criminological scholarship demonstrates the utility of traditional theories to improve our knowledge of cybercrimes. There are also clear limitations and shortcomings in these frameworks, which limit their applicability for certain offenses. While there is still a need for robust empirical assessment with various theories, populations, and measures, there may be value in developing new theoretical paradigms that incorporate aspects of the on and off-line experience more completely. In addition, **theoretical integration**, or syntheses of competing frameworks into a single model, may prove useful considering past research (e.g. Bossler & Burruss, 2011; Higgins & Marcum, 2011).

Integrated models

As noted previously, there is substantive value in including measures from both social learning and self-control theories in models of cybercrime offending. Recent research on digital piracy has extensively considered the relationship between differential associations, definitions, low self-control, and piracy behaviors (Higgins & Marcum, 2011). Some theorists have argued that the components of each theory must be included in order to avoid model misspecification (Higgins & Marcum, 2011; Pratt & Cullen, 2000; Pratt et al., 2009). It is unclear if this is an appropriate form of theoretical integration due to the evidence that there is a mediating effect of social learning between low self-control and cybercrime (Bossler & Holt, 2010; Burruss, Bossler, & Holt, 2013). Furthermore, the lack of empirical studies including full operationalizations of the social learning process call into question how these theories may interact when all variables are included in the same model.

One recent theoretical integration proposed to account for cybercrime victimization incorporates low self-control and routine activities variables in a single model (Schreck, 1999). While Gottfredson and Hirschi (1990) did not develop self-control theory as a means to understand victimization, there is a link between offending and victimization risk because both are viewed as a result of inadequate levels of self-control (pp.92–94). In fact, the behavioral correlates of low self-control may increase an individual's risk of victimization because individuals may place themselves in risky situations and engage in deviant or risky behaviors in close proximity to offenders who may select them as targets (e.g. Schreck, 1999; Schreck et al., 2002; Stewart et al., 2004).

These same factors may operate online, as individuals with low self-control likely engage in risky behaviors, such as digital piracy, which increase an individual's proximity to malicious software (e.g. Bossler & Holt, 2010; Higgins, 2005; Wolfe et al., 2008). Individuals with low self-control may also be more likely to divulge personal information to strangers in various social media and chat sites, thereby increasing the risk of harassment or cyberstalking (Stubbs-Richardson & May, 2014). Individuals with low self-control also have limited empathy, which increases the difficulty they may have engaging with others in online spaces where they must depend entirely on text-based communications in order to interact (e.g. Bossler & Holt, 2010). If they do not understand an individual or are easily frustrated by an online encounter, they may be more likely to lash out and increase their own risk of victimization. Finally, individuals with low self-control may increase their vulnerability to victimization because they may not take the time to understand how computers operate and utilize appropriate security tools to protect themselves (e.g. Bossler & Holt, 2010).

Empirical studies of the relationships between low self-control, routine activities, and cybercrime victimization suggest that there is an association, although it is conditioned by the type of victimization examined. Studies suggest that low self-control increases the risk of being harassed online, having computer passwords obtained, and having someone add, delete, or change information in one's computer files without their knowledge or permission (Bossler & Holt, 2010; Ngo & Paternoster, 2011; Van Wilsem, 2013a). A recent study by Van Wilsem (2013b) found that low self-control increased the risk of consumer fraud victimization in a sample of the Dutch general population. There is some evidence that low self-control is not associated with other forms of victimization, including electronic credit card theft (Bossler & Holt, 2010) and phishing attacks (Ngo & Paternoster, 2011) in college samples.

These mixed results may stem from differences in the nature of certain forms of victimization. For example, person-based forms of cybercrime (e.g. harassment) may be more directly influenced by peer associations than by low self-control. Bossler and Holt (2010) found that the effect of low self-control on hacking and online harassment victimization became non-significant when controlling for delinquent peer behavior. Thus, the effect of low self-control on online victimization may be indirect via peer relationships and proximity to motivated offenders.

For property or economically driven cybercrimes, such as credit card theft, self-control may be less pertinent as anyone may lose their personal information during a data breach of a corporate or business target. Thus greater research is needed to explore these relationships with diverse sample populations so as to understand both the prevalence of victimization and any potential relationships to individual-level traits.

Digital drift

Recently, Goldsmith and Brewer (2015) proposed that an older criminological theory initially designed to account for delinquency could be used in explaining crime on and off-line. The authors argue that Matza's (1964, 1969) drift theory may be practical in understanding the ways that individuals move in and out of criminal networks and thereby loosen controls on their behavior. Matza's (1964, 1969) theory argued that youth are not completely socialized into delinquent behaviors, as they can engage in both delinquent and non-delinquent behaviors depending on situational factors. The shift between conformity and delinquency is driven by exposure to delinquent peers and belief systems that enable them to justify or neutralize involvement in wrongdoing. They also perceive that the juvenile justice system does not reflect their beliefs and values, and has no ability to regulate or sanction behavior. In addition, punishments received from juvenile court judges are relatively lenient, suggesting there are no real consequences for offending. As a result, individuals are freed from societal norms and will act how they see fit depending on the circumstance and situation.

Using tenets of drift, Goldsmith and Brewer (2015) present the concept of **digital drift**. They state that they do not intend to account for hacking and other forms of cybercrime, but rather for the ways that technology creates opportunities to engage and disengage from criminal communities on and off-line. Access to and use of the Internet for personal communications exposes individuals to environments where they are disconnected from their actual identity. Anonymity frees individuals from a sense of responsibility, and may encourage or embolden individuals to act in ways they would otherwise not in the real world (Goldsmith & Brewer, 2015). The escapism provided by online games, chat, and other media also relaxes the need to conform to social norms and mores, which may encourage deviance. In fact, psychological research argues there is a disinhibition (Suler, 2004) or **deindividuation** effect (Hinduja, 2008) observed among Internet users. The asynchronous, faceless nature of online communications leads individuals to feel that behavioral norms are meaningless because they are disconnected from themselves and others. The absence of moral or social controls leads individuals to feel that they can behave in whatever way they see fit, and appears to have some association with digital piracy (e.g. Hinduja, 2008) and trolling behaviors (Bishop, 2013).

In this respect, Goldsmith and Brewer (2015) argue that the Internet facilitates the two conditions necessary for drift to occur: *affinity* (immediate rewards, awareness of others) and *affiliation* (means of hooking-up, deepening of deviant associations, skills, etc.). With respect to affinity, the content of the websites and other forms of CMC may surprise youth and expose them to criminal beliefs, behaviors, and justifications that can make criminality attractive. The same is true for social relationships cultivated on and off-line. For instance, increasing rates of viewing pornography and digital piracy among various age groups may present the notion that crime online is socially acceptable, and increase willingness to engage in other forms of online deviance as well.

Regarding affiliation, the more time individuals spend online, the more likely they are to be exposed to criminogenic pathways that may entice individuals to engage in various behaviors. Time spent on social media sites may expose individuals to new people they do not know off-line, who may be engaged in various forms of deviance on or off-line. The ability to access new social networks may increase exposure to criminal others and facilitate entry into deviant peer groups. In turn, these relationships may provide individuals with knowledge to justify and neutralize any sense of wrongdoing in criminal activity, creating what Matza (1964) argued were sources of reassurance that crime will neither be detected nor resolved. Since online relationships may or may not spill over into the real world, individuals can slip in and out of wrongdoing depending on their attitudes and perceptions of offending.

The arguments posed by Goldsmith and Brewer (2015) are interesting and demonstrate a potentially valid framework to understand cybercriminality. The fact that the authors indicate they are not interested in applying this perspective to more commonplace forms of cybercrime is unusual. Goldsmith and Brewer (2015) instead focus on acts of lone-wolf terrorism and pedophilia in the course of their work. The exchange of child pornography and pedophilic conversations do appear to have a direct tie to exposure to the Internet (e.g. Holt et al., 2010; Jenkins, 2001; Quayle & Taylor, 2002). Lone-wolf terrorism incidents are much less prevalent, and perhaps more appropriately characterized through radicalization frameworks rather than drift due to exposure to online content. They provide a few examples of recent incidents where individuals were radicalized to violence in part due to exposure to online content, though it is unclear how pertinent a role the Internet plays in terrorist-related violence (e.g. Chermak, Freilich, Parkin, & Lynch, 2012; Frielich, Chermak, Belli, Gruenewald, & Parkin, 2014). Thus, a great deal of additional research is needed with the concept of drift in order to fully determine its utility in an online context.

Space-transition theory

A second unique theory proposed to account for cybercrimes is K. Jaishankar's (2008) **space-transition theory**, which integrates various theoretical paradigms into a single model. This theory operates on the basic argument that people behave differently while online than they otherwise would in physical space, leading to different behavior patterns in online environments which are not identified by traditional theories of crime. Jaishankar presents seven basic propositions about behavior on and off-line:

1   Individuals who repress their desire to engage in crime in the real world due to either status or position have a propensity to engage in crimes online.
2   Offenders may be more likely to engage in cybercrime because of the ability to utilize various identities, hide their location, and the lack of deterrence in online spaces.
3   Crime in online spaces is likely to move into physical space, and vice versa.
4   Cybercriminals may have the opportunity to desist because of the temporary nature of the Internet and its spatio-temporal disconnect from the real world.
5   The nature of technology allows strangers to come together in cyberspace in order to plan and commit offenses in the real world, and those who know one another in the real world may partner in order to engage in cybercrimes.
6   Closed societies may produce greater levels of cybercrime than open societies due to the repressive nature of government regimes.
7   The disconnect between norms and values of a society in the real world and those of the Internet may lead some individuals to engage in cybercrime.

Scholars have not theoretically addressed or empirically tested space-transition theory's core propositions. In order to better understand the utility of this theory as a whole, additional research would be necessary to study the overlap between crime in the real and virtual worlds. Research studies examining the specific elements of this theory would be necessary in order to have a better understanding of its accuracy. For example, research on the life course of cybercriminals, including the desistance stage, would be necessary to provide support for proposition four.

Although several of the propositions are sensible and are supported by basic characteristics of the Internet (e.g. proposition two, focusing on the anonymity of the Internet), other propositions are somewhat difficult to test and may be contrary to either the current research on cybercrime, or be specific to a certain form of cybercrime. For proposition one to be supported, there would need to be a large subsection of individuals who commit cyber-deviance but do not commit deviance in the physical world because of their status. At this time, it would appear that many of the individuals who commit some forms of cyber-deviance (e.g. online harassment or cyberstalking) are the same individuals who commit traditional crime as well (Holt & Bossler, 2014).

Regarding proposition five, recent research has shown that American street gangs use the Internet for symbolic purposes (e.g. name recognition, status), and not for functional purposes to plan crimes in either the virtual or real world (Moule et al., 2014; Pyrooz et al., 2015). In addition, research is needed to examine whether rates of cybercrime vary based on the political landscape of the nation. Taken as a whole, actual empirical assessments are needed to validate this perspective before any sweeping statements can be made as to its legitimacy. A lesson of space-transition theory may be that it is difficult to create a theory that attempts to explain all forms of cybercrime. Their differences are greater than their similarities in some cases, indicating that this theory may only be successful in certain contexts.

Actor-network theory

As stated throughout this book, more complex forms of cybercrime have received less empirical attention than simpler forms. An example of an understudied problem among criminological scholarship is **botnets**, or networks of infected computers controlled by botherders or commanders (e.g. Symantec Corporation, 2014). This is an important issue considering that: (1) up to a quarter of computers may be a part of a botnet, with some botnets ranging up to millions of infected machines (Silva et al., 2013); and (2) botnets are used for a long list of serious offenses (e.g. online fraud, computer intrusions; denial of service attacks; see Bacher et al., 2005; Chu et al., 2010; Holt, 2013).

Van der Wagen and Pieters (2015) argue that **actor-network theory (ANT)**, a social constructionist approach that focuses on the role technologies or objects have in the course of various actions and does not prioritize human agency when analyzing behavior (Latour, 2005), would be most beneficial in the studying of botnets. In ANT, humans and non-humans deserve equal attention and either one can only be understood when viewed in relation to the other; thus their interaction is the unit of analysis in ANT. Van der Wagen and Pieters (2015) argue that botnets need to be viewed as a hybrid criminal network that is the result of mutual cooperation and interaction between humans and technology. In addition, they contend that most theories prioritize human agency and limit the role of technology to that of an instrument.

Van der Wagen and Pieters (2015) note that ANT is not a theory with causal arguments that can be tested, but rather a "sensitizing approach" to provide a different perspective on the interaction of humans and technology. They therefore consider a successful application of ANT to be one that provides a better understanding of botnets than a scholar would have had if using a conventional theory such as rational choice theory and routine activities theory in which human agency is central.

In order to illustrate their argument, they examined one complex botnet case from the Netherlands. They found that humans are not able to fully control technology, as illustrated by a botherder (individual controlling the botnet) who could not always predict how the interacting components of the network would operate. Van der Wagen and Pieters (2015) argue that without this theory, their analysis would have overemphasized the rational actor managing the network. Furthermore, they would have missed other actors who were either intentionally or unintentionally part of the network and thus a part of the criminal offense. Their role only became significant when viewed as part of a network. They also argue that the ANT approach allowed them to view offenders, victim, and defense (i.e. guardians) as intertwined rather than three separate elements, as is conceptualized in routine activities theory.

Van der Wagen and Pieters (2015) suggest that the ANT framework is not only appropriate for studying botnets but also for understanding how technology affects other forms of cybercrime as well. They conclude that the term *cyborg crime* should be considered for crimes that are heavily dependent on the agency of the systems and networks involved in the course of the offense. As a whole, Van der Wagen and Pieters (2015) provide an interesting framework that has yet to be examined in depth by criminologists. Many applications of criminological theories to cybercrime have not truly appreciated the role of technology in committing crime and have simply viewed it as a functional tool. Van der Wagen and Pieter's (2015) contribution may invigorate scholars to debate whether treating technological innovations as non-rational actors rather than as tools would lead to better insights and empirical testing of more complex forms of cybercrime.

Conclusions

This chapter has demonstrated that criminological theory has much to offer our understanding of both cybercrime offending and victimization. Certain theories, such as Akers's (1998) social learning theory, Gottfredson and

Hirschi's (1990) general theory of crime, and Cohen and Felson's (1979) routine activities theory, have received more empirical support to date than others. Thus, theories such as Agnew's (1992) general strain theory have received modest support and need more empirical testing to determine their utility.

In addition, the majority of empirical research has been conducted on various forms of piracy and online harassment, with an increasing amount on the correlates and causes of computer hacking and identity theft. Much less research has been conducted on more complex forms of cybercrime such as complex computer intrusions, malware infection distribution, and cyberterrorism. We believe that many of the limitations in the current cybercrime literature, including the lack of research on more complex cybercrime, are related more to methodological issues discussed in Chapter 2. Improvements to those methodological issues will address concerns and questions discussed throughout this chapter as well.

This chapter also demonstrated that cybercrime has unique characteristics that differentiate it from many traditional crimes. There are some offenses that have analogues in the real world (e.g. stalking, fraud, theft, etc.), referred to as "old wine" by Wall (1998). At the same time, new forms of crime, such as malware dissemination, were not possible before the advent of the Internet ("new wine"). Therefore, scholars need to consider carefully how concepts created to explain phenomena in the real world apply to the virtual world— the "new bottle." The unique characteristics of the Internet should make theorists consider whether new theories need to be created that focus on how cyberspace alters behavior. Innovative theory creation has largely been absent in the literature over the last decade. As Holt, Bossler, and Seigfried-Spellar (2015) note, the creation of new theories to explain offending and deviance in the virtual world may also lead to new insights about why individuals commit crime and deviance in the physical world as well.

Finally, there is a need to improve our body of cybercrime scholarship through collaboration between criminologists and scholars who are working in other fields, such as computer science, information technology, psychology, and political science. Although there are examples in the literature of criminologists working with individuals in other fields (e.g. Maimon et al., 2015), it is quite rare. Criminologists primarily only examine the commission of offending through a sociological lens. They almost always lack expertise in computer technology and often have limited knowledge on how global dynamics influence individual behavior. This type of collaboration will help the field move beyond analyses of cross-sectional data examining the effects of one or two criminological constructs on a specific type of cybercrime and may lead to alternative strategies to prevent offending and minimize the risk of victimization (see Chapter 5). Thus, the state of cybercrime literature may be dramatically different within the next decade, so long as researchers begin to address these gaps in our knowledge.

Key terms

Absence of a capable guardian
Actor-network theory (ANT)
Botnets
Celerity
Certainty
Classical School
Definitions
Deindividuation
Deterrence theory
Differential association
Differential reinforcement
Digital drift
General strain theory
General theory of crime
Imitation
Motivated offender
Positivist perspective
Rational choice theory
Routine activities theory
Self-control
Severity
Situational crime prevention
Social learning theory
Space-transition theory
Subcultural perspective
Suitable target
Theoretical integration

Chapter questions

1   Why is Cohen and Felson's (1979) routine activities theory more effective in explaining certain forms of cybercrime than others? Why are certain components (i.e. proximity to a motivated offender, absence of a capable guardian, and presence of a suitable target) more significantly correlated with certain cybercrimes than others?

2   Based on the routine activities literature summarized in this chapter, do you think that the findings are supportive or not supportive of Yar's (2005) critique of applying routine activities to cybercrime victimization?

3   Are cybercriminals more rational than traditional offenders? If so, does this mean that they are more deterrable? Does this vary by cybercrime type?

4   Why does social learning theory apply so well to various forms of cyber-crime? Which of the components has received the most support in predicting cybercrime? Least support?

5 Does it make conceptual sense that hackers could have low levels of self-control?

6 Why have strain theories not received more empirical research in attempting to predict various forms of cybercrime?

7 Of Goldsmith and Brewer's (2015) digital drift, Jaishankar's (2008) space-transition theory, or Van der Wagen and Pieters's (2015) use of actor-network theory, which theory holds the most promise for understanding current and new forms of cybercrime? Least promise?

8 Do scholars need to create new theories that specifically address cybercrime? Or should the focus be on better utilizing current theories?

References

Agnew, R. (1992). Foundation for a general strain theory of crime and delinquency. *Criminology*, 30, 47 87.

Agnew, R. (2001). Building on the foundation of general strain theory: Specifying the types of strain most likely to lead to crime and delinquency. *Journal of Research in Crime and Delinquency*, 38, 319–361.

Agnew, R., & White, H.R. (1992). An empirical test of general strain theory. *Criminology*, 30, 475–499.

Akers, R.L. (1998). *Social Learning and Social Structure: A General Theory of Crime and Deviance*. Boston: Northeastern University Press.

Akers, R.L., & Jensen, G.F. (2006). The empirical status of social learning theory of crime and deviance: The past, present, and future. In F.T. Cullen, J.P. Wright and K.R. Blevins (Eds.), *Taking Sock: The Status of Criminological Theory* (pp. 123–149). New Brunswick, NJ: Transaction Publishers.

Anderson, E. (1999). *Code of the Street: Decency, Violence, and the Moral Life of the Inner City*. New York: W.W. Norton & Company.

Bacher, P., Holz, T., Kotter, M., & Wicherski, G. (2005). *Tracking Botnets: Using Honeynets to Learn More About Bots*. The Honeynet Project and Research Alliance. www.honeynet.org/papers/bots/.

Bachmann, M. (2007). Lesson spurned? Reactions of online music pirates to legal prosecutions by the RIAA. *International Journal of Cyber Criminology*, 2, 213–227.

Bachmann, M. (2010). The risk propensity and rationality of computer hackers. *International Journal of Cyber Criminology*, 4, 643–656.

Beccaria, C. (1963). *On Crimes and Punishments*. Indianapolis, IN: Bobbs-Merrill.

Becker, G. (1968). Crime and punishment: An economic approach. *Journal of Political Economy*, 76, 169–217.

Bernard, T.J., Snipes, J.B., & Gerould, A.L. (2010). *Vold's Theoretical Criminology*. Sixth edition. Oxford University Press.

Bishop, J. (2013). *Examining the Concepts, Issues, and Implications of Internet Trolling*. Hershey, PA: Information Science Reference.

Blank, S. (2001). Can information warfare be deterred? In D.S. Alberts & D.S. Papp (Eds.). *Information Age Anthology, Volume III: The Information Age Military*. Washington, DC: Command and Control Research Program.

Blevins, K., & Holt, T.J. (2009). Examining the virtual subculture of johns. *Journal of Contemporary Ethnography*, 38, 619–648.

Bossler, A.M. & Burruss, G.W. (2011). The general theory of crime and computer hacking: Low self-control hackers? In T.J. Holt & B.H. Schell (Eds.), *Corporate Hacking and Technology-driven Crime: Social Dynamics and Implications* (pp. 38–67). Hershey, PA: ISI Global.

Bossler, A.M., & Holt, T.J. (2009). On-line activities, guardianship, and malware infection: An examination of routine activities theory. *International Journal of Cyber Criminology*, 3, 400–420.

Bossler, A.M., & Holt, T.J. (2010). The effect of self-control on victimization in the cyberworld. *Journal of Criminal Justice*, 38, 227–236.

Bossler, A.M., Holt, T.J., & May, D.C. (2012). Predicting online harassment victimization among a juvenile population. *Youth and Society*, 44, 500–523

Brake, M. (1980). *The Sociology of Youth Cultures and Youth Subcultures.* London: Routledge and Kegan Paul.

Brenner, S.W. (2007). "At light speed": Attribution and response to cybercrime/terrorism/ warfare. *The Journal of Criminal Law and Criminology*, 97, 379–475.

Brenner, S.W. (2011). Defining cybercrime: A review of federal and state law. In R.D. Clifford (Ed.), *Cybercrime: The Investigation, Prosecution, and Defense of a Computer-related Crime.* Third edition (pp. 15–104). Raleigh, NC: Carolina Academic Press.

Brezina, T. (1998). Adolescent maltreatment and delinquency: The question of intervening processes. *Journal of Research in Crime and Delinquency*, 35, 71–99.

Broidy, L. (2001). A test of general strain theory. *Criminology*, 39, 9–36.

Burruss, G.W., Bossler, A.M., and Holt, T.J. (2013). Assessing the mediation of a fuller social learning model on low self-control's influence on software piracy. *Crime & Delinquency*, 59, 1157–1184.

Business Software Alliance (2014). *The Compliance Gap: BSA Global Software Survey 2014.* globalstudy.bsa.org/2013/downloads/studies/2013GlobalSurvey_Study_en.pdf.

Buzzell, T., Foss, D., & Middleton, Z. (2006). Explaining use of online pornography: A test of self-control theory and opportunities for deviance. *Journal of Criminal Justice and Popular Culture*, 13, 96–116.

Cherbonneau, M., & Copes, H. (2006). "Drive it like you stole it": Auto theft and the illusion of normalcy. *British Journal of Criminology*, 46, 193–211.

Chermak, S.M., Freilich, J.D., Parkin, W., & Lynch, J.P. (2012). American terrorism and extremist crime data sources and selectivity bias: An investigation focusing on homicide events committed by Far-Right extremists. *Journal of Quantitative Criminology*, 28, 191–218

Choi, K.C. (2008). Computer crime victimization and integrated theory: An empirical assessment. *International Journal of Cyber Criminology*, 2, 308–333.

Chu, B., Holt, T.J., & Ahn, G.J. (2010). *Examining the Creation, Distribution, and Function of Malware On-line.* Washington, DC: National Institute of Justice. www.ncjrs.gov./pdffiles1/nij/grants/230112.pdf.

Clarke, R.V. (1983). Situational crime prevention: Its theoretical basis and practical scope. *Crime and Justice*, 4, 225–256.

Clarke, R.V. (Ed.) (1997). *Situational Crime Prevention: Successful Case Studies.* Monsey, NY: Criminal Justice Press.

Cohen, A.K. (1955). *Delinquent Boys: The Culture of the Gang.* Glencoe, IL: Free Press.

Cohen, L.E., & Felson, M. (1979). Social change and crime rates trends: A routine activity approach. *American Sociological Review*, 44, 588–608.

Collins, J.D., Sainato, V.A., & Khey, D.N. (2011). Organizational data breaches 2005–2010: Applying SCP to the healthcare and education sectors. *International Journal of Cyber Criminology*, 5, 794–810.

Cooper, J., & Harrison, D.M. (2001). The social organization of audio piracy on the Internet. *Media, Culture, and Society*, 23, 71–89.

Cornish, D.B., & Clarke, R.V. (1987). Understanding crime displacement: An application of rational choice theory. *Criminology*, 25, 933–948.

Cornish, D.B., & Clarke, R.V. (2003). Opportunities, precipitators and criminal decisions: A reply to Wortley's critique of situational crime prevention. *Crime Prevention Studies*, 16, 41–96.

Coupe, T., & Blake, L. (2006). Daylight and darkness targeting strategies and the risks of being seen at residential burglaries. *Criminology*, 44, 431–464.

Cromwell, P., & Olson, J.N. (2004). *Breaking and Entering: Burglars on Burglary*. Belmont, CA: Wadsworth.

Decary-Hetu, D., Morselli, C., & Leman-Langlois, S. (2012). Welcome to the scene: A study of social organization and recognition among warez hackers. *Journal of Research in Crime and Delinquency*, 49, 359–382.

Denney, A.S., & Tewksbury, R. (2013). Characteristics of successful personal ads in a BDSM on-line community. *Deviant Behavior*, 34, 153–168.

Denning, D.E. (2011). Cyber-conflict as an emergent social problem. In T.J. Holt & B. Schell (Eds.), *Corporate Hacking and Technology-Driven Crime: Social Dynamics and Implications* (pp. 170–186). Hershey, PA: IGI-Global.

Durkin, K.F., & Bryant, C.D. (1999). Propagandizing pederasty: A thematic analysis of the online exculpatory accounts of unrepentant pedophiles. *Deviant Behavior*, 20, 103–127.

Eck, R.V., & Clarke, J. (2003). *Becoming a Problem Solving Crime Analyst in 55 Small Steps*. London: University College London.

Fisher, B., Cullen, F., & Turner, M.G. (2000). *The Sexual Victimization of College Women*. National Institute of Justice Publication No. NCJ 182369. Washington: Department of Justice.

Foster, J. (1990). *Villains: Crime and Community in the Inner City*. London: Routledge.

Freilich, J.D., Chermak, S.M., Belli, R., Gruenewald, J., & Parkin, W.S. (2014). Introducing the United States Extremist Crime Database (ECDB). *Terrorism and Political Violence*, 26, 372–384

Gau, J.M. (2009). The empirical status of social learning theory: A meta-analysis. *Justice Quarterly*, 27, 765–802.

Geers, K. (2012). The challenge of cyber attack deterrence. *Computer Law and Security Review*, 26, 298–303.

Gibbs, J.P. (1975). *Crime, Punishment and Deterrence*. New York: Elsevier.

Goldsmith, A., & Brewer, R. (2015). Digital drift and the criminal interaction order. *Theoretical Criminology*, 19, 112–130.

Gordon, S., & Ma, Q. (2003). *Convergence of Virus Writers and Hackers: Factor or Fantasy*. Cupertino, CA: Symantec Security White Paper.

Gottfredson, M.R., & Hirschi, T. (1990). *A General Theory of Crime*. Stanford, CA: Stanford University Press.

Grabosky, P.N. (2001). Virtual criminality: Old wine in new bottles? *Social & Legal Studies*, 10, 243–249.

Grabosky, P.N., & Smith, R. (2001). Telecommunication fraud in the digital age: The convergence of technologies. In D. Wall (Ed.), *Crime and the Internet* (pp. 29–43). New York: Routledge.

Grov, C. (2004). Make me your death slave: Men who have sex with men and use the internet to intentionally spread HIV. *Deviant Behavior*, 25, 329–349.

Guitton, C. (2012). Criminals and cyber attacks: The missing link between attribution and deterrence. *International Journal of Cyber Criminology*, 6, 1030–1043.

Hay, C., Meldrum, R., & Mann, K. (2010). Traditional bullying, cyber bullying, and deviance: A general strain theory approach. *Journal of Contemporary Criminal Justice*, 26, 130–147.

Higgins, G.E. (2005). Can low self-control help with the understanding of the software piracy problem? *Deviant Behavior*, 26, 1–24.

Higgins, G.E. (2007). Digital piracy, self control theory, and rational choice: An examination of the role of value. *International Journal of Cyber Criminology*, 1, 33–55

Higgins, G.E., & Makin, D.A. (2004). Does social learning theory condition the effects of low self-control on college students' software piracy. *Journal of Economic Crime Management*, 2, 1–21.

Higgins, G.E. & Marcum, C.D. (2011). *Digital Piracy: An Integrated Theoretical Approach*. Durham, NC: Carolina Academic Press.

Higgins, G.E., Wilson, A.L., & Fell, B.D. (2005). An application of deterrence theory to software piracy. *Journal of Criminal Justice and Popular Culture*, 12, 166–184.

Hinduja, S. (2003). Trends and patterns among online software pirates. *Ethics and Information Technology*, 5, 49–61

Hinduja, S. (2008). Deindividuation and Internet software piracy. *Cyberpsychology & Behavior*, 11, 391–398.

Hinduja, S., & Ingram, J.R. (2008). Self-control and ethical beliefs on the social learning of intellectual property theft. *Western Criminology Review*, 9, 52–72.

Hinduja, S., & Kooi, B. (2013). Curtailing cyber and information security vulnerabilities through situational crime prevention. *Security Journal*, 26, 383–402.

Hinduja, S., & Patchin, J.W. (2008). Cyberbullying: An exploratory analysis of factors related to offending and victimization. *Deviant Behavior*, 29, 129–156.

Hinduja, S., & Patchin, J.W. (2009). *Bullying Beyond the Schoolyard: Preventing and Responding to Cyberbullying*. New York: Corwin Press.

Holt, T.J. (2007). Subcultural evolution? Examining the influence of on- and off-line experiences on deviant subcultures. *Deviant Behavior*, 28, 171–198.

Holt, T.J. (2009). Lone hacks or group cracks: Examining the social organization of computer hackers. In F. Smalleger and M. Pittaro (Eds.), *Crimes of the Internet* (pp. 336–355). Upper Saddle River, NJ: Pearson Prentice Hall.

Holt, T.J. (2013). Examining the forces shaping cybercrime markets online. *Social Science Computer Review*, 31, 165–177.

Holt, T.J., Blevins, K.R., & Burkert, N. (2010). Considering the pedophile subculture on-line. *Sexual Abuse: Journal of Research and Treatment*, 22, 3–24.

Holt, T.J., Blevins, K.R., & Kuhns, J.B. (2008). Examining the displacement practices of johns with on-line data. *Journal of Criminal Justice*, 36, 522–528.

Holt, T.J., Blevins, K.R., & Kuhns, J.B. (2014). Examining diffusion and arrest avoidance practices among johns. *Crime and Delinquency*, 60, 261–283

Holt, T.J., & Bossler, A.M. (2009). Examining the applicability of lifestyle-routine activities theory for cybercrime victimization. *Deviant Behavior*, 30, 1–25.

Holt, T.J., & Bossler, A.M. (2013). Examining the relationship between routine activities and malware infection indicators. *Journal of Contemporary Criminal Justice*, 29, 420–436.

Holt, T.J., & Bossler, A.M. (2014). An assessment of the current state of cybercrime scholarship. *Deviant Behavior*, 35, 20–40.

Holt, T.J., Bossler, A.M., & May, D.C. (2012). Low self-control, deviant peer associations, and juvenile cyberdeviance. *American Journal of Criminal Justice*, 37, 378–395.

Holt, T.J., Bossler, A.M., & Seigfried-Spellar, K.C. (2015). *Cybercrime and Digital Forensics: An Introduction.* Routledge: New York.

Holt, T.J., Burruss, G.W., & Bossler, A.M. (2010). Social learning and cyber deviance: Examining the importance of a full social learning model in the virtual world. *Journal of Crime and Justice*, 33, 15–30.

Holt, T.J., & Copes, H. (2010). Transferring subcultural knowledge on-line: Practices and beliefs of persistent digital pirates. *Deviant Behavior*, 31, 625–654.

Holt, T.J., & Graves, D.C. (2007). A qualitative analysis of advanced feed fraud schemes. *The International Journal of Cyber Criminology*, 1, 137–154.

Holt, T.J., & Kilger, M. (2008). *Techcrafters and Makecrafters: A Comparison of Two Populations of Hackers.* 2008 WOMBAT Workshop on Information Security Threats Data Collection and Sharing, 67–78.

Holt, T.J., & Kilger, M. (2012). Examining willingness to attack critical infrastructure online and offline. *Crime & Delinquency*, 58, 798–822.

Holt, T.J., Strumsky, D., Smirnova, O., & Kilger, M. (2012). Examining the social networks of malware writers and hackers. *International Journal of Cyber Criminology*, 6, 891–903.

Holt, T.J., & Turner, M.G. (2012). Examining risks and protective factors of on-line identity theft. *Deviant Behavior*, 33, 308–323.

Hutchings, A., & Holt, T.J. (2015). Crime script analysis and online black markets. *British Journal of Criminology*, 55, 596–614.

Ingram, J.R., & Hinduja, S. (2008). Neutralizing music piracy: An empirical examination. *Deviant Behavior*, 29, 334–365.

Jacobs, B.A. (1996). Crack dealers' apprehension avoidance techniques: A case of restrictive deterrence. *Justice Quarterly*, 13, 359–381.

Jacobs, B.A. (2000). *Robbing Drug Dealers: Violence Beyond the Law.* New York: Aldine De Gruyter.

Jaishankar, K. (2008). Space transition theory of cyber crimes. In F. Schmalleger & M. Pittaro (Eds.), *Crimes of the Internet* (pp. 283–301). Upper Saddle River, NJ: Prentice Hill.

Jenkins, P. (2001). *Beyond Tolerance: Child Pornography on the Internet.* New York: New York University Press.

Jordan, T., & Taylor, P. (1998). A sociology of hackers. *The Sociological Review*, 46, 757–780.

Khey, D.N., & Sainato, V.A. (2013). Examining the correlates and spatial distribution of organizational data breaches in the United States. *Security Journal*, 26, 367–382.

Kigerl, A. (2009). CAN SPAM Act: An empirical analysis. *International Journal of Cyber Criminology*, 3, 566–589.

Kigerl, A. (2012). Routine activity theory and the determinants of high cybercrime countries. *Social Science Computer Review*, 30, 470–486.

King, A., & Thomas, J. (2009). You can't cheat an honest man: Making ($$$s and) sense of the Nigerian e-mail scams. In F. Schmalleger & M. Pittaro (Eds.), *Crimes of the Internet* (pp. 206–224). Saddle River, NJ: Prentice Hall.

Kornblum, W. (1997). *Sociology in a Changing World.* Fourth edition. Fort Worth, TX: Harcourt Brace and Company.

Langlais, E. (2008). Detection avoidance and deterrence: Some paradoxical arithmetic. *Journal of Public Economic Theory*, 10, 371–382.

Latour, B. (2005). *Reassembling the Social: An Introduction to Actor-Network Theory.* Oxford: Oxford University Press.

Lee, G., Akers, R.L., & Borg, M.J. (2004). Social learning and structural factors in adolescent substance use. *Western Criminology Review*, 5, 17–34.

Maimon, D., Alper, M., Sobesto, B., & Culkier, M. (2014). Restrictive deterrent effects of a warning banner in an attacked computer system. *Criminology*, 52, 33–59.

Maimon, D., Kamerdze, A., Cukier, M., & Sobesto, B. (2013). Daily trends and origin of computer-focused crimes against a large university computer network. *British Journal of Criminology*, 53, 319–343.

Maimon, D., Wilson, T., Ren, W., & Berenblum, T. (2015). On the relevance of spatial and temporal dimensions in assessing computer susceptibility to system trespassing incidents. *British Journal of Criminology*, 55, 615–634.

Maratea, R. (2011). Screwing the pooch: Legitimizing accounts in a zoophilia on-line community. *Deviant Behavior*, 32, 918–943.

Marcum, C.D. (2010). Examining cyberstalking and bullying: Causes, context, and control. In T.J. Holt (Ed.), *Crime On-line: Correlates, Causes, and Context* (pp. 175–192). Raleigh, NC: Carolina Academic Press.

Marcum, C.D., Higgins, G.E., Ricketts, M.L., & Wolfe, S.E. (2014). Hacking in high school: Cybercrime perpetration by juveniles. *Deviant Behavior*, 35, 581–591.

Matza, D. (1964). *Delinquency and Drift.* Hoboken: John Wiley & Sons.

Matza, D. (1969). *Becoming Deviant.* Englewood Cliffs: Prentice Hall.

Maurer, D.W. (1981). *Language of the Underworld.* Louisville, KY: University of Kentucky Press.

Mazerolle, P., & Piquero, A. (1997). Violent responses to strain: An examination of conditioning influences. *Violence and Victims*, 12, 323–343.

Merton, R.K. (1938). Social structure and anomie. *American Sociological Review*, 3, 672–682.

Meyer, G.R. (1989) *The Social Organization of the Computer Underground.* Masters thesis, Northern Illinois University. csrc.nist.gov/secpubs/hacker.txt.

Miller, W.B. (1958). Lower class culture as a generating milieu of gang delinquency. *Journal of Social Issues*, 14, 5–19.

Mischel, W. (1968). *Personality and Assessment.* New York: John Wiley.

Moon, B., Hwang, H.W., & McCluskey, J.D. (2011). Causes of school bullying: Empirical test of a general theory of crime, differential association theory, and general strain theory. *Crime & Delinquency*, 57, 849–877.

Moon, B., McCluskey, J.D., & McCluskey, C.P. (2010). A general theory of crime and computer crime: An empirical test. *Journal of Criminal Justice*, 38, 767–772.

Moore, R., Guntupalli, N.T., & Lee, T. (2010). Parental regulation and online activities: Examining factors that influence a youth's potential to become a victim of online harassment. *International Journal of Cyber Criminology*, 4, 685–698.

Morris, R.G. (2011). Computer hacking and the techniques of neutralization: An empirical assessment. In T.J. Holt & B.H. Schell (Eds.), *Corporate Hacking and Technology-Driven Crime: Social Dynamics and Implications* (pp. 1–17). Hershey: IGI Global.

Morris, R.G., & Blackburn, A.G. (2009). Cracking the code: An empirical exploration of social learning theory and computer crime. *Journal of Crime and Justice*, 32, 1–32.

Moule, R.K., Pyrooz, D.C., & Decker, S.H. (2014). Internet adoption and online behaviour among American street gangs: Integrating gangs and organizational theory. *British Journal of Criminology*, 54, 1186–1206.

Mustaine, E.E. & Tewksbury, R. (1998). Predicting risk of larceny theft victimization: A routine activity analysis using refined lifestyle measures. *Criminology*, 36, 829–857.

Nagin, D.S. (1998). Criminal deterrence research at the outset of the twenty-first century. In M. Tonry (Ed.), *Crime and Justice: A Review of Research* (pp. 1–42). Chicago: University of Chicago Press.

Newman, G., & Clarke, R. (2003). *Superhighway Robbery: Preventing e-Commerce Crime*. Cullompton: Willan.

Newman, G., & Marongiu, P. (1990). Penological reform and the myth of Beccaria. *Criminology*, 28, 325–346.

Ngo, F.T., & Paternoster, R. (2011). Cybercrime victimization: An examination of individual and situational level factors. *International Journal of Cyber Criminology*, 5, 773–793.

Olsen, P. (2012). *We are Anonymous: Inside the Hacker World of LulzSec, Anonymous, and the Global Cyber Insurgency*. New York: Little, Brown, and Company.

Patchin, J.W., & Hinduja, S. (2011). Traditional and nontraditional bullying among youth: A test of general strain theory. *Youth and Society*, 43, 727–752.

Paternoster, R. (1987). The deterrent effect of the perceived certainty and severity of punishment: A review of the evidence and issues. *Justice Quarterly*, 4, 173–217.

Pogarsky, G. (2002). Identifying "deterrable" offenders: Implications for research on deterrence. *Justice Quarterly*, 19, 431–452.

Pratt, T.C., & Cullen, F.T. (2000). The empirical status of Gottfredson and Hirschi's general theory of crime: A meta-analysis. *Criminology*, 38, 931–964.

Pratt, T.C., Cullen, F.T., Blevins, K.R., Daigle, L.E., & Madensen, T.D. (2006). The empirical status of deterrence theory: A meta-analysis. In F.T. Cullen, J.P. Wright, & K.R. Blevins (Eds.), *Taking Stock: The Status of Criminological Theory* (pp. 367–396). New Brunswick, NJ: Transaction.

Pratt, T.C., Cullen, F.T., Sellers, C.S., Winfree, T., Madensen, T.D., Daigle, L.E., Fearn, N.E., & Gau, J.M. (2009). The empirical status of social learning theory: A meta-analysis. *Justice Quarterly*, 27, 765–802.

Pratt, T.C., Holtfreter, K., & Reisig, M.D. (2010). Routine online activity and Internet fraud targeting: Extending the generality of routine activity theory. *Journal of Research in Crime and Delinquency*, 47, 267–296.

Pratt, T.C., Turnanovic, J.J., Fox, K.A., & Wright, K.A. (2014). Self-control and victimization: A meta-analysis. *Criminology*, 52, 87–116.

Pyrooz, D.C., Decker, S.H., & Moule, R.K. (2015). Criminal and routine activities in online settings: Gangs, offenders, and the Internet. *Justice Quarterly*, 32, 471–499.

Quayle, E., & Taylor, M. (2002). Child pornography and the Internet: Perpetuating a cycle of abuse. *Deviant Behavior*, 23, 331–361.

Quinn, J.F., & Forsyth, C.J. (2005). Describing sexual behavior in the era of the Internet: A typology for empirical research. *Deviant Behavior*, 26, 191–207.

Rege, A. (2013). Industrial control systems and cybercrime. In T.J. Holt (Ed.), *Crime On-line: Causes, Correlates, and Context* (pp. 191–218). Raleigh, NC: Carolina Academic Press.

Reyns, B.W. (2013). Online routines and identity theft victimization: Further expanding routine activity theory beyond direct-contact offenses. *Journal of Research in Crime and Delinquency*, 50, 216–238.

Reyns, B.W., Burek, M.W., Henson, B., & Fisher, B.S. (2013). The unintended consequences of digital technology: Exploring the relationship between sexting and cybervictimization. *Journal of Crime & Justice*, 36, 1–17.

Reyns, B.W., Henson, B., & Fisher, B.S. (2011). Being pursued online: Applying cyberlifestyle-routine activities theory to cyberstalking victimization. *Criminal Justice and Behavior*, 38, 1149–1169.

Rid, T. (2013). *Cyber War Will Not Take Place*. London: Hurst & Company.

Roberts, J.W., & Hunt, S.A. (2012). Social control in a sexually deviant cybercommunity: A capper's code of conduct. *Deviant Behavior*, 33, 757–773.

Rosenmann, A., & Safir, M.P. (2006). Forced online: Pushed factors of Internet sexuality: A preliminary study of paraphilic empowerment. *Journal of Homosexuality*, 51, 71–92.

Sanchirico, C. (2006). Detection avoidance. *New York University Law Review*, 81, 1331–1399.

Schell, B.H., & Dodge, J.L. (2002). *The Hacking of America: Who's Doing it, Why, and How*. Westport, CT: Quorum Books.

Schreck, C.J. (1999). Criminal victimization and self control: An extension and test of a general theory of crime. *Justice Quarterly*, 16, 633–654.

Schreck, C.J., Wright, R.A., & Miller, J.M. (2002). A study of individual and situational antecedents of violent victimization. *Justice Quarterly*, 19, 159–180.

Short, J.F. (1968). *Gang Delinquency and Delinquent Subcultures*. Oxford: Harper & Row.

Silva, S.C., Silva, R.M.P., Pinto, R.C.G., & Salles, R.M. (2013). Botnets: A survey. *Computer Networks: The International Journal of Computer and Telecommunications Networking*, 57, 378–403.

Skinner, W.F., & Fream, A.M. (1997). A social learning theory analysis of computer crime among college students. *Journal of Research in Crime and Delinquency*, 34, 495–518.

Spano, R. & Nagy, S. (2005). Social guardianship and social isolation: An application and extension of lifestyle/routine activities theory to rural adolescents. *Rural Sociology*, 70, 414–437.

Spelman, W., & Eck, J.E. (1989). The police and the delivery of local government services: A problem-oriented approach. *Police Practice in the '90s: Key Management Issues*.

Steinmetz, K.F. (2015). Craft(y)ness: An ethnographic study of hacking. *British Journal of Criminology*, 55, 125–145.

Steinmetz, K.F., & Tunnell, K.D. (2013). Under the pixelated Jolly Roger: A study of on-line pirates. *Deviant Behavior*, 34, 53–67.

Stewart, E.A., Elifson, K.W., & Sterk, C.E. (2004). Integrating the general theory of crime into an explanation of violent victimization among female offenders. *Justice Quarterly*, 21, 159–181.

Stubbs-Richardson, M., & May, D.C. (2014). Predictors of adolescent online sexual behaviors. In E.C. Dretsch & R. Moore (Eds.), *Sexual Deviance Online: Research and Readings* (pp. 81–104). Raleigh NC: Carolina Academic Press.

Suler, J. (2004). The online disinhibition effect . *CyberPsychology & Behavior*, 7, 321–326.

Sutherland, E. (1947). *Principles of Criminology*. Fourth edition. Philadelphia: Lippincott.

Symantec Corporation (2014). *Symantec Internet Security Threat Report, Volume 18*. www.symantec.com/threatreport/.

Szor, P. (2005). *The Art of Computer Virus Research and Defense*. Addison-Wesley.

Taylor, P. (1999). *Hackers: Crime in the Digital Sublime*. London: Routledge.

Tewksbury, R. (2006). Click here for HIV: An analysis of Internet-based bug chasers and bug givers. *Deviant Behavior*, 27, 379–395.

Tittle, C.R. (1969). Crime rates and legal sanctions. *Social Problems*, 16, 409–423.

Van der Wagen, W., & Pieters, W. (2015). From cybercrime to cyborg: Botnets as hybrid criminal actor-networks. *British Journal of Criminology*, 55, 578–595.

Van Wilsem, J. (2011). Worlds tied together? Online and non-domestic routine activities and their impact on digital and traditional threat victimization. *European Journal of Criminology*, 8, 115–127.

Van Wilsem, J. (2013a). Hacking and harassment—do they have something in common? Comparing risk factors for online victimization. *Journal of Contemporary Criminal Justice*, 29, 437–453.

Van Wilsem, J. (2013b). "Bought it, but never got it": Assessing risk factors for online consumer fraud victimization. *European Sociology Review*, 29, 168–178.

Wall, D.S. (1998). Catching cybercriminals: Policing the Internet. *International Review of Law, Computers, & Technology*, 12, 201–218.

Wall, D. (2004). Digital realism and the governance of spam as cybercrime. *European Journal on Criminal Policy and Research*, 10, 309–335.

Whitty, M.T. (2013). Anatomy of the online dating romance scam. *Security Journal*, 28, 443–455.

Wolfe, S.E., Higgins, G.E., & Marcum, C.D. (2008). Deterrence and digital piracy: A preliminary examination of the role of viruses. *Social Science Computer Review*, 26, 317–333.

Wolfgang, M.E., & Ferracuti, F. (1967). *The Subculture of Violence: Toward an Integrated Theory in Criminology*. Tavistock Publications.

Wright, M.F., & Li, Y. (2013). The association between cyber victimization and subsequent cyber aggression: The moderating effect of peer rejection. *Journal of Youth and Adolescence*, 42, 662–674.

Wright, R., & Decker, S.G. (1994). *Burglars on the Job: Street Life and Residential Break-ins*. Boston, MA: Northeastern University Press.

Wright, R., & Decker, S. (1997). *Armed Robbers in Action*. Boston, MA: Northeastern University Press.

Yar, M. (2005). The novelty of "cybercrime": An assessment in light of routine activity theory. *European Journal of Criminology*, 2, 407–427.

Ybarra, M.L., Mitchell, K.J., Finkelhor, D., & Wolak, J. (2007). Internet prevention messages: Targeting the right online behaviors. *Archives of Pediatrics and Adolescent Medicine*, 161, 138–145.

Yu, J., & Liska, A. (1993). The certainty of punishment: A reference group effect and its functional form. *Criminology*, 31, 447–464.

Zhang, L., Welte, J.W., & Wiecxorek, W.F. (2001). Deviant lifestyle and crime victimization. *Journal of Criminal Justice*, 29, 133–143.

4 Issues in domestic and transnational cybercrime investigation

Chapter goals

- Examine the role of local law enforcement as first responders and their current capabilities
- Explore the need for specialized law enforcement units and trained officers to investigate cybercrime
- Assess the levels and causes of burnout and fatigue in digital forensic examiners
- Explore ways to improve inter-agency cooperation in investigating and preventing cybercrimes
- Discuss the fundamental obstacles that hinder transnational criminal investigations
- Compare and contrast cybercrime with cyberwar and understand the governmental response implications
- Provide qualitative and quantitative research ideas to further our knowledge of how we police cybercrime

Though the literature on cybercrime victimization and offending has increased (see Chapter 3), it may surprise some to learn that scholarly research on policing cybercrime has languished. There have been generally few studies of either police management or line officers regarding their views on cybercrime, and those that have been conducted are relatively limited in their generalizability. The bulk of the literature consists primarily of discussions on either the role of law enforcement in responding to cyber offenses or their inability to respond (e.g. Brenner, 2008; Goodman, 1997; Wall, 2001; Wall & Williams, 2013). As such, police perceptions of cybercrime, their experiences, and their insights on how best to respond may be some of the least studied but most essentially needed areas of scholarship.

One of the most well-referenced works in this area is by David Wall (2001), who explains the complex nature of cybercrime investigations in the real world. The framework he provides is valuable to understand the complexities of cybercrime for law enforcement and the gaps currently present in this literature. Wall (2001) argues that there are multiple actors and entities, legal and extralegal, who play a role in policing the Internet. The largest population of actors engaged in the identification of illegal activity online is **Internet users**. Due to the size of the World Wide Web and the various applications individuals use to communicate and share materials, it is virtually impossible for law enforcement to observe when most wrongdoing takes place online (Wall, 2001). As a result, the individuals actively engaged in online communities have the ability to observe and communicate when cybercrimes take place. They may not actively share this information with formal law enforcement agencies, however, which limits their efficacy in combating cybercrime.

Beyond end users, **Internet service providers**, or ISPs, play a critical role in dealing with cybercrime. Though they are primarily owned and operated as for-profit businesses, some ISPs may also be universities, public libraries, and other entities that may not be traditional businesses. ISPs play a twofold role in the identification and management of cybercrimes: (1) they host and provide access to online content and have a formal legal obligation to remove harmful material; and (2) they provide Internet connectivity for individuals and require that users comply with all applicable local and federal laws. ISPs have become a conduit for the identification of various forms of cybercrime, such as digital piracy, as they may be able to identify when individual users engage in file sharing or violate existing user agreements (e.g. Nhan, 2013).

Similar to ISPs, **corporate security personnel** are tasked with the protection and management of the assets of their organization, including sensitive information. Corporate security officers play a unique position as gatekeepers to law enforcement agencies in the event that either their organization is compromised or internal resources are used in the course of a cybercrime. For instance, security units within a company may have to cooperate with law enforcement agencies in order to provide access to servers or employee systems to allow for the seizure of digital evidence. Corporate security officers may be responsible for determining when their organization must make contact with law enforcement. Though laws are changing with respect to compliance in reporting data breaches and cybercrime incidents, it is still commonly argued that corporations tend to underreport cyber-attacks for fear of embarrassment or financial harm (e.g. Brenner, 2008; Wall, 2007).

Given that corporations and industry own much of the technological infrastructure used to engage in both commerce and cyber-attacks, there is no immediate way to guarantee compliance or cooperation between these entities, government, and law enforcement. A number of **non-governmental organizations (NGOs)** have emerged as a key link to promote synergy between various groups and government agencies (Wall, 2007). As NGOs have no formal responsibility to enforce laws, they instead serve as managerial and regulatory groups with ties to law enforcement agencies. A key example of NGOs involved in cybercrime investigation are **Computer Emergency Response Teams (CERTs)**, or Computer Incident Response Teams (CIRTs), which have an operational remit to provide coordinated response and investigative capabilities for incidents of hacking and malware attacks (Andress &

Winterfeld, 2013). CERTs are present in most major industrialized nations and publish information on vulnerabilities, known threats to networked systems, and perform analyses of malware and attack tools (e.g. FIRST, 2014). These organizations do not, however, specifically connect to law enforcement agencies and are a resource for coordinated responses to threats rather than legal action.

Wall (2001) also separates NGOs from **government-controlled organizations** that serve as regulatory bodies, but do not have the power to arrest or criminally sanction individual actors. In the US, a key example of such an entity is the Department of Energy (DOE), which regulates the operation and protection of energy programs and production in both public and private utilities. Since much of the US power infrastructure depends on control systems that can be connected through Internet connectivity, the threats posed by cyber-attacks have increased substantially. The DOE now operates the Office of the Chief Information Officer to provide information on key cyber-threats, protocols for computer security programs, and best practice guides to secure systems from external threats. There is, however, no formal police or regulatory entity within the DOE to either sanction corporations that do not conform to industry guidelines or arrest cybercriminals who harm energy systems (Andress & Winterfeld, 2013).

The breadth of groups involved in the informal policing of cyberspace demonstrates that traditional law enforcement agencies that are funded by governmental resources and mandated to enforce local laws are a small part of the response to cybercrime. The complex network of actors who must be incorporated into cybercrime investigations may account for the limited response of some law enforcement agencies to cybercrime calls for service. In fact, the literature with respect to policing cybercrime is limited relative to that of offending and victimization. As a result, this chapter will examine the literature regarding policing at various levels across the US. We will also identify key research questions that need to be addressed moving forward in order to improve our knowledge of the law enforcement response to cybercrimes generally.

Local law enforcement as first responders

Though there is generally little research on police responses to cybercrime, many scholars have clearly indicated that local law enforcement agencies should be prepared to respond to cybercrime calls for service. Not only are they the most common resource that a victim would recognize to contact in the event of an emergency, but local law enforcement agencies have substantive success in real world criminal investigations that should transfer to cybercrimes (Brenner, 2008; Goodman, 1997; Hinduja, 2007; McQuade, 2006; Stambaugh et al., 2001; Wall, 2007). Stambaugh and colleagues (2001) examined the need to prepare local law enforcement to respond to cybercrimes and highlighted ten key deficiencies that would need to be enhanced in order to improve their capability. To that end, the National Institute of Justice has developed various training manuals and resources oriented toward local officers to help them properly respond to cybercrime scenes and appropriately handle digital evidence as **first responders** (NIJ, 2008; Stambaugh et al., 2001).

There is, however, limited evidence of the capacities or efficacy of local agencies in responding to cybercrime, given the lack of statistical data on cybercrime-related calls for service or incidents cleared by arrest (see Chapter 2). One of the few attempts to estimate the capacities of local law enforcement to respond to cybercrime in the US was recently conducted by Holt, Burruss, and Bossler (2015). The authors used Law Enforcement Management and Administrative Statistics (LEMAS) survey data from 2003 and 2007 which included two questions related to an agency's role in cybercrime investigations. As of 2003, approximately 62 percent of municipal and county police departments, 56 percent of sheriffs' offices, and 53 percent of state agencies had primary responsibilities to investigate cybercrime. The size of the agency appeared to be a key factor in its role with respect to cybercrime, as larger agencies and those that served a larger population were more likely to have a primary investigative responsibility.

The survey also asked agencies to indicate the range of investigative resources they have available to deal with cybercrimes. This information helped to clarify the extent to which agencies technically dealt with cybercrime. Their analyses found that in 2003 there was a mix of resources available to deal with cybercrime, including specialized units (26 percent), dedicated personnel (29 percent), or simply having officers respond when called without a specialized unit or personnel (34 percent). This mix changed by 2007, with an increase in specialized units (37 percent) and dedicated personnel (31 percent). The number of agencies with no uniquely tasked personnel decreased to 23 percent, suggesting there is a transformation in the ways that local law enforcement agencies deal with cybercrime (Holt et al., 2015).

Though specialization appears to be the trend in law enforcement (see next section), it is pertinent to consider how agencies are dealing with cybercrime regardless of the presence of designated roles. Few studies have captured information on the types of cases handled by state and local law enforcement (Hinduja, 2004; Holt, Bossler, & Fitzgerald, 2010). Hinduja's (2004) analyses of Michigan law enforcement agencies found that the most prevalent crimes investigated were harassment/stalking (39.5 percent), child pornography (31.9 percent), forgery (19.2 percent), identity theft (17.4 percent) and e-commerce fraud (16.3 percent). It is important to note two issues with this study: (1) agencies could choose more than one "most prevalent" crime on the survey; and (2) the study technically used the term computer crime, though the offenses are comparable to what are currently referred to as cybercrimes.

A recent study by Holt, Bossler, and Fitzgerald (2010) developed a sample of 437 state and local law enforcement agents across the country and asked the respondents whether their agency investigated certain forms of crime. They found that the cybercrime the highest percentage of agencies had investigated was identity theft (79.2 percent), followed by fraud (71.9 percent), harassment (71.8 percent), child pornography (61.7 percent), solicitation of minors (51.7 percent), sex crimes (42 percent), and hacking (32 percent). Thus, a majority of these agencies had dealt with identity theft, fraud, and harassment, but less than a third had investigated computer intrusion cases. Additionally, 18.7 percent of the responding agencies had no cases that involved digital evidence, and 33.5 percent had not made an arrest based on digital evidence (Holt et al., 2010).

If local agencies are increasing their capability to respond to cybercrime, there is a need to understand what impact this is having on officers' perceptions of these offenses and their relevance compared with physical crimes. The majority of officers are likely to respond to calls for service involving traditional offenses, such as burglary, robberies, or assaults, though they may have limited familiarity with the unique aspects of cybercrime cases (e.g. Hinduja, 2007). The practices of a first responder are pivotal to the likelihood that a case is cleared by arrest (Hinduja, 2007), specifically with respect to the officer's ability to secure evidence, interview witnesses, and develop leads in the case (Bossler & Holt, 2012; Hinduja, 2007; NIJ, 2008; Stambaugh et al., 2001).

To that end, historical research indicates that training for front-line officers is inconsistent. For instance, a national sample of state and local police agencies developed in 1999 found that only 37 percent of agencies provided training for officers on digital evidence handling and collection (Stambaugh et al., 2001). Similarly, Holt and associates (2010) found that approximately 80 percent of agencies in their sample (n = 437) had less than 20 percent of their officers trained to handle digital evidence. It is unclear if those officers with training are relatively young and recent graduates from police academies. In fact, there is no research to date examining the extent to which cybercrime training has been integrated into police academy curricula across the US. Thus, it is unclear how officers are gaining exposure to cybercrime cases or appropriate resources for knowledge development.

The generally limited basis of knowledge with respect to police responses to cybercrime is exacerbated by the nature of scholarship in this space. An extremely limited body of research has developed over the last two decades examining how local police perceive various forms of cybercrime. The majority of these studies utilize samples of either police administrators or agency representatives which can give a sense of the managerial view of cybercrimes (Hinduja, 2004; Holt et al., 2010; Marcum, Higgins, Freiburger, & Ricketts, 2010; Stambaugh et al., 2001). The findings generally suggest local law enforcement agencies do not prioritize cybercrimes, with the exception of child exploitation (Hinduja, 2004; Stambaugh et al., 2001).

A small and recent set of research has sampled line officers within local law enforcement agencies to assess first responders' experiences with and perceptions of cybercrimes (Bossler & Holt, 2012; Holt & Bossler, 2012). A few studies have examined officers' perceptions of cybercrime, including its severity and frequency relative to traditional offenses (Holt et al., 2010; Holt & Bossler, 2012, Senjo, 2004). Senjo (2004) used a sample of Western police officers to conduct one of the first studies in this area. He asked officers to rank the severity of five computer crimes: (1) pedophilia, (2) credit card fraud, (3) electronic theft, (4) copyright infringement, and (5) espionage. Pedophilia was ranked as the most serious, followed by credit card fraud, computer espionage, electronic theft, and finally copyright infringement. This study, however, neither operationalized severity for respondents nor gave any frame of reference for their perceptions relative to traditional offenses.

Recently, Holt and Bossler (2012) developed a sample of officers from the Charlotte-Mecklenburg Police Department in Charlotte, North Carolina, and the Savannah-Chatham Metropolitan Police Department in Savannah, Georgia. They expanded on Senjo's (2004) work by asking respondents to rate the severity of 12 forms of crime: five traditional offenses (armed robbery, burglary, selling cocaine, shoplifting, and vandalism), and seven computer crimes (copyright infringement such as software and media piracy; credit card fraud; electronic theft of money from accounts; harassment over the Internet; identity theft; pedophilia on the Internet; viruses and malicious software infection). They also defined severity for the respondents based on the "financial and emotional harm to victims, and their threat to life, liberty, and personal property" (Holt & Bossler, 2012: 405).

The officers' responses fell into three specific categories, including both cyber and real-world crimes: (1) serious offenses: armed robbery, pedophilia, burglary, electronic theft, identity theft, selling cocaine, and credit card fraud; (2) moderately serious offenses: viruses and malicious software infection, and harassment over the Internet; and (3) less serious offenses: vandalism, copyright infringement, and shoplifting. Armed robbery was ranked as the most severe offense due most likely to the emotional and economic impact on victims, as well as its potential role in homicides. Pedophilia was viewed as the most serious form of cybercrime due to the violent and emotional harm caused to victims (see also Hinduja, 2004; Senjo, 2004; Stambaugh et al., 2001).

Property crimes were also grouped closely (burglary, identity theft, electronic theft of funds, and credit card fraud) due to the economic impact these crimes cause regardless of whether they occur on or off-line. The least serious offenses also shared some common elements, as they are all property crimes with a smaller impact on individual victims. Shoplifting, vandalism, and piracy all have a greater impact on businesses than persons, which reflects the nature of seriousness provided by the researchers (Holt & Bossler, 2012).

An extremely limited body of research has also examined the perceptions of specialized officers' perceptions of cybercrime. Two studies have utilized samples of respondents who have received specialized training from recognized training resources, including the Federal Law Enforcement Training Center (FLETC) (Holt et al., 2010) and the National White Collar Crime Center (NWC3) (Holt et al., 2015). Though there were minor differences in the types of crimes included in each survey, both allowed respondents to rank order a set of cyber and physical crimes on the basis of their perceived seriousness. There was relative parity between the samples, as both ranked child sex crimes as the most serious crimes overall (Holt et al., 2010; Holt et al., 2015), supporting previous research with samples of line officers (Holt & Bossler, 2012; Stambaugh et al., 2001).

Both sets also ranked terrorist attacks as the next most serious offense, though respondents in the sample of FLETC officers were presented with attacks against both physical targets (physical terrorism) and electronic targets (cyberterrorism) (Holt et al., 2010). They ranked physical attacks as the second most serious option, with cyberterrorism as the third. The sample of officers trained by the NWC3 was only presented with cyberterrorism as an option (Holt et al., 2015). Regardless, this is a strong indication of the increased prominence placed on terrorism incidents by local law enforcement agencies.

Additionally, both sets of respondents indicated that selling hard drugs was the next most serious criminal offense. This is a higher ranking than observed in prior research with patrol officers (Holt & Bossler, 2012). Software and media piracy were viewed as some of the least serious offenses overall, as was stealing something worth less than US$5 (see also Holt & Bossler, 2012; Holt et al., 2010).

Though survey research has proven valuable in identifying officers' perceptions of the seriousness of these offenses, there has been very little research examining the frequency in which officers respond to cybercrime calls for service. One of the only studies to date using a sample of line officers found that 62 percent of officers in two cities (Charlotte, NC, and Savannah, GA) had no experience with cybercrime calls for service (Bossler & Holt, 2012). Of those officers who have worked cybercrime cases, 44 percent were located in Savannah while only 33 percent were in Charlotte. This difference likely stems from the fact that Charlotte has a dedicated cybercrime unit which may often be directly tasked with these cases rather than randomly assigning them to patrol officers.

Officers in this study were also asked whether they agreed that cybercrime cases should be primarily investigated by local law enforcement. Only 18 percent of the respondents agreed with this sentiment, indicating there may be little interest in handling cybercrime cases among line officers (Bossler & Holt, 2012). The majority of respondents (73 percent) agreed that specialized units should be the primary responder to cybercrime incidents. As a result, local officers may have generally little concern for cybercrimes that occur in the populations that they serve. At the same time, officers who had experience with a cybercrime call were less likely to agree that a specialized unit should directly respond. Thus, officers may change their perceptions about cybercrime once they have handled a case.

If the results of this study are at all indicative of attitudes of local officers in other parts of the US, there may be substantial difficulties winning the hearts and minds of police to respond to cybercrimes. In fact, Bossler and Holt (2012) asked Savannah and Charlotte police officers their opinion on strategies to improve the response to cybercrime. Officers were presented with 15 survey items based on recommendations from the seminal Stambaugh et al. (2001) report, as well as recent recommendations from cybercrime scholars. Each officer was asked to rate each strategy from not important (1) to very important (5). The results demonstrated that officers felt the most important strategy was that Internet users needed to be more careful while online (Bossler & Holt, 2012). The following list includes all responses in descending rank order by mean score:

1   Internet users being more careful on the Internet (4.18);
2   more severe penalties for cybercriminals (4.14);
3   increased prosecutions of cybercriminals (4.08);
4   clearer legislation against cybercrimes to increase the success of prosecution and investigation (4.04);
5   special forensic tools and technologies (4.01);
6   increased funding for training law enforcement agencies (4.00);
7   creating and improving relationships with federal and state cybercrime task forces (3.99);
8   working with service providers (e.g. AOL) to "police" the Internet (3.97);
9   better education for the public concerning cybercrime (3.96);
10 cooperation with the business community (high-tech industries) to improve crime reporting and investigation (3.89);
11 structured local cybercrime units (3.80);
12 better methods for detecting cybercrime (3.80);
13 more computer training for line officers (3.73);
14 increased management to develop county- and regional-level cybercrime task forces (3.72); and
15 Working with citizens online to "police" the Internet (3.56).

Interestingly, the top four items did not immediately incorporate officers but rather affected citizens, the courts, and legislation. The concepts that had the greatest direct impact on local officers, particularly staffing local cybercrime units (11), training line officers (13), and working with citizens (15) were relatively low priority by comparison with other strategies. Since the scores were all between somewhat important and important (3–5), the findings demonstrated that officers did not dismiss any idea outright. Instead, it may be a general reflection of their lack of interest in direct engagement with cybercrime cases generally (e.g. Goodman, 1997).

These findings mirror a similar study of law enforcement representatives regarding Internet fraud (Burns et al., 2004). Almost all respondents (93 percent) felt that Internet laws, including those related to online fraud, should be handled by federal law enforcement. Some 70 percent of respondents also believed that state law enforcement agencies should have a role in investigating these crimes, though only 52 percent thought that local agencies should have a hand in these cases (Burns et al., 2004). At the same time, only 38 percent of respondents believed that federal agencies were actually enforcing these laws compared with 47 percent for local law enforcement. These findings generally demonstrate that there is a perception among first responders in the US that either local agencies are not prepared to handle cybercrime incidents or that there are more appropriate entities that should respond.

Specialization of law enforcement

Recognizing that local patrol officers may neither have experience with cybercrime cases nor have opinions about the appropriate agency to respond to them is valuable to our understanding of the growth of specialized units and officers dealing with cybercrime at the state and local levels. Cybercrimes can be extremely complex and require evidence collection techniques beyond what is available for traditional offenses. It is therefore not surprising that many police departments feel such cases are better suited for specialized units or **task forces**. These terms refer to distinct organizational forms, though they may have a common focus on a given form of crime. A special unit may serve a specific role in dealing with either single forms of crime or unique populations (e.g. juveniles). A task force, however, can incorporate officers from various agencies at the local, state, and/or federal levels to investigate crimes that cut across jurisdictional boundaries.

Cybercrimes are a key example of such offenses, as an offender may easily reside in a county or state far from their victim. Although local agencies do not typically investigate hacking cases (e.g. Hinduja, 2004; Holt et al., 2010), the jurisdictional issues regarding child exploitation cases may be less severe. Substantial resources have been invested in a unique task force strategy operating primarily at the local level. The creation of **Internet Crimes Against Children (ICAC) task forces** provide a mechanism for coordination of resources among local law enforcement, prosecutors, and federal agencies (ICAC, 2014).

The program began in 1998 under mandate from the Office of Juvenile Justice and Delinquency Prevention (OJJDP) to improve the resources available at all levels of law enforcement, including investigative resources, forensic and technological assistance, and prosecutorial guidance, to combat youth victimization. In fact, there is now a regular schedule of digital forensic and investigative training for ICAC investigators offered across the country, which are supported by various federal agencies (ICAC, 2014). The ICAC program currently comprises 61 task forces, operating in every state in the nation. Some states with larger populations and geography have multiple ICACs, such as Florida, California, and Texas (ICAC, 2014).

A positive movement across the US has been the apparent increase in the amount of local police department resources devoted to cybercrime investigations, especially those involving the exploitation of children (e.g. Marcum et al., 2010; Wolak, Finkelhor, & Mitchell, 2012). Marcum et al. (2010) found that of the 168 departments that responded to their national survey of law enforcement agencies, 30 percent had a dedicated task force or unit devoted to cybercrime and 41 percent provided department training for cybercrime investigation in 2007–08.

These extra resources, particularly the spread and presence of ICACs, have increased the number of arrests for child exploitation crimes across the country. For example, Marcum et al. (2010) found that having a task force increased the likelihood of investigating child pornography and making an arrest. Training, however, was only significantly related to increased child pornography arrests for one year of their study. Furthermore, a survey using a nationally representative sample of over 2,500 local and federal law enforcement agencies suggests that arrests for technology-facilitated child exploitation crimes have increased substantially since 2000 (Wolak et al., 2012). The number of arrests for child-related crimes increased threefold since 2000, from 2,577 arrests for child sexual exploitation crimes in 2000, to 8,144 in 2009 (Wolak et al., 2012). Similar evidence has been found within surveys of local law enforcement agencies, regardless of their relationship to an ICAC, indicating most cybercrime investigations at the local level focus on sexual offenses rather than financial or property-related crimes (Burns et al., 2004; Hinduja, 2004; Holt et al., 2010; Senjo, 2004).

Though ICACs appear to expand investigation of child exploitation crimes, few studies have considered how local and state agencies have responded to other forms of cybercrimes. Task forces are a logical solution to other forms of cybercrime as well, as they promote resource sharing and improve jurisdictional coordination for investigation. In fact, in 2001 the National Institute of Justice identified the formation of task forces as a critical priority to improve the capability of state and local cybercrime investigators (Stambaugh et al., 2001). Currently, it is unclear whether most local law enforcement agencies use these structures or simply designate officers to investigate these crimes with or without participation in informal working groups with agencies at different levels.

Improving the investigative capabilities of detectives and officers in local police agencies does not come cheaply. The material costs to establish a lab are prohibitive for most local agencies which must operate within limited budgets while also investigating traditional offenses that constitute the bulk of offenses made known to them (Britz, 2009, Stambaugh et al., 2001). Unique equipment is needed to capture bit for bit images of a hard drive or memory stick so that examiners can search the computer as it existed at the time of seizure (Britz, 2009, Ferraro & Casey, 2005; Hagy, 2007). Specialized software programs, such as EnCase or the ForensicToolKit (FTK), are also required in order to examine the image to determine the location and contents of files, Internet search histories, and other materials (Britz, 2009). A one-year site license and maintenance fee for EnCase and FTK are US$3,600 and $5,200, respectively (Mizota, 2013). This includes neither the costs for the computer equipment needed to install this software for use in analysis, nor all the peripheral equipment needed to seize forensic images of hard drives and mobile phones (Ferraro & Casey, 2005; Jones & Valli, 2011).

In addition, the costs for training and staffing a cybercrime or digital forensic unit may also exceed the budgetary capacity of local agencies (Ferraro & Casey, 2005; Jones & Valli, 2011; Senjo, 2004). Many of the officers assigned to investigate various cybercrimes go through extensive training in digital forensic evidence handling and analysis procedures which requires travel and financial investment on the part of their agency. For instance, a one-year training program for EnCase software costs $5,500 per person. Additional costs exist for any certifications that the officer or agency may want to indicate the user's mastery of the program (Guidance Software, 2014). These courses must be taken at an EnCase facility; at the time of writing, there were only four sites across the US. This increases the costs for training as the agency needs to pay for travel costs as well, including airplane tickets, hotel, ground transportation, and per diems.

Beyond the costs associated with both construction and staffing, there is the challenge in identifying officers who are either capable or interested in investigating cybercrime cases. Although officers may occasionally be exposed to cybercrime calls for service while on patrol, they generally will not have the appropriate skills, direct experience, or training to respond adequately. Thus, agencies should carefully identify which officers and detectives could serve in specialized roles to respond to and investigate various forms of cybercrime in order to ensure that any investment in training and staffing in specialized response roles is appropriately spent.

Few criminological studies have examined which officers have received digital evidence handling training and are interested in either general computer training or specialized cybercrime training (Holt & Bossler, 2012; Holt et al., 2015). Analyses of survey data collected from law enforcement officers who completed a digital forensics course from the NW3C indicated that younger, white officers who had more years of experience of handling digital evidence within larger police departments received more weeks of training than other officers (Holt et al., 2015).

Using data collected from patrol officers in the cities of Savannah, Georgia and Charlotte, North Carolina, Holt and colleagues found that there is relatively strong interest in receiving additional training, but only moderate interest in conducting cybercrime investigations. Some 62 percent of the officers were interested in receiving additional general computer training (Holt et al., 2015) and 57.7 percent were interested in cybercrime investigation training (Holt & Bossler, 2012); only 40 percent of the officers, however, expressed interest in conducting cybercrime investigations.

Officers who were interested in receiving general computer training tended to be older, believed that the Internet was not negatively impacting law enforcement, thought too many cybercrimes went unreported to the police, supported cybercrime investigations, and felt that cybercrime was going to dramatically change policing (Holt et al., 2015). Their current computer skill level was not related to their interest in additional computer training. Older officers with greater computer proficiency and no prior training expressed more interest in receiving cybercrime investigative training. They also found that officers who supported cybercrime investigations and thought that cybercrime was altering the role of policing were more likely to desire training and to participate in investigations (Holt & Bossler, 2012). Having previous exposure to cybercrime-related calls was not statistically related to an expressed interest in either training or investigation (Holt & Bossler, 2012).

Although the findings based on the Savannah/Charlotte data set (Holt & Bossler, 2012) may have limited generalizability beyond the geographic region, they demonstrate an important point regarding cybercrime training. Within policing agencies, individuals are typically placed into specialized roles on the basis of either seniority or perceived experience in the field. Though rank may be a pertinent factor in shaping officers' exposure to various crime types, it does not appear to be the most pertinent factor that should drive recruitment or staffing decisions for cybercrime training and investigations.

Instead, the abilities of the officer as well as his or her attitudes toward cybercrime investigations and how the Internet is altering policing should steer officer placement into cybercrime investigations as the technological complexities and laborious, mundane work posed by some cases may be extremely unattractive to officers. Finally, it should be noted that the substantial investment that agencies make in specialized cybercrime investigators may lead those officers with appropriate qualifications to pursue higher paying careers in the private sector (see Furnell, 2002; National Academy of Sciences, 2009). It is unknown how frequently staff turnover in specialized cybercrime roles occurs, though anecdotal evidence suggests this may have an impact on agency capacities.

The lack of research on both staffing decisions and officer interest in training must be addressed in order to improve our knowledge of policing cybercrime. Understanding what individual and structural factors attract officers to cybercrime investigative training may prove valuable to develop recruitment and retention strategies. Similarly, recognizing the conditions that decrease officer interest in cybercrime training is essential to improve the ways that agencies communicate the importance of cybercrime cases to rank and file officers.

Burnout and fatigue in digital forensics

The increasing move toward specialized units and personnel to investigate cybercrime, particularly those involving child victims, has led some researchers to consider how such roles impact the officers working in these positions (see Chapter 5; also Holt et al., 2015). Given that local law enforcement task forces and investigative units may handle a large number of child pornography and sexual exploitation cases, it is vital that police administrators, policymakers, and researchers consider how repeated exposure to this content may affect investigators. Investigators spend hours reviewing images, video, and audio files in an attempt to identify potential victims or evidence within this material (Perez et al., 2010). The psychological harm that may arise as a result of constant exposure to graphic, violent, or unnerving material of this sort cannot be understated. In fact, some law enforcement agencies mandate that officers attend counseling sessions after a set number of hours of exposure to child pornographic content or time on the job (Perez et al., 2010).

Consistent exposure to child pornography and emotionally trying content may lead officers to feel personal **stress, secondary trauma**, or emotional fatigue as a result of their job (Holt et al., 2015). Such experiences may substantially reduce workplace productivity, increase negative attitudes toward one's job (Holt & Blevins, 2012; Holt et al., 2012; Holt et al., 2015), and cause some to engage in negative coping behaviors such as drinking or smoking (Holt & Blevins, 2012; Holt et al., 2015).

A number of studies emerged over the last decade to examine these issues. Some of these studies provide qualitative assessments of officers' and examiners' experiences and reactions (e.g. Burns, Morley, Bradshaw, & Domene, 2008; Krause, 2009), while other researchers have developed samples of active examiners in the field to quantitatively assess the correlates of higher levels of stress (Holt & Blevins, 2012; Holt et al., 2012; Holt et al., 2015; Perez et al., 2010). Regardless of the methodology employed by the researchers, these studies demonstrate that between 25 and 50 percent of forensic investigators experience psychological harm as a result of dealing with child-related cases (Burns et al., 2008; Holt et al., 2015; Perez et al., 2010). A small proportion also report elevated levels of stress while on the job and diminished levels of satisfaction with their working experiences (Holt & Blevins, 2012; Holt et al., 2012; Holt et al., 2015).

The general findings of these studies indicate that there are some consistent factors associated with examiners who report higher levels of stress or psychological harm. In fact, some of these correlates are the same as those reported by line officers and other criminal justice system employees. One of the most prominent and consistently identified factors associated with stress and trauma is the way that an investigator perceives his or her job in terms of danger. Although digital forensics may not expose examiners to physical dangers, such as being shot at while on duty, the brutal pictures that investigators are exposed to create emotional and psychological damage (Burns et al., 2008; Krause, 2009; Perez et al., 2010; Stevenson, 2007). As a consequence, the digital forensics lab may create a "dangerous environment" in which their mental, emotional, and physical health is constantly being attacked (e.g. Burns et al., 2008; Perez et al., 2010).

Logically, digital investigators who felt their jobs were more dangerous were more likely to report higher levels of stress (Holt et al., 2012; Holt et al., 2015). This exposure to child pornography and other violent images increases individuals' levels of **burnout** and emotional fatigue in the course of their investigations (Holt et al., 2012; Holt et al., 2015). Therefore, an investigator's perception of the dangers of the job, along with the amount of child pornography images he or she is exposed to, increases his or her work stress level and decreases job satisfaction.

In addition, examiners who receive more support from their agency administrators have increased job satisfaction and reduced stress (Holt & Blevins, 2012; Holt et al., 2012; Holt et al., 2015; Senjo, 2004, Stambaugh et al., 2001). When managers fail to recognize the value of digital forensic investigation or the challenges of cybercrime cases, this can lead to a difficult working environment in which the investigators' hard work is under-appreciated and their stress underestimated. Investigators may therefore feel limited in their duties and possibly be encouraged to investigate certain offenses, such as child pornography cases, to the detriment of other digital evidence cases (Burns et al., 2008; Krause, 2009; Perez et al., 2010; Stevenson, 2007).

Third, although the evidence is mixed, examiners with more years of experience appear to report more stress and less satisfaction with their jobs. Two studies (Holt & Blevins, 2012; Holt et al., 2015) found that examiners who have worked longer in law enforcement reported greater work stress. Holt et al. (2012), however, found no relationship between examiner experience and their stress and satisfaction levels. Although this mixed evidence may be the result of sampling, the general literature on work experience in criminal justice agencies provides some support for the positive relationship between work experience and stress (Cullen et al., 1985; Cullen et al., 1989; Dowler, 2005; He et al., 2002). For digital forensic investigators, more years of service may simply equate to higher exposure levels to negative content over the course of their careers, increasing their potential for both burnout and secondary traumatic stress symptoms.

The limited body of research on digital evidence examiners indicates that the unique experiences of digital forensic investigation directly impacts their working and personal lives in ways that are both similar and different than traditional law enforcement. This body of scholarship, however, is still in its infancy. Greater study is sorely needed. A first step is to improve sampling in order to gather broader samples of officers with various ranges of experience in order to better understand the phenomena of stress, burnout, and trauma. In addition, both interviews and ethnographic research on the experiences of officers tasked with roles in special units like ICACs would be invaluable to expand our knowledge of the actual working lives of officers and demonstrate conditions that exacerbate levels of stress and secondary trauma. Similar research is common in the literature on policing generally and could prove exceedingly useful to explicate the relationship between exposure factors, working environments, and reported levels of stress.

The lack of inter-agency cooperation

In light of the limitations noted in local police agencies' response capabilities, and the jurisdictional issues evident in the nature of many cybercrimes, there is a need for clear inter-agency communication and investigative protocols. There is, however, limited evidence that law enforcement agencies have found successful ways to cooperate in order to combat cybercrime. To date, the best available evidence of cooperative relationships between agencies at the local, state, and federal levels involve child exploitation and pornography cases.

In the US, ICAC task forces provide a mechanism for coordination between local, state, and federal law enforcement and prosecutors (ICAC, 2014). The response to child pornography and exploitation cases requires multiple points of coordination and response. A successful investigation requires that arrests and takedowns occur as close together as is possible to avoid offenders realizing that they may be caught and attempting to flee or destroy evidence that may implicate them in criminal activity. Investigations that begin at the local level may also lead to evidence of criminal activity in other nations, which may increase the scope of agencies that need to become involved in order for arrests and prosecutions to be both legal and successful.

For other forms of cybercrime, such as hacking and fraud, there are fewer available resources to cooperatively investigate offenses. In the US, these crime types are largely investigated by either the Federal Bureau of Investigation (FBI) or the US Secret Service. There are minimal resources, working groups, and joint task forces that operate to transfer cases from either the federal level down to states or vice versa. There is also virtually no empirical research examining the flow of information between agencies or the decision-making process of agencies as to why or how cases are pushed from the local level to the federal level and vice versa.

Models that could be used to better understand inter-agency cooperation are the **US Internet Crime Complaint Center (IC3)** and UK Action Fraud Agency. Since these agencies take complaints directly from victims of cybercrime, they serve as a front-line reporting mechanism to triage cases to determine their veracity and potential for local, state, or federal investigation (see Chapter 2 for a discussion of the IC3). There has been virtually no assessment of either the total number of incidents that are directed toward law enforcement or the extent to which these cases are cleared by arrest. Thus, this is a key question that must be addressed in future studies as a means to understand how useful this sort of reporting mechanism is in the facilitation of inter-agency cooperation.

Instead, states have begun to develop their own information sources that may be used to communicate and investigate threat information. This has largely been facilitated through the concept of **fusion centers**. Fusion centers primarily operate at the state level and serve as a bridge to facilitate information sharing between federal and local agencies. They develop information and process leads in order to cultivate threat intelligence that may be of actionable value to law enforcement at the local, state, or federal levels. Fusion centers emerged in 2003 through collaboration between the Department of Homeland Security (DHS) and the Office of Justice Programs. Centers are designed to facilitate communication between law enforcement, as this was deemed a critical point of failure that enabled the 9/11 terrorist attacks to take place. Thus the initial remit of fusion centers is primarily regarding intelligence gathering on terrorist threats, though this has grown to include a range of crimes, including relevant cyber-threats.

While there is value in the concept of fusion centers, there are substantial criticisms over their actual value and utility (e.g. Chermak et al., 2013; Coburn, 2015; Levin & Coburn, 2012). An analysis by the US Senate (Coburn, 2015) found that fusion centers often produced no actionable intelligence leads and may have violated civil rights of individuals. Though it is unclear how many fusion centers have generated information on cyber-threats, a notable failure has been brought to light regarding an analysis from the Illinois fusion center. A water pump failed in a local Illinois water district's SCADA system in 2011 which analysts attributed to Russian hackers (Zetter, 2012). The report was, however, derided by DHS as false, which was corroborated by an analysis of data obtained by the FBI. Despite the erroneous information generated, the report was moved forward as valid intelligence to Congress and the Intelligence community as a whole. The confusion and fear generated by a factually inaccurate report was, however, deemed a success by DHS because it "generated interest" in incidents and intelligence generally (Zetter, 2012).

If fusion centers are a potentially failed model for inter-agency cooperation, then it is unclear what may supplant their role in the field. There is a need for resources to be identified that may otherwise link agencies together in a meaningful way. There is virtually no assessment of these resources or their impact on cognizance and cooperation between agencies. Thus, future research is needed to examine these issues in detail to better understand and develop models for inter-agency cooperation.

Transnational criminal investigation

Similar to efforts made in the US, the focus of transnational investigations and agency cooperation has led to working groups that exist to coordinate transnational responses to child exploitation. An example of a task force that was created to provide coordinated responses to multinational child exploitation investigations is the **Virtual Global Taskforce (VGT)**. The VGT was established in 2003 and has linked law enforcement agencies at the national level with private industry sources, such as ISPs, to identify, investigate, and respond to incidents of child exploitation (VGT, 2014). Currently, national law enforcement agencies in Australia, Canada, Italy, Indonesia, South Korea, the Netherlands, New Zealand, the United Arab Emirates, the UK, and the US, as well as Europol and Interpol, all cooperate with the VGT (VGT, 2014). The power of this model lies in its ability to link agencies cross-nationally, along with their local counterparts, to generate investigations and arrests. In fact, they have conducted over 1,000 investigations of child pornography and exploitation, leading to hundreds of arrests globally.

Though such a model is sensible for person-based child pornography and exploitation cases, there is no analogous entity for hacking and identity fraud cases. In fact, serious hacking and data breach incidents are a notable example of the failure of transnational law enforcement. Over the last decade, the number of high-profile data breaches has increased in the US. In fact, at least seven breaches occurred during a 14-month period from 2013 to 2014, resulting in the loss of millions of customer records in each attack (Higgins, 2014; Pauli, 2014; Seals, 2014).

Despite the growth in breaches, there has not been a concurrent increase in the number of arrests associated with these incidents. Arrests are infrequent and tend to occur in clusters surrounding long-term investigations of online markets and actors associated with the theft or sale of data. This may stem from the substantive difficulty agencies have in developing identity information on market participants and the need for insider access in order to determine the location of actors. This is best exemplified by the takedown of the ShadowCrew forum, known for trading personal information and related services to engage in fraud and identity crimes (Peretti, 2009). The investigation began in part due to the arrest of Albert Gonzales, a US hacker who was arrested after being observed attempting to use multiple debit cards to withdraw money from an ATM at one time in New York City (Zetter, 2013). He became an informant for the US Secret Service shortly thereafter, providing access to the virtual private network (VPN) used by key members of the group to obfuscate their IP addresses and minimize the likelihood of identification.

Subsequently, the Secret Service in conjunction with other law enforcement agencies in Europe and South America arrested members of the group and took down the website itself. The total number of arrests reported varies between 21 and 28 individuals, depending on news sources and their location, whether in Europe or the US (Peretti, 2009; Zetter, 2013). Regardless, 19 individuals were indicted in the US on multiple counts of various violations of the Computer Fraud and Abuse Act.

The majority of individuals who have been successfully prosecuted lived either in the US or in Western Europe, or traveled to a nation with friendly extradition relationships to the US (Zetter, 2013). For instance, Aleksi Kolorov, a Bulgarian national, was initially indicted but not arrested due to his residence in a country with ineffectual relations to support an extradition (Zetter, 2013). He was only brought to the US in 2013 after being arrested in Paraguay in 2011. Kolorov was initially arrested on unrelated fraud charges involving misuse of credit and debit card data at Paraguayan financial institutions. Once in custody, Kolorov was brought to the attention of US prosecutors who were able to successfully negotiate a transfer after two years of detention in Paraguay. Three of the individuals who were originally indicted are still at large and all were thought to reside in Russia at the time of the takedown (Zetter, 2013).

This incident points to several factors that hinder the potential for transnational cooperation for economic-based cybercrimes. First, there is a substantial degree of difficulty for law enforcement agencies to develop accurate actor attribution in transnational hacking and identity fraud cases. While individuals involved in some forms of child sexual exploitation may appear in photos or media enabling physical identification, that likelihood is absent in hacking incidents. Instead, IP addresses must be used as an initial point of identification; however, they are not necessarily accurate as an attacker may use proxies or victim machines in order to facilitate their attacks. Similarly, individuals who attempt to purchase or sell stolen personal information via forums and Tor-based markets use handles that cannot be immediately or easily tied to a real identity.

Gaining access to and using insiders of cybercrime groups also presents its own set of risks for law enforcement. For instance, Albert Gonzales, who was pivotal in the takedown of the ShadowCrew, was not indicted due to his cooperation in the investigation. Instead, he continued to engage in serious data breaches while serving as a confidential informant for the Secret Service. Gonzales served a key role in the massive data breaches of both TJX Corporation and Heartland Payment Systems in the US between 2005 and 2007 (Zetter, 2013). These incidents led to the loss of over 170 million credit and debit card records, and eventually Gonzales receiving a 20-year federal prison sentence in the US. There is a need to carefully weigh the utility of such an investigative tactic in light of the potential harms that may otherwise result.

The ShadowCrew investigation also demonstrates the substantial challenge agencies may face when dealing with offenders who reside in nations that have no real extradition relationship to the victim country. Cybercrime researchers have called for revision to extradition relationships for the last two decades in order to improve the success of investigations and prosecutions (e.g. Brenner, 2008; Holt & Smirnova, 2014; Smith et al., 2004; Wall, 2007). There has been minimal change in the relationships between countries that are thought to have active cybercriminal communities, such as China and Russia, relative to commonly targeted nations such as Canada, the US, and UK. As a result, there may be a perception among cybercriminals in these nations that targeting any foreign government may be the best way to offend with minimal sanctions or risk of arrest. This may embolden actors to continue to target specific nations as their home government may otherwise turn a blind eye to their actions.

Given the limited capacities of law enforcement to combat certain forms of international cybercrime, a number of private businesses and organizations have begun to act in order to fill this gap. For instance, the Recording Industry Association of America (RIAA) and the UK's Federation Against Copyright Theft (FACT) work in conjunction with ISPs to send cease and desist letters to individuals who are thought to have illegally downloaded media without payment through torrent file sharing (Nhan, 2013). This is a relatively non-invasive practice based on the civil and financial interests of the copyright holders in order to deter further piracy by individuals in the general public. The Motion Picture Association of America (MPAA) also hired the private firm Aiplex Software to engage in targeted denial of service attacks against torrent sharing websites like the Pirate Bay (Whitney, 2010). The MPAA justified this practice on the grounds that these websites facilitated criminal activity with direct financial harm to copyright holders and were non-compliant to threats of legal action (Nhan, 2013). The attacks were relatively unsuccessful and actually led to targeted attacks against the MPAA and various recording artists' websites by hackers and piracy groups alike (Nhan, 2013).

These extralegal sanctions are indicative of a growing trend in industry attempts to affect cybercrime on their own. For instance, Microsoft has attempted to proactively combat cybercrime with some cooperation from law enforcement through the creation of their Digital Crimes Unit in 2013 (Adhikari, 2013). Though the unit works with law enforcement, their efforts are somewhat questionable, as demonstrated by one of their first campaigns against a botnet operator. Initially, Microsoft filed a civil lawsuit against the ZeroAccess botnet malware operator in an attempt to disrupt their practice. The suit was dropped after the company was able to connect with law enforcement agencies in the US and Europe to directly identify the IP addresses of infected systems. From this point, the company directly pushed security updates to patch the infected systems and remove them from the larger network of zombie computers (Adhikari, 2013).

Similar strategies are increasingly employed by both public and private computer security firms in an attempt to not only mitigate the size of botnets, but disrupt the practices of botnet operators as a whole (NASK, 2013; Sancho & Link, 2013). The practices of these entities are drawing criticism as to the role of industry in proactively policing the Internet and the legal risks presented by these activities. Private industry has no necessary duty or legal authority to protect the general public or to arrest or deter cybercriminals. In addition, disrupting a botnet by mitigating infections on user systems may seem beneficial to the victim as individuals may not have known they were infected, but directly identifying the IP addresses of private citizens may, however, appear to be an overreach of user agreements and an invasion of individual privacy (Adhikari, 2013).

Attempts to disrupt malware infections may also lead to the recovery of sensitive personal data, such as usernames, passwords, and financial data that could be maintained or archived by an industry source. Finally, techniques to disrupt infected systems may actually harm legitimate computer users whose systems were not infected but were associated with the infected nodes (Adhikari, 2013). Thus, there is a substantial demand for research examining the ethical implications of such work, its perceived deterrent effect by botnet operators, its overall effectiveness, and its potential impact on the perceived legitimacy and capabilities of law enforcement as a whole.

Cybercrime versus cyberwar

A final issue complicating the process of policing cybercrime is the fact that some parts of the Internet are increasingly transforming into a militarized environment. Nation-states have begun to utilize hacking techniques in support of their political and national interests, which may at first appear to resemble a criminal hack or attack. The ability to use proxy tools and mechanisms to minimize the likelihood of actor attribution means that nations may operate with some degree of impunity against electronic targets. In fact, most industrialized nations have come to view cyberspace as a new operational domain for warfare, in the same sense as air, sea, and land (Andress & Winterfeld, 2013; Rid, 2013).

These developments have led to the growth of the term **cyberwarfare**, referencing the use of attacks against electronic targets and/or infrastructure via various mechanisms by individuals tied to a nation-state. Such attacks often employ the same hacking techniques as that employed by cybercriminals, such as the creation of backdoors in systems, the capture of sensitive data, or disruption of critical network services. There is a difference, however, in the nature of the attack, the goal of the attackers, and the prospective targets that may be impacted.

A nation has the capacity to exert influence over their citizens and other nations through force in order to further their own interests. A nation-state is defined by three factors: (1) sovereignty, (2) territoriality, and (3) abstract organization (Creveld, 1999). Sovereignty recognizes that an individual or government has the authority and power to rule an area and make and enforce its own laws. Territoriality is also required as it defines the boundaries and borders of that state's sovereignty (Creveld, 1999). Finally, "abstract organization" recognizes that a state has an independent persona from the culture of its people. In this respect, a nation may have a democratic government, constitutional monarchy, or dictatorship, but the culture of its people may be based on ethnic origins or other sets of norms defined by the citizenry (Creveld, 1999).

Acts of **cyberwar** are performed by individuals who are tied to a nation-state in some fashion, whether through military deployments or individuals acting as proxies for government interests. As a result, some cyber-attacks may be referred to as nation-state sponsored because the actors may be given indirect economic support, but are not acting on direct orders that can be linked to government or military agencies.

Because of the substantive resources that a nation-state may be able to leverage to engage in cyber-attacks, their actions may be much more sophisticated than that of the standard attack by cybercriminals. In fact, there are several noteworthy incidents that may be tied to nation-state-sponsored actors over the last two decades. One of the most recent instances involved the identification of a piece of malware called Stuxnet operating within the Natanz and Busheir uranium enrichment facilities in Iran (Clayton, 2010;

Kerr et al., 2010). The code was designed to target a specific type of Programmable Logic Controller (PLC) used to operate centrifuges within these plants (Clayton, 2010; Kerr et al., 2010).

Once installed within computers connected to the SCADA systems of the plant, the code would enable an attacker to remotely command the PLCs, while projecting an image of a normally functioning device to plant control systems. This enabled attackers to cause the centrifuges to operate beyond maximum capacity for periods of time such that they would then catastrophically fail, while giving the operators no clue as to the source of systemic errors and device failures. It is thought that the malware was able to operate undetected for months and damage at least 1,000 centrifuges and substantially delay the functionality of the plant by months, if not years (Kerr et al., 2010; Sanger, 2012).

The complexity of the attack, coupled with the specialized knowledge needed to create this malware, indicate that it was unlikely to have been created by a single individual, or even a small team of actors. The fact that the attack neither generated economically viable information nor was used to blackmail the plant also demonstrates that this attack was not likely to have come from a traditional criminal actor.

Stuxnet appears to have been created by the US under the Bush Administration as part of a larger campaign of targeted attacks meant to hinder the development of nuclear weapons in Iran. This program continued under President Obama and was implemented in the field as it was thought to be a way to affect the Iranian program without causing collateral or physical damage through a bombing campaign or with the direct implication of US forces in the region (Sanger, 2012). In addition, the use of this code was thought to have reduced the likelihood of a conventional military strike by Israel which would have dangerous consequences for the region as a whole.

The US has neither confirmed nor denied its role in the creation or release of the Stuxnet malware. If the allegations are true, this begs the question of how this act may be defined. Some may argue this is a state crime, as the US violated the sovereignty of another nation and utilized criminal techniques to compromise sensitive and protected computer systems (e.g. Ross, 2000). Others may consider this to be an act of cyberwar based on existing definitions of physical or terrestrial wars. Though there is no single definition of war, there is an historical literature on warfare and tactics that provides a series of operational characteristics associated with armed conflicts. Typically, they involve acts of force or physical violence that compel the target, or opponent, to fulfill the will of the aggressor or victor (Andress & Winterfeld, 2013; Brenner, 2008; Schwartau, 1996).

In a virtual context, the potential for physical violence is questionable, though the outcome is to affect or control the activities of an opposing force. Brenner (2008: 65) defined cyberwarfare as nation-states' "use of military operations by virtual means ... to achieve essentially the same ends they pursue through the use of conventional military force." The creation and implementation of Stuxnet is an excellent example of an operation to specifically affect the practices of an opposing nation. In this case, the US developed a cyber-weapon that would hinder the capacities of a nuclear facility in the same way that a targeted tactical assault would with conventional weapons. Though the malware did not cause catastrophic damage to either the physical structure of the plants or individual employees in the way that a missile strike might have, it was able to surreptitiously degrade and disrupt the manufacturing capabilities of the plants through targeted damage to key equipment.

The use of Stuxnet raises a critical question as to the legitimacy of the term "cyberwarfare" because of the lack of physical harm and its ability to be used against nations which may not otherwise be engaged in direct conflicts. The scant criminological literature on this issue has largely focused on the definitional issues inherent in both cyberwar and cyberterrorism (e.g. Brenner, 2008; Furedi, 2005). Research in this space is largely informed by political science, military research, and legal scholars debating the ethical implications of cyber-attacks (e.g. Brenner, 2008; Denning, 2011), or the extent to which nation-state attacks may be deterred (Rid, 2013). What criminological scholarship does exist tends to take a more critical perspective that incidents of cyberterrorism and warfare are abstract concepts designed to promote fear and foster greater state control absent actual capacities for attack (Furedi, 2005; Yar, 2013). These studies are emboldened by the lack of clarity over what incidents constitute acts of war relative to espionage or other phenomena.

One of the most cogent discussions of these issues is presented by Rid (2013), a researcher in war studies, in his book *Cyber War Will Not Take Place*. The hypothesis of this work is that various forms of cyber attack cannot be considered acts of war because they neither involve physical acts of violence nor create true harm to individuals in the form of loss of life. Rid (2013) argues that cyber-attacks are not inherently violent as they target electronic resources predominantly controlled by government or industry. Instead, the outcomes of cyber-attacks are largely meant to destabilize governments or affect trust in organizations and entities.

While there have been noteworthy incidents that cause financial harm to wider populations, Rid notes that there has been no evidence of violent outcomes generated by an attack. He presents various noteworthy cyber-attacks that occurred over the last decade in a similar fashion to presentations from other scholars (Brenner, 2008; Denning, 2011). For instance, the serious financial harms Russian actors caused the nation of Estonia through denial of service attacks are a critical example of an incident that some label cyberwar (Rid, 2013). Similarly, various US companies lost sensitive intellectual property as a consequence of Chinese hackers launching a series of attacks in 2010 (Denning, 2011).

Rid (2013) cites these and other attacks as evidence that physical violence and harm is incidental to cyber-attacks rather than a specific goal. Instead, malicious software and hacks can be thought of as offensive cyber weapons because they have the ability to damage computer systems and networks. Their ability to cause direct collateral damage to persons or places is, however, inherently limited and unlikely. Rid makes an essential argument that the increasing availability of technological access and hacking tools should lead to general reductions in the use of violence by nation-states and extremist groups as a whole.

This is an interesting assertion, and one that may be applicable to certain circumstances as an electronic attack may be more difficult to detect and attribute to a nation-state or state-sponsored actor. Furthermore, the ability to use social media and various online outlets to communicate may dilute the messages of extremist groups and complicate their ability to radicalize individuals to a single perspective. As a result, the increased dependence on technology may increase the number of ideological movements, but minimize the likelihood of physical violence generally.

Though this work is a very well-reasoned and justified examination of cyberwar, there is an inherent limitation that is not given much redress by the author. Rid (2013) asserts that sabotage, espionage, and subversion activities in online spaces are neither acts of cybercrime nor cyberwar. There is no clear explanation as to why these activities, when performed by individuals, are not cybercrimes even though almost all nations have criminalized these activities. Furthermore, these are three forms of cyber-attack that have been explicitly identified by the US Department of Defense as behaviors which may generate a military response of some type (Department of Defense, 2011).

As such, these behaviors must fall into a category of some sort, which may depend on the target of the attack. In the US for instance, attacks against civilian or industry targets would largely fall under the jurisdiction of law enforcement for criminal investigation, while attacks against military networks and infrastructure would be handled by the Department of Defense or related entity. The incident may be treated as a crime if it appears to originate from an individual, though it may be handled differently if it appears to originate from a nation-state.

To that end, military and intelligence agencies are increasingly structured to accomplish network-based offensive and defensive operations (see Andress & Winterfeld, 2013). In the US, the Pentagon established a new United States Cyber Command (USCYBERCOM) in 2009 within the larger United States Strategic Command (USSTRATCOM) to expressly manage the defense of US cyberspace and critical infrastructure (Andress & Winterfeld, 2013). Since all branches of the US armed forces have some capacity for offensive and defensive operations in cyberspace, the USCYBERCOM now serves as a point of coordination for and oversight of networks and devices that touch Department of Defense-operated networks. Similar organizations can be found in virtually all industrialized nations, such as the Australian Cyber Security Operations Centre (CSOC), the Chinese Information Warfare Militia Units, Technical Reconnaissance Bureaus (TRB), the General Staff

Department (GSD), and Russian Federal Guard Service (Andress & Winterfeld, 2013).

As the discussion above demonstrates, scholars have debated both the definitions of cybercrime and cyberterrorism and how computer intrusions may be categorized. Many may see this as an abstract academic debate that does not apply to the "real world" where crimes have to be investigated and people's lives and computer systems have to be protected. This discussion is, however, a key question to understand what level of government is responsible for investigating the offense and attempting to prevent future similar events. If the offense is viewed as a crime, law enforcement agencies at local, state, and federal levels will be assigned the responsibility. If the offense is categorized as cyberwarfare, then various military branches will investigate and respond with cyber-attacks or escalate the response to include traditional military responses, such as missile strikes or troops on the ground. As a result, definitions are a critical factor in the cybercrime debate and will likely continue to be so as time progresses.

Summary and conclusion

In general, this chapter demonstrated the lack of empirical research on the ways law enforcement agencies have responded to cybercrime and the inadequate nature of capabilities. While there is a robust literature with respect to police decision making, staffing, and practice for real-world crimes, there is generally little by comparison to cybercrime. A partial explanation for this scant literature is because of both the relatively recent emergence of cybercrime as a law enforcement concern and the challenges that researchers have in gaining access to law enforcement agencies. Unfortunately, there are also two other explanations for the lack of research on this topic: (1) minimal interest in policing cybercrimes by criminologists and criminal justice researchers generally; and (2) an overreliance in the field of criminology on analyzing secondary data sets rather than collecting primary data. The lack of new data collection leads to gaps in our knowledge of both criminal justice agencies (e.g. law enforcement) and emerging issues (e.g. cybercrime).

Regardless of the amount of weight that is placed upon each of the above explanations for the current state of the literature, the gaps identified above must be addressed through both qualitative and quantitative studies in order to expand our knowledge of law enforcement responses to cybercrime. First, the clear variations identified in the preparedness of local law enforcement and their capacity to respond to various forms of cybercrime demand further inquiry. Virtually all the studies conducted to date are too geographically limited and temporally bound to provide generalizable findings. Research is needed that taps into diverse samples of officers and administrators of small, medium, and large agencies, in both the US and around the world, to quantify both their experiences with cybercrime calls for service and the perceived importance of these cases relative to traditional offenses.

Capturing data from police management is essential to understand the extent to which agencies communicate the severity and importance of cyber-crimes relative to street crimes. Such data can also provide a valuable point of comparison to line officer samples to identify whether officer attitudes stem from experiences with citizens, a lack of communication from command staff, or both. Sampling from agencies that serve rural, urban, and suburban populations is also critical to improve our knowledge of the extent to which the size of the agency and the nature of the population served may shape the perceptions of law enforcement to cybercrimes in their area.

Second, there is a need for research assessing the extent to which cyber-crime training is provided in both academic settings and police academies. Since law enforcement agencies at all levels have increasingly valued officers with university degrees, prospective officers may have had some practical exposure to cybercrime during their education. Such content may not be covered during police academy training, and there is minimal scholarship addressing the extent to which such content is delivered or the quality of the information. Thus, research addressing this topic could improve our knowledge of the ways that officers are gaining some background information on cybercrime and digital evidence prior to their experience in the field.

Third, robust qualitative scholarship exploring the experiences of officers serving in specialized units or roles tasked with the investigation of cyber-crime is necessary. Since specialized unit staffing is increasingly common at the state and local levels, there is no real information available as to how officers are selected for these positions. There is also minimal knowledge of the extent to which experiences with cybercrime cases and digital forensic investigations affect officers' perceptions of their jobs. For instance, seminal studies of policing argue that there is a subculture of policing which encourages officers to behave in certain roles depending on situational encounters with citizens and others on and off the job. There is no research to date that considers the subculture of specialized officers who deal with cybercrime cases and the extent to which their values deviate from those of the larger body of line officers dealing with street crime. Such research would greatly improve our knowledge of the practicalities of cybercrime investigation for officers on a daily basis, and the ways that their jobs differ from street-based policing.

There is also a need for research assessing the ways that cybercrime cases are triaged and the points where an incident may be diverted from a local agency to a federal body, from a federal law enforcement agency to a military body, or assigned to an existing task force or an ad hoc group. This sort of study could be achieved in various ways, ranging from interviews with active and former law enforcement agents to content analyses of policies and procedures within various agencies. Such information could expand our knowledge of the ways that cybercrime case handling has changed historically and identify thresholds for error and miscommunication between agencies. A "best practices" study of this kind is vital within the policing cybercrime literature, detailing how the correct agencies are notified and how they then participate in the investigation and prevention of specific forms of cybercrime.

These are just a few of the potential research questions that should be addressed in future research. Given that the current literature is sparse, any attempts to expand this field of study through empirical analysis should be encouraged. The rich tradition of policing research should be able to inform not only methodological decisions, but provide a wealth of insights into the ways that policing cybercrime may be similar to other offenses. Without this line of inquiry, the field stands to suffer and stagnate in tandem with police strategies to investigate cybercrimes and aid victim populations.

Key terms

Burnout
Computer Emergency Response Teams (CERTs)
Corporate security personnel
Cyberwar
Cyberwarfare
First responders
Fusion centers
Government-controlled organizations
Internet Crimes Against Children (ICAC) task forces
Internet service providers (ISPs)
Internet users
Non-governmental organizations (NGOs)
Secondary trauma
Stress
Task forces
US Internet Crime Complaint Center (IC3)
Virtual Global Taskforce (VGT)

Discussions questions

1   Do you think that local law enforcement should be first responders to most cybercrimes? Why or why not? Regardless of your answer, how can we alter local law enforcement officers' attitudes toward being first responders?
2   Should local departments spend more resources on training officers in digital evidence handling considering its expense, the department's budget, and the fact that there is always additional training needed to deal with traditional issues, such as use of force?
3   How do task forces address some of the obstacles that hinder inter-agency cooperation?
4   What are the major obstacles that obstruct successful transnational criminal investigations? Considering that many cybercrimes originate in

nations with which the US and many Western countries do not have strong ties, how can we improve transnational investigations?
5 How clear is the difference between "cybercrime" and "cyberwarfare"? How comfortable are you with the military rather than national law enforcement agencies taking on larger roles in investigating and preventing cyber attacks?
6 What area of research do you think is most needed to improve our understanding of how we police cybercrime?

References

Adhikari, R. (2013). Microsoft's ZeroAccess Botnet takedown no "mission accomplished". *TechNewsWorld*, December 9. www.technewsworld.com/story/79586.html.

Andress, J., & Winterfeld, S. (2013). *Cyber Warfare: Techniques, Tactics, and Tools for Security Practitioners*. Second edition. Waltham MA: Syngress.

Bossler, A.M., & Holt, T.J. (2012). Patrol officers' perceived role in responding to cybercrime. *Policing: An International Journal of Police Strategies & Management*, 35, 165–181.

Brenner, S.W. (2008). *Cyberthreats: The Emerging Fault Lines of the Nation State*. New York: Oxford University Press.

Britz, M.T. (2009). *Computer Forensics and Cyber Crime*. Second edition. Upper Saddle River, NJ: Prentice Hall.

Burns, C.M., Morley, J., Bradshaw, R., & Domene, J. (2008). The emotion impact on and coping strategies employed by police teams investigating Internet child exploitation. *Traumatology*, 14, 20–31.

Burns, R.G., Whitworth, K.H., & Thompson, C.Y. (2004). Assessing law enforcement preparedness to address Internet fraud. *Journal of Criminal Justice*, 32, 477–493.

Chermak, S., Carter, J., Carter, D., McGarrell, E.F., & Drew, J. (2013). Law enforcement's information sharing infrastructure: A national assessment. *Police Quarterly*, 2, 211–244.

Clayton, M. (2010). Stuxnet malware is "weapon" out to destroy ... Iran's Bushehr Nuclear Plant. *Christian Science Monitor*, September 21. www.csmonitor.com/USA/2010/0921/Stuxnet-malware-is-weapon-out-to-destroy-Iran-s-Bushehr-nuclear-plant.

Coburn, T. (2015). *A Review of the Department of Homeland Security's Missions and Performance*. Washington, DC: US Senate.

Creveld, M.V. (1999). *The Rise and Decline of the State*. Cambridge: Cambridge University Press.

Cullen, F.T., Lemming, T., Link, B.G., & Wozniak, J.F. (1985). The impact of social supports on police stress. *Criminology*, 23, 503–522.

Cullen, F.T., Lutze, F., Link, B.G., & Wolfe, N.T. (1989). The correctional orientation of prison guards: Do officers support rehabilitation? *Federal Probation*, 53, 33–42.

Denning, D.E. (2011). Cyber-conflict as an emergent social problem. In T.J. Holt & B. Schell (Eds.), *Corporate Hacking and Technology-Driven Crime: Social Dynamics and Implications*. (pp. 170–186). Hershey, PA: IGI-Global.

Department of Defense (2011). *Department of Defense Strategy for Operating in Cyberspace*. Washington, DC. www.defense.gov/news/d20110714cyber.pdf.

Dowler, K. (2005). Job satisfaction, burnout, and perception of unfair treatment: The relationship between race and police work. *Police Quarterly*, 8, 476–489.

Ferraro, M., & Casey, E. (2005). *Investigating Child Exploitation and Pornography: The Internet, the Law, and Forensic Science.* New York, NY: Elsevier Academic Press.

FIRST (2014). *Global Initiatives.* www.first.org/global.

Furedi, F. (2005). *Politics of Fear: Beyond Left and Right.* London: Continuum Press.

Furnell, S. (2002). *Cybercrime: Vandalizing the Information Society.* London: Addison-Wesley.

Goodman, M.D. (1997). Why the police don't care about computer crime. *Harvard Journal of Law and Technology*, 10, 465–494.

Guidance Software (2014). *Guidance Software Products.* www.guidancesoftware.com/p roducts/Pages/default.aspx.

Hagy, D.W. (2007). *Digital Evidence in the Courtroom: A Guide for Law Enforcement and Prosecutors.* Washington, DC: US Department of Justice.

He, N., Zhao, J., & Archbold, C.A. (2002). Gender and police stress: The convergent and divergent impact of work environment, work-family conflict, and stress coping mechanisms of female and male police officers. *Policing: An International Journal of Police Strategies & Management*, 25, 687–708.

Higgins, K.J. (2014). Target, Neiman Marcus data breaches tip of the iceberg. *Dark Reading*, January 13. www.darkreading.com/attacks-breaches/target-neiman-ma rcus-data-breaches-tip-o/240165363.

Hinduja, S. (2004). Perceptions of local and state law enforcement concerning the role of computer crime investigative teams. *Policing: An International Journal of Police Strategies and Management*, 3, 341–357.

Hinduja, S. (2007). Computer crime investigations in the United States: Leveraging knowledge from the past to address the future. *International Journal of Cyber Criminology*, 1, 1–26.

Holt, T.J., & Blevins, K.R. (2012). Examining job stress and satisfaction among digital forensic examiners. *Journal of Contemporary Criminal Justice*, 27, 230–250.

Holt, T.J., Blevins, K.R., & Burruss, G.W. (2012). Examining the stress, satisfaction, and experiences of computer crime examiners. *Journal of Crime and Justice*, 35, 35–52.

Holt, T.J., & Bossler, A.M. (2012). Predictors of patrol officer interest in cybercrime training and investigation in selected United States Police Departments. *Cyberpsychology, Behavior, and Social Networking*, 15, 464–472.

Holt, T.J., Bossler, A.M., & Fitzgerald, S. (2010). Examining state and local law enforcement perceptions of computer crime. In T.J. Holt (Ed.), *Crime On-line: Correlates, Causes, and Context* (pp. 221–246). Raleigh NC: Carolina Academic Press.

Holt, T.J., Burruss, G.W., & Bossler, A.M. (2015). *Policing Cybercrime and Cyberterror.* Raleigh, NC: Carolina Academic Press.

Holt, T.J., & Smirnova, O. (2014). *Examining the Structure, Organization, and Processes of the International Market for Stolen Data.* Washington, DC: US Department of Justice. www.ncjrs.gov/pdffiles1/nij/grants/245375.pdf.

ICAC (Internet Crimes Against Children Task Force) (2014). *Internet Crimes Against Children Task Force Program.* www.icactaskforce.org/Pages/ICACTFP.aspx.

Jones, A., & Valli, C. (2011). *Building a Digital Forensic Laboratory: Establishing and Managing a Successful Facility.* New York: Butterworth-Heinemann.

Kerr, P.K., Rollins, J., & Theohary, C.A. (2010). *The Stuxnet Computer Worm: Harbinger of an Emerging Warfare Capability.* Washington, DC: Congressional Research Service.

Krause, M. (2009). Identifying and managing stress in child pornography and child exploitation investigators. *Journal of Police and Criminal Psychology*, 24, 22–29.

LEMAS (2010). *Law Enforcement Management and Administrative Statistics 2010*. Washington DC: United States Department of Justice, Office of Justice Statistics.

Levin, C., & Coburn, T. (2012). *Federal Support For and Involvement in State and Local Fusion Centers*. Washington, DC: US Senate.

McQuade, S. (2006). Technology-enabled crime, policing and security. *Journal of Technology Studies*, 32, 32–42.

Marcum, C., Higgins, G.E., Freiburger, T.L., & Ricketts, M.L. (2010). Policing possession of child pornography online: Investigating the training and resources dedicated to the investigation of cyber crime. *International Journal of Police Science & Management*, 12, 516–525.

Mizota, K. (2013). Unbiased testing confirms: EnCase Forensic is fastest. *Digital Forensics Today*, May 14. encase-forensic-blog.guidancesoftware.com/2013/05/unbia sed-testing-confirms-encase_14.html (accessed July 2, 2014).

NASK (2013). NASK shuts down dangerous Virut botnet domains. 18 January. www. nask.pl/press_infoID/id/828.

National Academy of Sciences (2009). *Strengthening Forensic Science in the United States: A Path Forward*. Washington, DC: US Department of Justice.

Nhan, J. (2013). The evolution of online piracy: Challenge and response. In T.J. Holt (Ed.), *Crime On-line: Causes, Correlates, and Context* (pp. 61–80). Raleigh, NC: Carolina Academic Press.

NIJ (National Institute of Justice) (2008). *Electronic Crime Scene Investigations: A Guide for First Responders*. Second edition. NCJ 219941. Washington, DC: National Institute of Justice.

Pauli, D. (2014). Oz privacy comish says breaches could be double this year. *The Register*, October 20. www.theregister.co.uk/2014/10/20/2014_a_bumper_year_for_a ussie_breaches/.

Peretti, K.K. (2009). Data breaches: What the underground world of "carding" reveals. *Santa Clara Computer and High Technology Law Journal*, 25, 375–413.

Perez, L.M., Jones, J., Engler, D.R., & Sachau, D. (2010). Secondary traumatic stress and burnout among law enforcement investigators exposed to disturbing media images. *Journal of Police and Criminal Psychology*, 25, 113–124.

Rid, T. (2013). *Cyber War Will Not Take Place*. London: Hurst & Company.

Ross, J.I. (2000), *Varieties of State Crime and its Control*. Monsey: Criminal Justice Press.

Sancho, D., & Link, R. (2013). Trend Micro sinkholes and eliminates a ZeuS botnet C&C. *Security Intelligence Blog*. blog.trendmicro.com/trendlabs-security-intelli gence/trend-micro-sinkholes-and-eliminates-a-zeus-botnet-cc/.

Sanger, D.E. (2012). *Confront and Conceal: Obama's Secret Wars and Surprising Use of American Power*. New York: Crown Publishing.

Schwartau, W. (1996). *Information Warfare*. Second edition. New York: Thunder's Mouth Press.

Seals, T. (2014). 2014 so far: The year of the data breach. *Infosecurity Magazine*, August 12. www.infosecurity-magazine.com/news/2014-the-year-of-the-data-breach/.

Senjo, S.R. (2004). An analysis of computer-related crime: Comparing police officer perceptions with empirical data. *Security Journal*, 17, 55–71.

Smith, R., Grabosky, P., & Urbas, G. (2004). *Cyber Criminals on Trial*. Cambridge: Cambridge University Press.

Stambaugh, H., Beaupre, D.S., Icove, D.J., Baker, R., Cassady, W. and Williams, W.P. (2001). *Electronic Crime Needs Assessment for State and Local Law Enforcement.* Washington, DC: National Institute of Justice, NCJ 186276.

Stevenson, J. (2007). *Welfare Considerations for Supervisors Managing Child Sexual Abuse on Line Units.* Unpublished doctoral dissertation, Middlesex University, London, UK.

VGT (Virtual Global Task Force) (2014). *VGT Making a Difference.* www.virtualgloba ltaskforce.com/what-we-do/.

Wall, D.S. (2001). Cybercrimes and the Internet. In D.S. Wall (Ed.), *Crime and the Internet* (pp. 1–17). New York: Routledge.

Wall, D.S. (2007). *Cybercrime: The Transformation of Crime in the Information Age.* Cambridge: Polity Press.

Wall, D.S., & Williams, M.L. (2013). Policing cybercrime: Networked and social media technologies and the challenges for policing. *Policing and Society,* 23, 409–412.

Whitney, L. (2010). 4chan takes down RIAA, MPAA sites. *CNet,* September 20. www. cnet.com/news/4chan-takes-down-riaa-mpaa-sites/.

Wolak, J., Finkelhor, D., & Mitchell, K. (2012). *Trends in Law Enforcement Responses to Technology-facilitated Child Sexual Exploitation Crimes: The Third National Juvenile Online Victimization Study (NJOV-3).* Durham, NH: Crimes against Children Research Center.

Yar, M. (2013). *Cybercrime and Society.* Second edition. London: SAGE Publications.

Zetter, K. (2012). DHS issued false "water pump hack" report; called it a "success." *Wired,* October 2. www.wired.com/2012/10/dhs-false-water-pump-hack/.

Zetter, K. (2013). 9 years after ShadowCrew, Feds get their hands on fugitive cyber-crook. *Wired,* July 1. www.wired.com/2013/07/bulgarian-shadowcrew-arrest/.

5 Issues in the prevention of cybercrime

Chapter goals

- Explore the challenges of preventing cybercrime
- Compare and contrast threats affecting corporations and enterprises with those affecting individuals
- Critique the attempts to increase the effort required to offend
- Explain methods to increase the perceived risks of offending
- Assess the mechanisms designed to reduce the rewards of offending
- Describe techniques to remove excuses for offenders and victims

As noted throughout the previous chapters, our understanding of cybercrime is growing and provides some direction for theory and policymakers. The literature on offending and victimization provides some consistent findings regarding the nature of cybercrime, but calls into question how we may more effectively deter offenders and insulate victims from risk. The behavioral, attitudinal, and demographic correlates of offending and victimization identified in the existing literature can provide substantive direction for crime-prevention techniques (Clarke, 1983; Cornish & Clarke, 1987, 2003). In fact, the implications of these studies may be used to help inform situational crime-prevention frameworks for cybercrime (Collins, Sainato, & Khey, 2011; Hinduja & Kooi, 2013; Newman & Clarke, 2003). This criminological perspective combines rational choice theory along with routine activities perspectives (Clarke & Felson, 1993; Cohen & Felson, 1979), crime pattern theories (Spelman & Eck, 1989), and the problem analysis triangle (Braga, 2002), to help shape problem-oriented policing strategies (Braga, 2002; Clarke & Eck, 2007).

As noted in Chapter 3, situational crime prevention views offenders as active thinkers who make choices to engage in crime based on their assessment of perceived risks, potential rewards, and situational factors such as environmental cues (Cornish & Clarke, 1987, 2003). Situational crime prevention focuses on five categories designed to impact both offenders and victims by identifying strategies that directly influence opportunities to offend by: (1) making it more challenging to engage in crime; (2) increase the risk of detection; (3) reduce the rewards that may result from offending; (4) reduce provocations to offend; and (5) remove excuses for offending (Clarke, 1983, 1995, 1997; Cornish & Clarke, 2003). Within each category, there are five techniques that can be applied to affect the likelihood of crime, such as target hardening to increase the effort offenders must exert, using place managers to increase the risk of detection, concealing targets to reduce the potential rewards of offending, and posting clear rules for behavior to remove excuses for criminality (Cornish & Clarke, 2003). From this perspective, offenders may reduce their overall criminal behavior as a function of a perceived cumulative fear of apprehension, minimized conditions or opportunities to offend, or decreased rewards resulting from offending.

There is generally little empirical research applying situational crime prevention (SCP) to different forms of cybercrime. Most of these studies utilize aspects of SCP to examine a specific crime type (e.g. Collins et al., 2011; Khey & Sainato, 2013) or provide summary overviews of existing knowledge within an SCP framework (e.g. Hinduja & Kooi, 2013; Rege, 2013). There is, however, a substantial literature on cybercrime offending and prevention from both criminological and computer science research.

This chapter will provide a synthesis of the current research literature on preventing cybercrime from a situational crime prevention perspective. We focus primarily on acts of cyber-trespass and deception/theft as they have generated the largest overall body of research on why individuals commit these offenses and attempts to minimize the likelihood of victimization.

Using these offenses, we first discuss differences in the landscape of threats to corporations and organizations relative to individuals. We then consider the empirical research on cybercrimes using four of the five categories of techniques of situational crime prevention: (1) increasing the difficulty of offending; (2) increasing risks of offending; (3) mechanisms to reduce rewards of involvement in cybercrime; and (4) removing excuses for offenders and victims. This is not meant to be a completely comprehensive analysis of all 25 techniques of crime prevention, but rather a survey of the current state of research. In fact, we do not consider techniques to reduce provocations for involvement in cybercrime as our understanding of some of the triggering factors for offending is still in its infancy. Finally, we will discuss whether this framework has substantive value to affect the practices of both cybercriminals and their victims.

The challenge of preventing cybercrime

Corporations and enterprise-level issues

When considering the threats to corporations, universities, governments, and other large-scale organizations, there is a distinct difference in the nature of actors who may attempt to compromise their resources. These are two types of attackers that affect corporate targets: **internal** and **external attackers**

(Brenner, 2008; Furnell, 2002). An external attacker is an individual who does not have an existing relationship with network owners, has no authorized access to systems or resources, and operates completely outside the network. Internal attackers are individuals who have authorized and legitimate access to computers, networks, and certain data stored on corporate systems. They typically misuse their credentials and exceed what access they have by guessing a password or exploiting knowledge of system-level vulnerabilities in order to gain access to various resources.

In the 1980s and early 1990s, external attacks were a relatively small proportion of all incidents experienced at the enterprise level. As Internet connectivity increased in the mid-1990s and computer technology became more user-friendly, external attacks became much more common. Now, internal attacks are a small proportion of all incidents reported on a yearly basis (Ponemon Institute, 2015; Symantec Corporation, 2014).

The scope of internal attacks is much more limited compared with external attacks. Research involving case studies of insider attacks suggest that hackers may operate within secure environments as trusted system administrators or security professionals (Cappelli, Moore, Shimeall, & Trzeciak, 2006; Dhillon & Moores, 2001; Shaw, Ruby, & Post, 1998). The actions employees take to misuse or misappropriate resources may go unnoticed, particularly by individuals with root administrative privileges as there are few others with greater credentials who would monitor their activities (Cappelli et al., 2006; Dhillon & Moores, 2001). Insiders may surreptitiously steal information or place backdoors in programs which can be accessed to cause damage in case they are fired or mistreated (see Cappelli et al., 2006; Shaw et al., 1998). Insiders may operate along a continuum of technical sophistication since insider attacks have been both simple and complex depending on the types of services that have been exploited across industries (Cappelli et al., 2006). They may also have flexible ethical outlooks, wherein they view any piece of data or file that has not been properly secured as a potential target for attack (Shaw et al., 1998). Finally, insiders tend to be loners who are dependent on or addicted to computers and online communications (see Shaw et al., 1998).

By contrast, external attackers are driven by various motivations which could influence the resources they target within organizations (Holt & Kilger, 2012; Kilger, 2011). For instance, a financially motivated hacker may target customer databases and point-of-sale terminals to acquire financial data that can be resold to others. Hackers seeking profits may also offer **botnets** and denial of service attack services for hire against either corporate targets or leveraging their infrastructure to facilitate attacks (Holt, 2013; Motoyama et al., 2011). Hackers motivated by ego, social causes, or entertainment may attempt to deface a corporate website to send a message or demonstrate their skills to the public. A politically motivated or nation-state-sponsored attacker may seek intellectual property stored within company computers or servers for subsequent use by their government (Holt & Kilger, 2012). Alternatively, nation-state-sponsored actors may slowly gain access to a network and acquire individual user credentials so that they can surreptitiously use organizational resources over time. Such methods minimize their risk of detection and increase the potential quantity of data, confidential or otherwise, that they can acquire (Denning, 2011; Mandiant, 2013).

Guarding against all of these threats makes it virtually impossible to defend all sectors equally. Enterprise-level companies have greater resources available to protect their infrastructure, from intrusion detection systems (IDS) that identify and block threats when they happen to large-scale email spam filters. Various security tools can also be installed on individual computer systems, like antivirus software, to help minimize the likelihood of successful malware infections. Small to medium-sized businesses may not have the same degree of recognition and implementation of software tools. They may neither have the budget to support implementing security tools nor the comprehension needed to do so effectively. As a result, there are substantial inconsistencies in the security posture of businesses.

Regardless of resource access, the greatest weaknesses across all organizations are the individual users who have access to systems and resources. If an individual does not understand the threats they face from different forms of attack, or does not utilize the security tools available, they exponentially increase the risk of a successful attack. One key way attackers prey upon user populations is through the use of **social engineering**, where they attempt to build and leverage trust with potential victims in order to gain sensitive information or unauthorized access privileges (Furnell, 2002; Huang & Brockman, 2010; Mitnick & Simon, 2002). Social engineering is most evident in the massive quantity of spam emails sent every day. It is easy for senders to claim to be trusted agents within an organization and demand that the recipients provide personal login credentials (Mitnick & Simon, 2002). The sender can then use the credentials to gain insider access to data and networks.

Non-technical attacks involving social engineering are a vital tool in the arsenal of hackers and attackers because it is virtually impossible to inoculate all individuals against responding to such messages (Huang & Brockman, 2010; Mitnick & Simon, 2002). Even though companies constantly attempt to communicate risks to their employees, there is no guarantee that this messaging is effective. Attackers have also adjusted their techniques to include so-called spear **phishing**, where email messages are sent to a select number of recipients rather than large masses (FireEye, 2012). These messages are more personalized, and typically include external web links or attachments that would be of interest to the recipient. These links will lead the unsuspecting user to malicious software that can provide an initial point of access for an attacker to gain entry into larger networks.

A well-known example of spear phishing was observed in the computer security incident dubbed **Operation Aurora** by the security vendor McAfee (Schmugar, 2010). In 2009, a group of sophisticated Chinese hackers compromised multiple high-level corporations, including Google, Adobe, Yahoo,

Symantec, and Dow Chemical, by sending messages to select employees with links to websites hosting malware which would attack the Internet Explorer web browser and infect the user system (Schmugar, 2010; Zetter, 2010). From there, the attackers used infected systems as launch points to identify and compromise source code repositories and establish backdoors in the system (Markoff & Barboza, 2010; Zetter, 2010).

Individuals and end users

The threats facing the general public are somewhat different from those facing corporations. For instance, it is unlikely that the average person is running their own website or server that would be compromised by hackers. They are also unlikely to be the direct target of a denial of service attack. An individual's computer system is a valuable resource, however, which individual hackers would want to access and control. Home computers store sensitive user details, like passwords and banking information, which have monetary value on the black market. Similarly, home computers can be used as launch points for attacks that would anonymize a hacker's location or serve as a force multiplier.

As a result, individuals are more likely to face threats from cybercrimes like malware, phishing, fraud, and counterfeiting issues. These are difficult threats to block, as attackers target as many individuals as is possible to increase their likelihood of success. Many of these threats may come from phishing emails or spam that is generic in nature and targeting customers at major banks or retailers. Alternatively, hackers have come to depend on botnet malware which can be sent to a victim through an email attachment or through browser infections as noted in the Operation Aurora incident described above (Bacher, Holz, Kotter, & Wicherski, 2005; Symantec Corporation, 2014). Once the program is installed, it enables the computer to connect to an Internet Relay Chat (IRC) channel in order to receive commands and be controlled by a bot master, or herder (Bacher et al., 2005). The victim machine becomes part of a larger network of infected systems creating a **botnet**, or network of remotely controlled machines (Bacher et al., 2005). This form of malware is often very easy to control through the use of sophisticated interfaces, enabling bot masters to use their network to send spam, engage in distributed denial of service (DDoS) attacks, or commit various other forms of cybercrime.

Many of the threats that end users face can be avoided through the use of antivirus software and other protective programs. There is, however, generally little knowledge of how many end users employ these tools properly, or understand how they operate. Furthermore, many end users do not fully understand how the technologies they use and depend on operate. This creates a substantial threat to the safety of their devices, as they do not recognize scam or spam emails when they are received in their inbox. They may not also realize when an infection has occurred, or realize the risk of downloading tools or programs from unknown websites. All of these behaviors increase both the risk of victimization and the ease with which offenders can actively compromise systems.

Attempts to increase the effort required to offend

One of the primary foci of SCP with immediate applicability to cybercrime involves **target hardening** strategies that make it more difficult for offenders to access a target, specifically increasing protections for computer users, systems, and personal data (see Newman & Clarke, 2003). As mentioned above, one of the most common mechanisms used to protect computer systems are software suites that increase the difficulty offenders experience in attempting to compromise computer systems (Bossler & Holt, 2009; Choi, 2008; Holt & Bossler, 2009; Holt & Turner, 2012; Ngo & Paternoster, 2011). There are a range of tools designed to reduce the likelihood of malicious software infections through the use of definition-based system scans, including **antivirus software**, anti-spyware, and adware programs (PandaLabs, 2007; Symantec Corporation, 2014). These software programs can be configured to identify malicious files while they are being downloaded, and remediate infected or corrupted files after an infection is attempted (PandaLabs, 2007; Symantec Corporation, 2014).

The utility of antivirus tools to impact the risk of victimization is debatable. For instance, Choi (2008) found users with computer security software had a reduced risk of malware victimization, while Ngo and Paternoster (2011) found users with protective software were more likely to report infections. At the same time, Bossler and Holt (2009) found no relationship between security programs and risk of infection. These contradictory findings may stem from the fact that victims may only know that a compromise has occurred due to an alert provided by antivirus software (Symantec Corporation, 2014). In addition, malware infections can occur even in the presence of antivirus tools, suggesting they have limited utility to affect the risk of victimization (PandaLabs, 2007; Symantec Corporation, 2014).

The value of protective software as a target hardening mechanism against other forms of cybercrime is mixed. For example, protective software is related to a decreased risk of online identity theft victimization (Holt & Turner, 2012). This is sensible as keylogging malware and Trojan Horse programs can easily acquire personally identifiable information to facilitate identity crimes (e.g. Chu, Holt, & Ahn, 2010; Franklin, Paxon, Perrig, & Savage, 2007; Holt & Lampke, 2010; James, 2005). Studies of online harassment suggest that antivirus tools have no relationship to the risk of victimization (Holt & Bossler, 2009; Marcum, 2013). This relationship may stem from the fact that these tools cannot block mean or threatening emails and instant messages.

Protective software suites designed for parents to regulate the amount of time youths spend online and the types of content that can be accessed may minimize exposure to pornographic content and potentially block unwanted programs (Bossler & Holt, 2010; Ngo & Paternoster, 2011; Symantec Corporation, 2014). Assessments of these programs suggest they have minimal impact on the risk of bullying, harassment, and unwanted sexual solicitation (see Marcum, 2013). For instance, Moore and colleagues (2010) found that parental regulation of Internet usage did not significantly affect online harassment victimization. Similarly, evidence from nationally representative samples of youth suggests that the risks of various forms of person-based cybercrime victimization are high despite the presence of parental filtering and protective software in the home (Jones et al., 2012).

An additional target-hardening strategy oriented toward individual computer users is the development of computer skills (Bossler & Holt, 2009; Bossler, Holt, & May, 2012; Holt & Bossler, 2009). It is thought that individuals with a substantive understanding of technology may be more likely to determine if their computer has been compromised and identify scam emails and risky attachments that may otherwise harm their devices and data (Mitnick & Simon, 2002; Symantec Corporation, 2014). Personal computer skills do not have a consistent relationship to any diminished risk of malware infections (Bossler & Holt, 2009; Ngo & Paternoster, 2011). Victims may not know that they have been attacked since malicious software infections can mimic failing computer systems and hardware (Bossler & Holt, 2010, 2009; Symantec Corporation, 2014). Some hacking techniques may also become known to the victim after sensitive information has been removed or corrupted in some fashion (Wall, 2007). In addition, computer skill was nonsignificant in predicting phishing victimization in a college sample (Ngo & Paternoster, 2011). Computer skill also appears to have a mixed impact on the risk of harassment victimization (Bossler et al., 2012; Holt & Bossler, 2009). In some instances, those with greater computer proficiency may have an increased risk of harassment victimization, due to their involvement in cybercrime or spending time in online spaces that increase their risk of victimization (Bocij, 2004; Holt & Bossler, 2009). Thus, current empirical evidence has not supported general computer skills as an effective protective measure for individual computer users.

One of the greatest limitations of computer security affecting both individuals and corporations alike is the issue of **password** security. Almost every system, from web-based email to internal database logins, requires the use of a username and password to authenticate the user and provide a modicum of protection to that resource. Passwords have historically been weak due to the difficulty end users have in managing multiple passwords for various systems. Individuals may choose to use the same password across multiple accounts so that they can be more easily recalled. They may also use relatively simple passwords, including "123456," and "password" (Condliffe, 2015).

All of these issues create substantial opportunities for attackers to gain access to sensitive data and resources. An effective phishing campaign that leads an attacker to gain access to an individual's username and password credentials may provide them with subsequent access to other email accounts and other resources the individual maintains. As a result, some corporations are attempting to innovate in this space by finding alternative strategies to serve as user authentication which are much more difficult to circumvent. The recent development of touch-screen interfaces enables the use of passwords that are non-alphanumeric, such as distinct swipe patterns (Diepe, 2012). Android cell phones, for instance, utilize this sort of password for user access to the device. These passwords may be somewhat more difficult to defeat through dictionary attacks leveraged by hackers, though they may be determined if screens are not cleaned regularly (Diepe, 2012).

Some companies have begun to integrate **biometric security** measures into their products in order to authenticate the user as well. For instance, Apple recently integrated a fingerprint sensor into the home button of their smartphones which provided a unique degree of security. Additional biometric measures are being developed for use in smartphones, such as heartbeat sensors. The company Nymi has developed a wearable wristband that connects wirelessly to a cell phone and only allows the device to be used by an individual whose heartbeat matches the wearer's pattern (Kelly, 2014). Similarly, an app developed for Android phones by Descartes Biometrics maps where the human ear comes into contact with the phone's screen. The earprint then serves as a biometric authentication measure that can be used to unlock the phone (Kelly, 2014). Such an application could be expanded to authenticate users when completing financial transactions and other sensitive sign in services. It is important to note that much of the innovation in this space is associated only with mobile devices. Such technology has yet to be integrated or implemented successfully into traditional PC processes, limiting their utility.

Methods to increase the perceived risks of offending

Situational crime prevention researchers frequently consider various forms of surveillance when considering methods to increase an offender's risk of detection (e.g. Clarke, 1997; Newman & Clarke, 2003). Regarding cybercrime, there is mixed evidence concerning the utility of surveillance and guardianship techniques to increase the risk of offending. One key resource used to increase the risk of detection for acts of cyber-trespass are **Intrusion Detection Systems**, or **IDS**. One of the first publications on the use of a model for anomaly detection was published by Dorothy Denning (1986), which served as a basis for many modern IDS in use today. Modern systems involve a variety of software tools that actively monitor system logs and network traffic and apply detection algorithms to identify when a behavior is either legitimate use or constitutes a potential attack against the network (Denning, 1986). Computer science research on IDS focuses on their use in identifying two patterns of traffic: (1) misuse of resources based on general signatures of known malware or abuse (Debar, Dacier, & Wespi, 1999; Lee & Stolfo, 2000); and (2) anomalies that are deviations from standard patterns of use which suggest network abuse may be in progress (Debar et al., 1999; Patcha & Park, 2007). Thus, IDS have value in limiting both external attacks and internal actors who abuse company Internet use policies or attempt to misuse corporate resources.

Intrusion detection systems are extremely valuable as they operate differently from antivirus tools and firewalls (Scarfone & Mell, 2010). While antivirus tools are signature based, they do not provide information on the entire traffic patterns of a given network and only stop attacks on a single system if set to proactively scan for threats. Firewalls also limit access to various network resources coming from outside the network boundaries, but give no information on insider threats and provide no warning when threats are detected. Additionally, IDS can also be designed to operate passively, where the IDS alerts operators to potential problems, or proactively, which gives the system the ability to respond to threats automatically (Scarfone & Mell, 2010).

Though IDS provide a necessary layer of protection to network infrastructure, they are limited by various factors, such as how frequently they are updated to include new signatures (Elhag, Fernandez, Bawakid, Alshomrani, & Herrera, 2015). Furthermore, they may be unable to identify unknown or rare exploits and attack techniques because there is limited knowledge of the processes involved (Khor, Ting, & Phon-Amnuaisuk, 2012). **Anomaly detection** may prove valuable to offset this limitation, by identifying aberrations from usual patterns of use. The system managers must be able to identify when anomalous activity occurs and be willing to accept the potential for false positives based on user activities in general. Finally, the size and scope of network use means that IDS operators must have the ability to interpret potential intrusions quickly, and implement protocols either to limit access or block an individual from the network entirely (Gacto, Alcala, & Herrera, 2011).

These challenges mean that IDS are not a perfect tool to prevent attacks, though they may increase the difficulty offenders have in gaining access and raise the likelihood that an attack may be identified (Singh, Lambert, Ganacharya, & Williams, 2010). Attackers have found ways to minimize the likelihood of detection by changing processes of an attack so as to reduce the likelihood that it will conform to a known pattern of an incident. For instance, an attacker can send a Trojan or piece of malicious code through a different port on a system or use proxies to minimize the likelihood that the source of an attack is identified by IDS (Singh et al., 2010). In fact, IDS researchers continuously publish new methods to improve detection protocols and algorithms to identify malicious behavior (e.g. Elhag et al., 2015). Thus, IDS are just one potential tool that can increase the risk of detection in cybercrime incidents.

Several formal mechanisms have developed over the last two decades through the adoption of distinct undercover investigative techniques by law enforcement agencies to disrupt underground communities involved in various forms of cybercrime (Chu et al., 2010; Franklin et al., 2007; Hinduja, 2007; Poulsen, 2012). Police agencies recognize the importance of the Internet, chatrooms, and instant messaging systems for sex offenders, and have developed **undercover operations** to target those who solicit children or trade child pornography online with some degree of success (e.g. Hinduja, 2007; Jenkins, 2001; Wolak, Finkelhor, & Mitchell, 2012). In fact, the number of arrests concerning the production and/or consumption of child pornography has increased substantially over the last decade at both the local and federal levels in the US (Wolak et al., 2012). These arrests stem from more proactive police operations, rather than a necessary increase in the production of child pornography generally (Wolak et al., 2012).

Federal law enforcement agencies around the world have also infiltrated forums and IRC channels engaged in the sale of stolen data to identify buyers and data thieves and to disrupt the markets (Franklin et al., 2007; Holt & Lampke, 2010; Poulsen, 2012). Though market disruption is often viewed as a technique to reduce the rewards derived from offending (e.g. Cornish & Clarke, 2003), the mechanisms employed to disrupt markets also fit within an increased risk framework because of the methods used by law enforcement to monitor participants. This was evident in the 2004 bust of the international carding group called the **ShadowCrew**, where agents from the US Secret Service, Federal Bureau of Investigation (FBI), the UK's National Hi-Tech Crimes Unit, the Royal Canadian Mounted Police, and Europol used insiders in order to disrupt the network (see Chapter 4 for additional discussion; Holt & Lampke, 2010; Peretti, 2009; Poulsen, 2012).

In the wake of this operation, data thieves began to eschew the use of certain resources like virtual private networks (VPNs) as they were used by law enforcement to identify the location of market participants. A more complicated investigation began in 2006, when an FBI agent operating undercover as a hacker and using the name Master Splynter began to participate in a forum called **DarkMarket** (Poulsen, 2012). The forum was established by Renukanth Subramaniam, a UK citizen, who ran the site from an Internet café under the name Jilsi. The site sold all manner of personal data and credit card information, and had participants from Canada, Germany, France, Russia, Turkey, the UK, and the US. Master Splynter actively participated on the forum almost every day, eventually becoming a trusted member of the site. He even persuaded Jilsi to allow him to become an administrator of the site, and host it on a covert FBI-controlled server (Mills, 2009). As a result, the FBI was able to dismantle the group through joint operations around the world, leading to the arrest of 60 individuals including Jilsi.

The DarkMarket investigation is an excellent demonstration of the depths that underground stings must go to in order to be effective. These investigations are critical to develop substantive evidence against the participants, and sow distrust between market actors based on fear they may be a member of law enforcement. Such complex investigative techniques appear only to be possible at the national level because of jurisdictional challenges and the general resources available for investigation. As noted in Chapter 4, local agencies have limited capacity for hacking and data theft cases (e.g. Holt et al., 2010; Stambaugh et al., 2001). Thus, there is some limited evidence that the investigative capabilities of law enforcement may have generally no impact on the perceived risk of offending.

There is also limited empirical evidence that cybercriminals who are arrested and prosecuted do not receive punishments or sanctions that are commensurate with the scope of their offenses (Smith, Grabosky, & Urbas, 2004). Individuals in multiple nations appear to receive short prison sentences and fines that comprise a fraction of the total economic harm caused to financial institutions, corporations, and individual computer users generally (Smith et al., 2004). Beyond this research, there is generally little information on the prosecution and pursuit of cybercriminals at the local, state, or national level generally (see Holt, 2013; Wall, 2007). As a result, the lack of information regarding the criminal justice system response to cybercrime may actually embolden rather than deter offenders.

Due to the potential limitations of law enforcement agencies in combating transnational cybercrimes, a number of computer security firms have begun to engage in informal means of disruption of cybercriminal activities. Antivirus vendors and security companies take various steps, from publishing reports on active threats to actively policing corporate boundaries, in order to increase the perceived risk of offending. The security firm Mandiant (2013) published one of the most highly publicized reports in the last decade—a highly detailed investigation of the attacks and tradecraft of a single unit of the **People's Liberation Army (PLA)** of China which was previously unidentified in public documents. The report included targets that the unit actively attacked across various industry sectors, including companies managing electricity grids, and oil and gas pipelines. Mandiant also included the domain names, IP addresses, and malware signatures used by this unit, and referred to their attacks as **Advanced Persistent Threats (APT)** due to the persistent and effective attacks launched.

Making a report of this nature available to the general public was a departure from the company's usual policy with respect to disclosure of sensitive attack information. In fact, Mandiant (2013: 6) included a statement in the report describing its decision to make this information available, stating:

> there are downsides to publishing all of this information publicly ... When Unit 61398 changes their techniques after reading this ... they will undoubtedly force us to work harder to continue tracking them with such accuracy ... this report can temporarily increase the costs of Unit 61398's operations and impede their progress ...

Mandiant recognized the tensions affecting their decision-making process. This statement also illustrates an important issue that has become apparent over the last decade: the value of industry sources in deterring hackers and cybercriminals (see Chapter 4 for additional discussion). Given that industry sources have no necessary obligation to the general public, and can operate with much greater impunity and speed than law enforcement, there is a possibility that they may be more effective at increasing the perceived risk of engaging in cybercrime. The fact that a group's activities may be made public or otherwise detected by industry sources may be sufficient to make them seek alternative targets or practices.

The company **CrowdStrike** recently claimed that their presence within a company's network was sufficient to deter a group of Chinese hackers from completing an attack. CrowdStrike claims that a group called Hurricane Panda had successfully attacked a company in April 2014 (Shalal, 2015). CrowdStrike was hired to respond to that breach, and identified the vulnerability that enabled Hurricane Panda to gain access to the network. After reporting this vulnerability to Microsoft and acquiring a patch that secured the network, CrowdStrike was able to bar the hackers from subsequent access (Shalal, 2015).

In January 2015, CrowdStrike was hired by a second company which was being attacked by what was revealed to be the same group of hackers. The company expelled the hackers from this new network, and the hackers attempted to gain access through an alternative form of attack. After gaining initial access, CrowdStrike claims that the hackers scanned for the presence of their company's software on the victim network (Shalal, 2015). After Hurricane Panda members found CrowdStrike software, they exited the system and made no subsequent attempts to gain access. The co-founder of the company, Dmitri Alperovitch, claimed that the hacker group "realized that we had raised the cost and given the time and money wasted on a previous 0-day [exploit used on the first victim network], decided it wasn't worth it" (Shalal, 2015).

If this story is indeed accurate, it demonstrates that the risk of formal sanctions from law enforcement may be less significant for some hackers than those of informal sanctions that can be leveraged by industry sources. If an attack can be successfully terminated, then the effort spent by a hacker group is wasted and their methods for infiltration may be better understood and blocked in the future. Thus, there is a need to consider how an increased presence of industry in detection and mitigation of cybercriminal activity may affect not only the behavior of hackers, but the perceived legitimacy of law enforcement agencies as a whole.

The recording industry has also begun to partner with Internet service providers (ISPs) to engage in informal surveillance to increase the risks of digital piracy. The Recording Industry Association of America (RIAA) and other groups track downloading through torrent seeding programs and work with ISPs to identify the individual users responsible (Bachmann, 2007; Nhan, 2013). The individual user associated with the IP address and user account receives a **cease and desist letter** in order to help slow down the volume of pirated materials traded online (Nhan, 2013). In fact, the RIAA began to distribute letters to Internet users in the US who were thought to have engaged in illegal file sharing in order to pay settlements for their copyright violations in 2007 (Nhan, 2013). The letters indicated that individuals can pay with a credit card through the website p2plawsuits.com. This was thought to be a way to directly reduce the legal costs the RIAA incurred as a result of pursuing settlements against file sharing (Bachmann, 2007). It is unclear if this strategy has been successful, though it may have less severe consequences than their more invasive attempts to disrupt the flow of pirated materials (see Chapter 4 for discussion).

The development of both formal and informal self-reporting resources for victims of cybercrime is also essential to improve our knowledge of the prevalence of cybercrime and increase the risk of prosecution (Bossler & Holt, 2012; Wall, 2007). There are now two national-level models for information sharing and victim reporting for online fraud. The **US Internet Crime Complaint Center (IC3)** operates as a reporting resource for crime victims, consumers, and researchers to understand the scope of various forms of online fraud (Internet Crime Complaint Center, 2012). Victims can contact the agency through an online reporting form to indicate what type of crime they experienced, with the most common complaints associated with auction fraud, advance fee fraud victimization, and other forms of spam-based cybercrime (Internet Crime Complaint Center, 2012). In turn, victims may be directed to the appropriate investigative resources to further handle complaints. The UK operates a similar resource called **UK Action Fraud** which allows victims to report their experiences with fraud and triage the incident to an appropriate law enforcement agency (Action Fraud, 2015). There is minimal information available as to the number of complaints received that successfully lead to arrest. These mechanisms are a key starting point to improve victim reporting and awareness of online fraud.

Similarly, social media sites like Facebook, Instagram, Twitter, and YouTube, now provide internal reporting mechanisms for users to report inappropriate behavior. Since there are millions of active accounts on these platforms, it is virtually impossible for the operators to police all content that is posted. This may lead some offenders to feel that they can abuse these resources to send spam, hurtful content, or engage in various types of abuse with impunity. The development of reporting resources can increase the perceived risk of operating on these sites by enabling the user population to actively police this space.

A key example of the reporting process involves Facebook's report service. Facebook provides users with various resources to maintain the security of their account, including the ability to unfriend someone and block individuals from viewing their page. In the event that hate speech, hurtful messages, or pornographic content are found, or that someone notices their account has been taken over by a third party, they provide a Report button on user pages which brings the incident to the attention of the Facebook security team.

A recent report published by the Facebook Safety Group (Facebook Tools, 2012) indicated that filing a complaint is just the start of an extremely complex process. The nature of the complaint determines which of four

Operations groups handles the incident: Safety, Hate & Harassment, Abusive Content, and Access. For instance, hacking complaints go to the access group, while threats of vandalism, violence, or drug use go to the safety team. In the event that an incident leads to credible evidence that an individual is going to do harm to themselves, or to others (via hate speech or violence), Facebook will coordinate a response with an appropriate law enforcement agency. In addition, the individual against whom the complaint has been filed (i.e. the reportee) will receive a message from Facebook regarding their behavior. In some cases, the reportee may have their account terminated or shut down.

Facebook and other social media sites provide virtually no information on how many incidents lead to a response of some type. There is also minimal detail provided as to how many complaints are received each year, making the utility of these programs unclear. They do, however, provide a potential mechanism for informal monitoring and management of user behaviors online.

Mechanisms designed to reduce the rewards of offending

Research examining techniques to reduce the rewards of offending in real-world crimes typically focuses on techniques designed either to remove potential targets from the view of offenders or disrupt markets where products can be sold (Clarke, 1997). There are various technological mechanisms that can be deployed in the field to deny cybercriminals rewards for their actions, particularly those offenses involving deception and theft (Newman & Clarke, 2003). For example, the use of **honeypots** in corporate and organizational networks may prove valuable in reducing the rewards of offending. As noted in Chapter 2, honeypots mimic actual user systems in networked environments in order to entice attackers into attempts to gain access to data and resources (The Honeynet Project, 2003). In actuality, they provide a way to monitor attacker behavior and do not contain user data or sensitive information. Honeypots may be useful in lulling attackers into a false sense of successful penetration and provide information on attacker behavior that is critical for enterprise-level security. In fact, honeypots can be used as an additional means of threat intelligence by capturing attacker behavior in the event they have been able to evade IDS detection (The Honeynet Project, 2003; Riebach, Rathgeb, & Toedtmann, 2005). Since honeypots can be detected and avoided by skilled hackers, they are only one potential solution to minimize the rewards an offender may gain in the course of an attack.

If an attacker has successfully breached an organization, they are likely to seek out sensitive data that can be resold or used for economic advantage by a nation-state. One of the key ways to help minimize the rewards from a network intrusion or malicious insider is to utilize **data obfuscation**, or **data masking** techniques to hide database information (Fujinkoki, 2015; Oracle, 2013). The development of the Internet and the World Wide Web has transformed the quantity of data now available by retailers, organizations, and government sources. Large-scale data repositories are now commonplace, which creates ample opportunities for misuse and fraud if an individual is able to gain access to sensitive information that may be stored either on servers in the cloud or internally behind network boundaries (Fujinkoki, 2015). Nations have also begun to mandate that data be secured from outsiders to ensure individual privacy and security, as with the US **Health Insurance Portability and Accountability Act (HIPAA)** regarding healthcare data (Collins et al., 2011; Oracle, 2013).

As a result, data obfuscation techniques are necessary to maintain the privacy and integrity of data from individuals who are not otherwise supposed to access this information. There are a range of techniques that can be applied to mask data, which typically focus on either code or data. **Code-based obfuscation** involves techniques to hide the meaning in activities used to search and operate data queries. Such techniques make it difficult for an attacker or insider to determine the functions needed to actually use data maintained in a repository (Oracle, 2013). At the same time, data obfuscations are designed to hide information in the data, and can take multiple forms ranging from simple substitution of values to encryption of database information which can only be decrypted using a specific cipher key.

The inherent value of obfuscation techniques to better protect information in large databases is obvious. There are weaknesses in the techniques used to mask data which can easily be subverted by attackers. For instance, the use of some code obfuscations techniques may be defeated by malicious insiders who can monitor and log the queries used by individuals in order to reverse engineer the meaning of the codes (Fujinkoki, 2015). In addition, the use of obfuscation techniques can actually limit the usability of databases for end users and employees. This may account for the fact that many retailers use only the bare minimum encryption standards on their databases of information as required by law in their nation (e.g. Oracle, 2013). As a whole, data obfuscation techniques are not a perfect solution, but create some potential challenges for cybercriminals when attempting to gain access to information that could be used to engage in fraud or theft.

An additional technique designed to both protect consumers and increase the difficulty offenders have in manipulating and acquiring rewards from stolen data is the use of "**Chip and PIN**" or **EMV (Europay, MasterCard, and Visa)** technologies. Card-issuing financial institutions provide account holders with cards that have an integrated circuit or computer chip which authenticates a transaction at point of sale terminals and ATMs (Pavia, Veres-Ferrer, & Foix-Escura, 2012). These cards require that the user insert their card into a specially designed point of sale terminal which connects the chip on the card to the payment system. The account holder must then enter a **Personal Identification Number (PIN)** which authenticates the card, the chip, and the PIN through bank servers (Pavia et al., 2012). These technologies provide a greater degree of security for the account holder, as the magnetic strip data on the card may be captured but not the actual integrated chip. As a result, fraudsters who acquire data from EVM or Chip and PIN cards are unable to use them to engage in transactions at point of sale terminals (Pavia et al., 2012; Sullivan, 2013; Wilson, 2012).

The adoption of Chip and PIN technologies in Europe suggests they have a direct impact on fraud losses. For instance, Chip and PIN technology was rolled out across the UK in 2003, and there was a direct reduction in fraud losses in 2005 (Hayashi & Sullivan, 2013). It was thought that this was due to the increased difficulty offenders had in using stolen data at point of sale terminals. Fraudsters instead began to use data acquired through breaches and other means to make purchases online and over the phone due to weaker security protocols (Hayashi & Sullivan, 2013). In fact, trend analyses suggest fraud losses increased dramatically between 2005 and 2008, when the deployment of Chip and PIN technologies were almost complete across the UK. These estimates began to decline, as security protocols were increased in these environments making it more difficult for offenders to acquire funds from stolen data (Hayashi & Sullivan, 2013).

Since the US has experienced a massive increase in mega-breaches, losing millions of cards at a time, there has been a concurrent increase in the amount of fraud completed due to counterfeit card use (Sullivan, 2014). In fact, this category is now the top method used to engage in fraud generally. As a result, financial institutions across the country began to issue Chip and PIN cards to customers starting in late 2014 to help minimize the likelihood of successful use in fraud (Sullivan, 2013). Researchers estimate we may see similar declines in fraud to the UK and France, though it will depend entirely on customer education and the ways that authorization and authentication protocols are implemented. There is also a need to dramatically improve our reporting systems for fraud and identity crimes so as to increase our ability to recognize when and how fraud is taking place and the total amount of fraud losses experienced from different payment categories (Hayashi & Sullivan, 2013; Wilson, 2012).

There have also been various attempts to deny pirates' access to various forms of illegally copied media by tracking and disrupting international file-sharing networks. As noted in Chapter 4, companies have been hired in order to poison torrent networks with corrupted files. Recently, Sony Pictures Entertainment began a similar campaign of placing fake "seed" files, which appear to contain media files but have no actual content. This tactic was employed after a hacker collective called the **Guardians of Peace (GoP)** leaked files and films, some of which were not released to the public yet, as part of a campaign to threaten Sony not to release a film mocking North Korea (Gallagher, 2014). The company was able to distribute such a large number of fake seeds that they were able to make it difficult for pirates to identify the real files from the fake ones. Similarly, several countries now allow ISPs to block users from accessing websites known for sharing pirated materials (Stone, 2015). These tactics have not diminished the prevalence of pirated media, but demonstrate that creative extra-legal solutions to piracy may be employed without legal challenges to the industry's methods (Nhan, 2013).

A final technique employed to reduce the rewards of cybercrime offending involves affecting the payment mechanisms used by offenders to pay for goods and services in the underground economy for hacking and data. There are a range of **online payment systems** used by market actors to pay for various services, including WebMoney, Bitcoin, Yandex, and other digital currencies. Law enforcement agencies may be able to initiate investigations against payment providers with more efficiency than attempts to disrupt the networks of market actors (Franklin et al., 2007; Holt & Smirnova, 2014). By eliminating payment providers, law enforcement agencies would be able to produce a short-term impact on the practices of stolen data vendors and buyers by increasing the difficulty associated with sending and receiving payments. This strategy could have a relatively equal effect on all markets because of their dependence on online currencies and payment providers (e.g. Franklin et al., 2007; Holt, 2013; Motoyama et al., 2011).

There are two recent examples of such a disruption strategy, including the US-based prosecution of the **e-Gold** payment processor on four charges of money laundering due in part to its use by data thieves in the early 2000s (Holt & Lampke, 2010; Peretti, 2009; Surowiecki, 2013). The service provided a digital gold-backed currency that was known to be used by members of the carding group the ShadowCrew to send and receive payments for stolen data (Peretti, 2009). This investigation forced market actors to transition to other payment systems, and affected the practices of buyers and sellers (Krebs, 2013). Similarly, the payment processor LibertyReserve was shut down in 2013 by the US government on charges of money laundering and operating an unlicensed financial transaction company (Surowiecki, 2013). Anecdotal evidence suggests that market actors lost thousands of dollars individually as a result of this takedown (Krebs, 2013).

It is necessary to note that this tactic is not a panacea, as it will only slow the flow of money while buyers and sellers adapt to different strategies (Holt & Lampke, 2010; Krebs, 2013). There are myriad forms of currency that could be used by market actors if one payment service is eliminated. At the same time, the short-term benefits afforded by this sort of enforcement strategy may be of substantive value to reduce the rewards of cybercrime. There is a need for greater research in this area to evaluate the impact of such disruption strategies on cybercrime behaviors.

Techniques to remove excuses for offenders and victims

Situational crime prevention scholars typically focus on offenders when considering techniques to remove excuses and justifications for involvement in crime. For example, clear guidelines for behavior including speed limit signs and parking instructions reduce an individual's ability to say they were unaware that their actions violated the law (Cornish & Clarke, 2003). In addition, offenders may also utilize techniques of neutralization in order to justify or excuse their actions in some fashion (Newman & Clarke, 2003).

One key way to remove any excuses that individuals may have for cyber-crime is to inform them of what behaviors are acceptable in online environments (Newman & Clarke, 2003). Many companies, universities, publicly accessible Wi-Fi hotspots operated by companies, and even public libraries, provide information to individual users about what behaviors will not be tolerated while online through **Internet Use Policies (IUPs)** or **Fair Use Policies** (Sommestad, Hallberg, Lundholm, & Bengtsson, 2014). These policies are typically posted when an individual attempts to log in to a network, and the user must agree to abide by these policies in order to use the service (Young & Case, 2004). IUPs also tend to focus on deterrence through the use of fear of sanctions from either the organization or law enforcement, depending on the behavior (Li, Sarathy, & Zhang, 2010; Pahnila et al., 2007).

It is important to note that the publication of acceptable and unacceptable behaviors fits into traditional deterrence theory from a criminological perspective (see Chapter 3). The majority of research in this area, however, is informed by information security and computer science, limiting our understanding of this phenomenon from a social science perspective. With this caveat in mind, the larger body of research on IUPs suggests they may be generally unsuccessful in reducing misuse on corporate-controlled networks (e.g. Li et al., 2010). There are also inconsistent findings as to the factors that affect individual compliance with a particular IUP. A recent meta-analysis of 29 studies on this issue found that over 60 variables have been included in research designs, with no one factor accounting for the majority of compliance or non-compliance (Sommestad et al., 2014). Furthermore, the way that variables have been measured is extremely inconsistent which renders it difficult to say that one factor, such as individual moral beliefs, is more likely to increase compliance overall (Sommestad et al., 2014).

It is also unclear as to the ways that individual and organizational factors interact to increase or decrease compliance (Sommestad et al., 2014). For instance, there is limited evidence that individuals who are inclined to abuse network policies tend to have loose moral beliefs that enable them to feel little sense of culpability (D'Arcy et al., 2009). Those who conform to policies also tend to view the guidelines as morally responsible and in line with their own value systems (Li et al., 2010; Tyler, 2006; Tyler et al., 2007). At the same time, the perceived fairness of a formal or informal organizational punishment for violations of IUPs appears to directly affect compliance (Li et al., 2010).

Taken as a whole, there is a need for greater research on the utility of IUPs from a criminological perspective. It is possible that factors beyond perceptual deterrence, such as individual levels of self-control, and their ability to rationally comprehend the meaning of IUPs may have a greater influence on individual willingness to comply than perceptual deterrence factors. Whether or not IUPs work to deter behavior, it is vital that they continue to be used in order to provide warnings to both employees and users that there are potential punishments for wrongdoing. Without this information, a person could easily claim that they had no idea what they were doing was wrong or a violation of corporate policy.

One of the more prominent factors that affects individual involvement in offending is their acceptance of justifications for deviant and criminal activity (Cornish & Clarke, 1987; Newman & Clarke, 2003). Attempts to target offenders' ability to excuse or justify their activities can be pivotal in preventing offending over the long term. To that end, there is a substantial body of research on the impact that justifications and neutralizing definitions for cybercrime have on individual behavior (see Higgins & Marcum, 2011; Holt & Bossler, 2014; Skinner & Fream, 1997). The belief that it is acceptable to engage in various forms of deviance, and that the online environment is a generally lawless and unpoliced space, may increase individual willingness to engage in cybercrimes.

Peer associations are pivotal in introducing individuals to techniques of neutralization to excuse or justify malicious or unethical behaviors online (Bossler & Burruss, 2011; Holt et al., 2012; Holt et al., 2010; Skinner & Fream, 1997). Computer hackers consistently report maintaining peer relationships with other hackers, whether on or off-line (Holt, 2009; Holt & Kilger, 2012; Schell & Dodge, 2002). Peers may provide a source of imitation and expose individuals to the perception that hacking does not harm individuals (Gordon & Ma, 2003). They may also lead the hacker to blame their victims for having poor skills or security to prevent victimization (Jordan & Taylor, 1998; Taylor, 1999). Social relationships are also an important predictor for involvement in digital piracy of media and software (Higgins, 2005; Higgins & Marcum, 2011; Higgins, Marcum, Freiburger, & Ricketts, 2012; Hinduja & Ingram, 2008; Holt et al., 2012; Skinner & Fream, 1997). Positive reinforcement for participation in software piracy (Holt & Copes, 2010; Ingram & Hinduja, 2008) and the presence of sources of imitation for pirating behaviors increase the likelihood that an individual will engage in piracy (Holt et al., 2010; Ingram & Hinduja, 2008; Skinner & Fream, 1997).

Individual participation in cybercrimes also appears to increase the risk of cybercrime victimization, especially malicious software infections (Bossler & Holt, 2009; Choi, 2008; Holt & Copes, 2010; Wolfe, Higgins, & Marcum, 2007). Downloading movies or media from untrustworthy online sources greatly increases individual proximity to infected files, as does access to pornographic photos and video (Bossler & Holt, 2009; Choi, 2008). Engaging in cyberbullying, online harassment, and other forms of cybercrime also increase the risk of various forms of online victimization (Holt & Bossler, 2009; Holt et al., 2012; Hinduja & Patchin, 2009; Ybarra et al., 2007).

As a result, there is a need to identify and target strategies that deter offenders by removing the influence of techniques of neutralization or justifications for deviant behavior in order to reduce their risk of harm. Limited research suggests public awareness campaigns regarding various forms of cybercrime are generally ineffective at reducing rates of offending. A number of campaigns concerning the illicit nature of digital piracy have been created and implemented in the field, including messages against piracy at the start of major movies, television, and video games (e.g. Nhan, 2013). Their implementation produces a general reduction in piracy, though it is short-lived and does not generally affect rates of piracy in a practical fashion (Bachmann, 2007).

The Motion Picture Association of America has also developed educational programs aimed at youth, such as a "Respect Copyrights" patch that Boy Scouts could receive for completing an educational program (Verrier, 2013). The Center for Copyright Information also sponsored the iKeepSafe program, targeting students from kindergarten through high school with messaging about copyright laws and the notion of intellectual property (iKeepSafe, 2015). The language in these programs is meant to teach youth what copyright means, what value intellectual property has (through ideas about drawing and stories they may write), and how stealing property negatively affects others. It is unclear how well children actually understand these messages, or the extent to which they fundamentally affect their views on illegal file sharing. Thus, there is a need for increased research to evaluate anti-piracy programs and the extent to which they inhibit the formation of justifications for piracy (see also Holt & Copes, 2010).

Recent legal innovations have also been implemented that are designed to remove excuses from corporations not reporting data breaches and major incidents affecting the safety and security of citizens' identities. Most states in the US now have laws that require corporations to notify consumers when personal information has been harmed, to increase liability for the data holder, and improve victim agency in the event they are compromised (Holt & Schell, 2013; National Conference of State Legislatures, 2012). Breaches can directly affect millions of consumers depending on the scope of a breach, often through no fault of the consumers. **Data breach notification** laws remove the ability of companies to hide major incidents from the public while at the same time removing any excuses from victims that they were not aware their data were lost.

The first US state to develop a breach notification law was California, with the **California Security Breach Notification Act of 2003** (Cal. Civil Code). This law mandated that any entity that experienced a database compromise must notify victims in the event that the loss of data led to the loss of an individual's first and last name along with any of the following information: (1) social security number; (2) driver's license number or California State ID card number; or (3) an account, debit, or credit card number in combination with any security information that could be used to authorize a transaction, such as the three-digit security code on the card.

There are currently 46 states in the US with mandatory data breach notification laws, as well as the District of Columbia, Guam, Puerto Rico, and the Virgin Islands (National Conference of State Legislatures, 2012). A similar set of laws were recently implemented in the European Union (EU) through the E-Privacy Directive 2009/136/EC, requiring telecommunications companies and ISPs to report a data breach within 24 hours of its discovery (Ashford, 2013). There is also a regulatory requirement within the EU, called the Draft Data Protection Regulation, requiring businesses to report data breaches to the general public (Ashford, 2013). Similar draft legislation is being developed in Asia and South America, suggesting that this may remove excuses for businesses not to promote greater protection of personal data from hackers and data thieves (Newman & Clarke, 2003).

Despite the growth in data breach notification laws, there are still a substantial number of breaches that occur each year. There is also some evidence that breaches are not reported consistently across industries, leading to difficulties in understanding the scope of harm caused by each incident (Collins et al., 2011). In fact, some breaches are brought to the public's knowledge before the victim company has actually disclosed the incident based on state laws (Collins et al., 2011). For instance, the home improvement chain Home Depot experienced a data breach during the summer of 2014. The noted security reporter Brian Krebs reported on September 2 that banks were seeing massive quantities of data being sold through an online forum which appeared to come from Home Depot stores (Krebs, 2014a). The company issued a press release and began customer notifications on September 18 (Krebs, 2014b). Thus, data breach laws may have limited utility in encouraging industry to report victimization to the general public.

Additional laws have developed that reduce the ability of victims to claim that they were unaware their personal information was lost or that they have experienced identity theft (Holt & Schell, 2013; Newman & Clarke, 2003). For instance, the **Fair and Accurate Credit Transactions Act of 2003** in the US provides multiple protections to help reduce the risk of identity theft, and assist victims to repair their credit in the event of identity theft (Holt & Schell, 2013). This law required businesses to remove customer credit card information (except the last four digits) from receipts to minimize exposure of personal information. The law also gives consumers the right to request a copy of their credit report at no charge every year from the three major credit bureaus in the US (Equifax, Experian, and TransUnion) to assist in the identification of fraudulent transactions or potential identity theft (Brenner, 2011). Finally, the Act provided mechanisms for consumers to place and receive alerts on their credit file to reduce the risk of fraudulent transactions (Brenner, 2011). Similar legislation exists in the UK; European data and identity protection laws generally help to minimize the risk of loss from cybercriminals (Brenner, 2011; Holt & Schell, 2013; Newman & Clarke, 2003).

Summary and conclusions

Taken as a whole, this chapter demonstrates the breadth of research and policy initiatives designed to affect cybercrime. The range of scholarship has identified a number of key factors that affect the success of offending, harden prospective targets, and reduce the likelihood of obtaining funds or utilizing data acquired. Reviewing this literature also demonstrates a number of limitations and failures in current strategies to prevent cybercrime.

One of the clearest deficiencies in strategies to affect cybercrime is targeted at the end user, as they are the weakest link in the security chain. Enterprises can employ various tools to detect attacks, such as IDS, and provide resources to limit the likelihood of infections and phishing campaigns. If the individual users within that environment do not utilize them properly, are negligent in using basic security strategies, or misuse resources in violation of IUPs, then those tools are completely nullified. In response to this problem, the US Department of Defense recently attempted to implement a whole-of-government approach to "cyber-hygiene" by treating computer security as a public health issue (Department of Defense, 2011). The use of simple techniques that are easy comparisons to real-world health, such as comparing antivirus software to tooth brushing to decrease cavities, may be instrumental in increasing the general security of sensitive networks and better network protection as a whole (Department of Defense, 2011). Such strategies may decrease the likelihood of success that an attack will be effective, particularly simple-to-defeat, low-level attack tools like botnets that create stable attack platforms (Bacher et al., 2005; Chu et al., 2010; Department of Defense, 2011).

There is no way to completely harden end users from compromise since attackers utilize zero-day exploits against commonly used software and operating systems (Chu et al., 2010; Symantec Corporation, 2014). As a result, some argue that vendors should proactively identify as many vulnerabilities as possible prior to a product launch in the market to ensure a more secure product from the outset (Hinduja & Kooi, 2013; Newman & Clarke, 2003). This issue is important as consumer electronic devices are increasingly designed to be successfully used out of the box with minimal technical skill, particularly tablet computers and cell phones.

The lack of pre-installed security tools on certain devices also demonstrates the need for solutions that harden devices in a relatively seamless and easy-to-use fashion. For instance, most mobile device providers (Apple, Android, Kindle, etc.) do not come installed with protective software, despite the fact that the browser and other common applications may be compromised (see Chu et al., 2010; Symantec Corporation, 2014). Similarly, the ability to download third-party applications through markets outside the regulated Android marketplace means that cell phones and tablets using this operating system platform require security tools (Symantec Corporation, 2014).

The absence of security tools makes it difficult to promote their necessity to unskilled computer users, and creates large populations of vulnerable targets for attackers. Making antivirus suites part of operating systems that function across laptop and mobile platforms rather than stand-alone services may prove essential to increase security. Such a measure could also ensure silent updates to vulnerable system protocols and antivirus suites without the need for user intervention, ensuring greater security overall. These strategies can remove excuses for both victims and attackers, thereby increasing the risk of detection while decreasing the likelihood of success (e.g. Newman & Clarke, 2003).

In order to further deter offenders through increased risk of detection and removal of excuses for both prospective victims and attackers, there is a need for clearly defined, strategic policy initiatives that affect offenders locally and nationally (see Brenner, 2008; Holt et al., 2010; Wall, 2007). Local agencies have been given substantially increased responsibilities to respond to cyber-crime and terrorist attacks, though their capabilities vary based on budgets and staffing (see Chapter 4; Stambaugh et al., 2001). In addition, the jurisdictional duties of local agencies relative to federal law enforcement may not be clearly elaborated, thereby limiting the perception among local agencies that they should respond to cybercrimes (see Bossler & Holt, 2012).

As a consequence, offenders may believe that they can operate with impunity and affect whatever citizens and countries they choose. This creates tacit nation-level approval for cyber-attacks against US resources while limiting the deterrent impact of any sanction (Andress & Winterfeld, 2011; Chu et al., 2010). Victims may feel more disenfranchised by the local response and not report incidents, thereby reducing the perception that incidents may be pursued (see Wall, 2007). Thus, there is a need to increase the training and resources of law enforcement agencies, and promote the reporting of cyber-crimes among local victims to police in order to better document the prevalence of these offenses (Brenner, 2008; Department of Defense, 2011; Stambaugh et al., 2001).

There may also be some value in legislation designed to sanction businesses in the event of a data breach or hacking incident, as a vulnerability in an industry source can affect a massive victim population with greater speed and efficiency than targeting individual end users. Legislation designed to mandate data breach reporting is an important step in order to increase recognition of this threat among the general public (Collins, Sainato, & Khey, 2011; Khey & Sainato, 2013). Evidence suggests that data breaches are clustered in states with the most punitive laws and sanctions for both industries and offenders (Khey & Sainato, 2013). As a result, there may be limited utility in attempting to deter offenders through legal strategies alone.

There is also a need for clearly defined roles and collaborative efforts between local and federal governmental agencies, public and private companies, and law enforcement in order to secure critical infrastructure from cyber-attacks (Andress & Winterfeld, 2011; Rege, 2013). This is particularly difficult as much of the telephony, financial, and power system equipment in the US is owned by private industry, but regulated in part by government entities. As a consequence, any attempt to standardize security protocols or response/incident management between industry and government may be met with resistance, or may not be completely adopted across an industry (Brodscky & Radvanovsky, 2011; Kilger, 2011).

The increasing militarization of cyberspace by nation-states may also be effective in order to deter certain forms of cyber-attack. For instance, the US Department of Defense detailed their new policies treating cyberspace as a protected domain in the same way as physical environments (Andress & Winterfeld, 2011; Department of Defense, 2011). There is substantive emphasis placed on sanctions for three forms of attack: theft of data, destructive attacks to degrade network functionality, and denial of service attacks (Department of Defense, 2011). This is due to the direct threat these forms of hacking attacks can cause to the communications capabilities of the nation and the maintenance of secrecy and intellectual property. Similar policies and strategic plans are emerging in developed nations around the world, from Canada, to South Korea, to the UK (Andress & Winterfeld, 2011). The development and publication of these policies helps to illustrate the sanctions that will result from attacks and generally increase the risk of serious response to targeted attacks (Andress & Winterfeld, 2011; Brenner, 2008).

The development of training and education programs that promote ethical computer use among youth may be invaluable in reducing long-term rates of offending and increasing the reporting of offending to law enforcement (Brenner, 2008; Hinduja & Patchin, 2009; Wall, 2001). There are a number of ethical education programs currently being implemented across the globe, though there are few attempts to evaluate their utility or impact on behavior. Thus, consistent research is needed to assess the influence that education and awareness programs will have on youth behavior over time. In fact, there have been few attempts to evaluate cybercrime prevention and enforcement strategies in various contexts. Thus, criminologists must begin to address this gap in the research literature and improve our knowledge of the utility of existing techniques to affect cybercrimes (Rege, 2013; Newman & Clarke, 2003). In turn, more effective prevention techniques may be deployed in order to reduce the number of cybercrimes committed worldwide.

Finally, there is a need to focus on techniques to deter and detect insider abuse and crime. While most of the techniques outlined in this chapter focus on external threats, misuse of resources by insiders is still a credible threat to corporate security. There is a need to develop security policies and programs with specific emphasis on the malicious insider in order to increase the perceived risk of detection and remove their ability to justify wrongdoing (Collins et al., 2011). One way to improve on existing policies and procedures is to develop them in tandem with crime scripts of malicious insiders (Sainato, 2009; Willison & Siponen, 2009). As noted in Chapter 2, crime script analyses focus on the process of offending from start to finish, including methods of infiltration and justification of actions (e.g. Hutchings & Holt, 2015). The findings from script analyses can then be used to develop countermeasures for each technique and minimize the likelihood of success throughout the process, including IDS signatures, user policies, and procedures within human resource programs to effectively sanction wrongdoing (Sainato, 2009; Willison & Siponen, 2009). In turn, such techniques may prove invaluable to strengthen corporate defenses against both internal and external threats.

Key terms

Advanced Persistent Threats (APTs)
Anomaly detection
Antivirus software
Biometric security
Botnet
California Security Breach Notification Act of 2003
Cease and desist letter
Chip and PIN
Code-based obfuscation
CrowdStrike
DarkMarket
Data breach notification
Data masking
Data obfuscation
e-Gold
Europay, MasterCard, and Visa (EMV)
External attackers
Fair and Accurate Credit Transactions Act of 2003
Fair Use Policies
Guardians of Peace (GoP)
Health Insurance Portability and Accountability Act (HIPAA)
Honeypots
Internal attackers
Internet Use Policies
Intrusion detection systems (IDS)
Online payment systems
Operation Aurora
Password
People's Liberation Army (PLA)
Personal Identification Number (PIN)
Phishing
ShadowCrew
Social engineering
Target hardening
UK Action Fraud
Undercover operations
US Internet Crime Complaint Center (IC3)

Discussion questions

1 Which combination of prevention strategies do you think will have the greatest success in reducing the likelihood of external attackers? Do they need to differ from that of internal attackers, and why?

2 If the greatest threat to Internet security is the individual, what kinds of messaging and strategies need to be used in order to harden them from attack? How can we make cybersecurity a real concern for the common person?

3 Will we ever be able to truly eliminate the threat of some forms of cybercrime? How could this be achieved? If not, why not?

4 Why do you think Internet User Agreements are unsuccessful in limiting wrongdoing on corporate networks? What individual factors may lead individuals to either ignore these agreements or take them seriously?

References

Action Fraud (2015). National fraud & cyber crime reporting centre report it. www. actionfraud.police.uk.

Andress, J., & Winterfeld, S. (2011). *Cyber Warfare: Techniques, Tactics, and Tools for Security Practitioners.* Waltham, MA: Syngress.

Ashford, W. (2013). EU data breach disclosures to be enforced soon. *Computer Weekly.* www.computerweekly.com/news/2240203760/EU-data-breach-disclosures-to-be-enforced-soon (accessed 1 September 2013).

Bacher, P., Holz, T., Kotter, M., & Wicherski, G. (2005). *Tracking Botnets: Using Honeynets to Learn More About Bots.* The Honeynet Project and Research Alliance. www.honeynet.org/papers/bots/.

Bachmann, M. (2007). Lesson spurned? Reactions of online music pirates to legal prosecutions by the RIAA. *International Journal of Cyber Criminology* 2, 213–227.

Bocij, P. (2004). *Cyberstalking: Harassment in the Internet Age and How to Protect Your Family.* Westport, CT: Praeger Publishers.

Bossler, A.M. & Burruss, G.W. (2011). The general theory of crime and computer hacking: Low self-control hackers? In T.J. Holt & B.H. Schell (Eds.), *Corporate Hacking and Technology-Driven Crime: Social Dynamics and Implications* (pp. 38–67). Hershey, PA: ISI Global.

Bossler, A.M., & Holt, T.J. (2009). On-line activities, guardianship, and malware infection: An examination of routine activities theory. *International Journal of Cyber Criminology*, 3, 400–420.

Bossler, A.M., & Holt, T.J. (2010). The effect of self-control on victimization in the cyberworld. *Journal of Criminal Justice*, 38, 227–236.

Bossler, A.M., & Holt, T.J. (2012). Patrol officers' perceived role in responding to cybercrime. *Policing: An International Journal of Police Strategies and Management*, 35, 165–181.

Bossler, A.M., Holt, T.J., & May, D.C. (2012). Predicting online harassment among a juvenile population. *Youth and Society*, 44, 500–523.

Braga, A.A. (2002). *Problem-oriented Policing and Crime Prevention.* Monsey, NY: Criminal Justice Press.

Brenner, S.W. (2008). *Cyberthreats: The Emerging Fault Lines of the Nation State.* New York: Oxford University Press.

Brenner, S.W. (2011). Defining cybercrime: A review of federal and state law. In R.D. Clifford (Ed.), *Cybercrime: The Investigation, Prosecution, and Defense of a Computer-related Crime.* Third edition (pp. 15–104). Raleigh, NC: Carolina Academic Press.

Brodscky, J., & Radvanovsky, R. (2011). Control systems security. In T.J. Holt & B. Schell (Eds.), *Corporate Hacking and Technology-Driven Crime: Social Dynamics and Implications* (pp. 187–204). Hershey, PA: IGI-Global.

Cappelli, D., Moore, A., Shimeall, T.J., & Trzeciak, R. (2006). *Common Sense Guide to Prevention and Detection of Insider Threats.* Carnegie Mellon Cylab.

Choi, K.C. (2008). Computer crime victimization and integrated theory: An empirical assessment. *International Journal of Cyber Criminology,* 2, 308–333.

Chu, B., Holt, T.J., & Ahn, G.J. (2010). *Examining the Creation, Distribution, and Function of Malware On-line.* Washington, DC: National Institute of Justice.

Clarke, R.V. (1983). Situational crime prevention: Its theoretical basis and practical scope. *Crime and Justice,* 4, 225–256.

Clarke R.V. (1997). *Situational Crime Prevention: Successful Case Studies.* Second edition. Guilderland, NY: Harrow and Heston.

Clarke, R.V., & Eck, J.E. (2007). *Crime Analysis for Problem Solvers in 60 Small Steps.* Washington, DC: US Department of Justice, Office of Community Oriented Policing Services. www.popcenter.org/Library/RecommendedReadings/60Steps.pdf.

Clarke, R.V., & Felson, M. (1993). *Routine Activity and Rational Choice.* Advances in Criminological Theory, Vol. 5. New Brunswick, NJ: Transaction Books.

Cohen, L.E., & Felson, M. (1979). Social change and crime rate trends: A routine activity approach. *American Sociological Review,* 44, 588–608.

Collins, J.D., Sainato, V.A., & Khey, D.N. (2011). Organizational data breaches 2005–2010: Applying SCP to the healthcare and education sectors. *International Journal of Cyber Criminology,* 5, 794–810.

Condliffe, J. (2015). The 25 most popular passwords of 2104: We're all doomed. *Gizmodo,* January 20. gizmodo.com/the-25-most-popular-passwords-of-2014-were-all-doomed-1680596951.

Cornish, D., & Clarke, R.V. (1987). Understanding crime displacement: An application of rational choice theory. *Criminology,* 25, 933–947.

Cornish, D.B., & Clarke, R.V. (2003). Opportunities, precipitators and criminal decisions: A reply to Wortley's critique of situational crime prevention. *Crime Prevention Studies,* 16, 41–96.

D'Arcy, J., Hovav, A., & Galletta, D. (2009). User awareness of security countermeasures and its impact on information systems misuse: A deterrence approach. *Information Systems Research,* 20, 79–98.

Debar, A., Dacier, J., & Wespi, C. (1999). Towards a taxonomy of intrusion-detection systems. *Computer Networks,* 31, 805–822.

Denning, D.E. (1986). An intrusion detection model. Proceedings of the Seventh IEEE Symposium on Security and Privacy. May, 119–131.

Denning, D.E. (2011). Cyber-conflict as an emergent social problem. In T.J. Holt & B. Schell (Eds.), *Corporate Hacking and Technology-Driven Crime: Social Dynamics and Implications* (pp. 170–186). Hershey, PA: IGI-Global.

Department of Defense (2011) *Department of Defense Strategy for Operating in Cyberspace.* Washington, DC. www.defense.gov/news/d20110714cyber.pdf.

Dhillon, G., & Moores, S. (2001). Computer crimes: Theorizing about the enemy within. *Computers and Security*, 20, 715–723.

Diepe, F. (2012). Your finger swipe could become your password. *Technewsdaily*, 2 October. www.technewsdaily.com/6300-your-finger-swipe-could-become-your-password.html.

Elhag, S., Ferndandez, A., Bawakid, A., Alshomrani, S., & Herrera, F. (2015). On the combination of genetic fuzzy systems and pairwise learning for improving detection rates on intrusion detection systems. *Expert Systems with Applications*, 42, 193–202.

Facebook Tools (2012). *Safety*. www.facebook.com/safety/tools/.

FireEye (2012). Spear phishing attacks—Why they are successful and how to stop them. Combatting the attack of choice for cybercriminals. www.locked.com/sites/default/files/Spear-Phishing-Attacks-White-Paper.pdf.

Franklin, J., Paxson, V., Perrig, A., & Savage, S. (2007). An inquiry into the nature and cause of the wealth of Internet miscreants. Paper presented at CCS07, October 29–November 2, in Alexandria, VA.

Fujinkoki, H. (2015). Designs, analyses, and optimizations for attribute-shuffling obfuscation to protect information from malicious cloud administrators. *Security and Communications Networks*, 8, 3045–3066.

Furnell, S. (2002). *Cybercrime: Vandalizing the Information Society*. London: Addison-Wesley.

Gacto, M., Alcala, R., & Herrera, A.F. (2011). An overview of ensemble methods for binary classifiers in multi-class problems: Experimental study on one-vs-one and one-vs-all schemes. *Pattern Recognition*, 44, 1761–1776.

Gallagher, S. (2014). Sony fights spread of stolen data by using "bad seed" attack on torrents. *Ars Technica*, December 11. arstechnica.com/techpolicy/2014/12/11/sony-fights-spread-of-stolen-data-by-using-bad-seed-attack-on-torrents/.

Gordon, S., & Ma, Q. (2003). *Convergence of Virus Writers and Hackers: Fact or Fantasy?* Cupertino, CA: Symantec.

Hayashi, F., & Sullivan, R.J. (2013). Fees, fraud, and regulation: Forces of change in the payment card industry. *Payment Systems Research Briefing*. Federal Reserve Bank of Kansas City. www.kc.frb.org/publicat/psr/briefings/psr-briefingapr2013.pdf.

Higgins, G.E. (2005). Can low self-control help with the understanding of the software piracy problem? *Deviant Behavior*, 26, 1–24.

Higgins, G.E., & Marcum, C.D. (2011). *Digital Piracy: An Integrated Theoretical Approach*. Raleigh, NC: Carolina Academic Press.

Higgins, G.E., Marcum, C.D., Freiburger, T.L., & Ricketts, M.L. (2012). Examining the role of peer influence and self-control on downloading behavior. *Deviant Behavior*, 33, 412–423.

Hinduja, S. (2004). Perceptions of local and state law enforcement concerning the role of computer crime investigative teams. *Policing: An International Journal of Police Strategies and Management*, 27, 341–357.

Hinduja, S. (2007). Computer crime investigations in the United States: Leveraging knowledge from the past to address the future. *International Journal of Cyber Criminology*, 1, 1–26.

Hinduja, S., & Ingram J.R. (2008). Self-control and ethical beliefs on the social learning of intellectual property theft. *Western Criminology Review*, 9, 52–72.

Hinduja, S., & Kooi, B. (2013). Curtailing cyber and information security vulnerabilities through situational crime prevention. *Security Journal*, 26, 383–402.

Hinduja, S., & Patchin, J.W. (2009). *Bullying Beyond the Schoolyard: Preventing and Responding to Cyberbullying*. New York: Corwin Press.

Holt, T.J. (2007). Subcultural evolution? Examining the influence of on- and off-line experiences on deviant subcultures. *Deviant Behavior*, 28, 171–198.

Holt, T.J. (2009). Lone hacks or group cracks: Examining the social organization of computer hackers. In F. Schmalleger & M. Pittaro (Eds.), *Crimes of the Internet* (pp. 336–355). Upper Saddle River, NJ: Pearson Prentice Hall.

Holt, T.J. (2013). Examining the forces shaping cybercrime markets online. *Social Science Computer Review*, 31, 165–177.

Holt, T.J., & Bossler, A.M. (2009). Examining the applicability of lifestyle-routine activities theory for cybercrime victimization. *Deviant Behavior*, 30, 1–25.

Holt, T.J., & Bossler, A.M. (2014). An assessment of the current state of cybercrime scholarship. *Deviant Behavior*, 35, 20–40.

Holt, T.J., Bossler, A.M., & Fitzgerald, S. (2010). Examining state and local law enforcement perceptions of computer crime. In T.J. Holt (Ed.) *Crime On-line: Correlates, Causes, and Context* (pp. 221–246). Raleigh NC: Carolina Academic Press.

Holt, T.J., Bossler, A.M., & May, D.C. (2012). Low self-control deviant peer associations and juvenile cyberdeviance. *American Journal of Criminal Justice*, 37, 378–395.

Holt, T.J., Burruss, G.W., & Bossler, A.M. (2010). Social learning and cyber deviance: Examining the importance of a full social learning model in the virtual world. *Journal of Crime and Justice*, 33, 15–30.

Holt, T.J., & Copes, H. (2010). Transferring subcultural knowledge online: Practices and beliefs of persistent digital pirates. *Deviant Behavior*, 31, 625–654.

Holt, T.J., & Graves, D.C. (2007). A qualitative analysis of advanced fee fraud schemes. *The International Journal of Cyber-Criminology*, 1, 137–154.

Holt, T.J., & Kilger, M. (2012). *The Social Dynamics of Hacking*. Know Your Enemy Series. The Honeynet Project. honeynet.org/papers/socialdynamics.

Holt, T.J., & Lampke, E. (2010). Exploring stolen data markets on-line: Products and market forces. *Criminal Justice Studies*, 23, 33–50.

Holt, T.J., & Schell, B.H. (2013). *Hackers and Hacking: A Reference Handbook*. Santa Barbara, CA: ABC-CLIO.

Holt, T.J., & Smirnova, O. (2014). *Examining the Structure, Organization, and Processes of the International Market for Stolen Data*. Washington, DC: US Department of Justice. www.ncjrs.gov/pdffiles1/nij/grants/245375.pdf.

Holt, T.J., & Turner, M.G. (2012) Examining risks and protective factors of on line identity theft. *Deviant Behavior*, 33, 308–323.

The Honeynet Project (2003). The Honeynet Project: Trapping the hackers. *IEEE Security and Privacy*, 1, 15–23.

Huang, H., & Brockman, A. (2010). Social engineering exploitations in online communications examining persuasions used in fraudulent emails. In T. Holt (Ed.), *Crime On-line: Correlates, Causes and Context* (pp. 87–111). Durham, NC: Carolina Academic Press.

Hutchings, A., & Holt, T.J. (2015). Crime script analysis and online black markets. *British Journal of Criminology*, 55, 596–614.

iKeepSafe (2015). *Educator Curriculum*. www.ikeepsafe.org/copyright/.

Ingram, J.R., & Hinduja, S. (2008). Neutralizing music piracy: An empirical examination. *Deviant Behavior*, 29, 334–366.

Internet Crime Complaint Center (2012). *2011 Internet Crime Report*. www.ic3.gov/media/annualreport/2011_IC3Report.pdf.

James, L. (2005). *Phishing Exposed*. Rockland: Syngress.

Jenkins, P. (2001). *Beyond Tolerance: Child Pornography on the Internet*. New York: New York University Press.

Jones, L.M., Mitchell, K.J., & Finkelhor, D. (2012). Trends in youth Internet victimization: Findings from three youth Internet safety surveys 2000–2010. *Journal of Adolescent Health*, 50, 179–186.

Jordan, T., & Taylor, P. (1998). A sociology of hackers. *The Sociological Review*, 46, 757–780.

Kelly, H. (2014). 5 biometric alternatives to the password. *CNN*, April 4. www.cnn.com/2014/04/04/tech/innovation/5-biometrics-future/.

Khey, D.N., & Sainato, V.A. (2013). Examining the correlates and spatial distribution of organizational data breaches in the United States. *Security Journal*, 26, 367–382.

Khor, K.C., Ting, C.Y., & Phon-Amnuaisuk, S. (2012). A cascaded classifier approach for improving detection rates on rare attack categories in network intrusion detection. *Applied Intelligence*, 36, 320–329.

Kilger, M. (2011). Social dynamics and the future of technology-driven crime. In T.J. Holt & B. Schell (Eds.), *Corporate Hacking and Technology-Driven Crime: Social Dynamics and Implications* (pp. 205–227). Hershey, PA: IGI-Global.

Krebs, B. (2013). Underweb payments, post-liberty reserve. May 30. krebsonsecurity.com/2013/05/underweb-payments-post-liberty-reserve/.

Krebs, B. (2014a). Banks: Credit card breach at Home Depot. September 2. krebsonsecurity.com/2014/09/banks-credit-card-breach-at-home-depot/.

KrebsB. (2014b). Home Depot: 56M cards impacted, malware contained. September 18. krebsonsecurity.com/2014/09/home-depot-56m-cards-impacted-malware-contained/.

Lee, W., & Stolfo, S. (2000). A framework for constructing features and models for intrusion detection systems. *ACM Transactions on Information Systems and Security*, 3, 227–261.

Li, H., Sarathy, R., & Zhang, J. (2010). Understanding compliance with internet use policy from the perspective of rational choice theory. *Decision Support Systems*, 48, 635–545.

Mandiant (2013). APT1: Exposing one of China's cyber espionage units. *Mandiant*. intelreport.mandiant.com.

Marcum, C.D. (2013). Assessing sex experiences of online victimization: An examination of adolescent online behaviors utilizing Routine Activity Theory. *Criminal Justice Review*, 35, 412–437.

Markoff, J., & Barboza, D. (2010). Two China schools said to be linked to online attacks. *The New York Times*. www.nytimes.com/2010/02/19/technology/19china.html.

Mills, E. (2009). Q&A: FBI agent looks back on time posing as a cybercriminal. *cNet*May 7. www.cnet.com/news/q-a-fbi-agent-looks-back-on-time-posing-as-a-cybercriminal/.

Mitnick, K.D., & Simon, W.L. (2002). *The Art of Deception: Controlling the Human Element of Security*. New York: Wiley Publishing.

Moore, R., Guntupalli, N.T., & Lee, T. (2010). Parental regulation and online activities: Examining factors that influence a youth's potential to become a victim of online harassment. *International Journal of Cyber Criminology*, 4, 685–698.

Motoyama, M., McCoy, D., Levchenko, K., Savage, S., & Voelker, G.M. (2011). An analysis of underground forums. *IMC'11*, 71–79.

National Conference of State Legislatures (2012). *State Security Breach Notification Laws*. www.ncsl.org/issues-research/telecom/security-breach-notification-laws.aspx.

Newman, G., & Clarke, R. (2003). *Superhighway Robbery: Preventing e-Commerce Crime.* Cullompton: Willan.

Ngo, F.T., & Paternoster, R. (2011). Cybercrime victimization: An examination of individual- and situational-level factors. *International Journal of Cyber Criminology,* 5, 773–793.

Nhan, J. (2013). The evolution of online piracy: Challenge and response. In T.J. Holt (Ed.), *Crime On-line: Causes, Correlates, and Context* (pp. 61–80). Raleigh, NC: Carolina Academic Press.

Oracle (2013). *Data Masking Best Practice.* An Oracle White Paper. www.oracle.com/us/products/database/data-masking-best-practices-161213.pdf.

Pahnila, S., Siponen, M., & Mahmood, A. (2007). Employees' behavior towards IS security policy compliance. In *System Sciences* (pp. 156b–156b). HICSS 2007. 40th Annual Hawaii International Conference, January. IEEE.

PandaLabs (2007). Malware infections in protected systems. research.pandasecurity.com/blogs/images/wp_pb_malware_infections_in_protected_systems.pdf.

Patcha, A., & Park, J.M. (2007). An overview of anomaly detection techniques: Existing solutions and latest technological trends. *Computer Networks,* 51, 3448–3470.

Pavia, J.M., Veres-Ferrer, E.J., & Foix-Escura, G. (2012). Credit card incidents and control systems. *International Journal of Information Management,* 32, 501–503.

Peretti, K.K. (2009). Data breaches: What the underground world of "carding" reveals. *Santa Clara Computer and High Technology Law Journal,* 25, 375–413.

Ponemon Institute (2015). *2014 Cost of Cyber Crime Study.* Traverse City, MI: Ponemon Institute.

Poulsen, K. (2012). *Kingpin: How One Hacker Took Over the Billion Dollar Cybercrime Underground.* New York: Broadway.

Rege, A. (2013). Industrial control systems and cybercrime. In T.J. Holt (Ed.), *Crime On-line: Causes, Correlates, and Context.* Second edition (pp. 191–218). Raleigh, NC: Carolina Academic Press.

Riebach, S., Rathgeb, E.P., & Toedtmann, B. (2005). Efficient deployment of honeynets for statistical and forensic analysis of attacks from the Internet. *Networking,* 3462, 756–767.

Sainato, V. (2009) *Situational Surveillance Control.* New York: City University of New York.

Scarfone, K., & Mell, P. (2010). *Guide to Intrusion Detection and Prevention Systems (IDPS): Recommendations of the National Institute of Standards and Technology.* NIST Special Publication 800–894. Washington, DC: National Institute of Standards and Technology, US Department of Commerce.

Schell, B.H., & Dodge, J.L. (2002). *The Hacking of America: Who's Doing it, Why, and How.* Westport, CT: Quorum Books.

Schmugar, C. (2010). More details on "Operation Aurora." *McAfee Security Blog.* www.avertlabs.com/research/blog/index.php/2010/01/14-more-details-on-operation-aurora/.

Shalal, A. (2015). U.S. firm CrowdStrike claims success in deterring Chinese hackers. *Business Insider,* April 13. www.businessinsider.com/r-us-firm-crowdstrike-claims-success-in-deterring-chinese-hackers-2015-4.

Shaw, E., Ruby, K., & Post, J. (1998). The insider threat to information systems: The psychology of the dangerous insider. *Security Awareness Bulletin,* 2, 1–10.

Singh, A., Lambert, S., Ganacharya, T.A., & Williams, J. (2010). Evasions in intrusion prevention/detection systems. *Virus Bulletin,* March 1. www.virusbtn.com/virusbulletin/archive/2010/04/vb201004-evasions-in-IPS-IDS.

Skinner, W.F., & Fream, A.F. (1997). A social learning theory analysis of computer crime among college students. *Journal of Research in Crime and Delinquency*, 34, 495–518.

Smith, R.G., Grabosky, P., & Urbas, G. (2004). *Cyber Criminals on Trial*. Cambridge: Cambridge University Press.

Sommestad, T., Hallberg, J., Lundholm, K., & Bengtsson, J. (2014). Variables influencing information security policy compliance: A systematic review of quantitative studies. *Information Management and Computer Security*, 22, 42–75.

Spelman, W., & Eck, J. (1989). Sitting ducks, ravenous wolves, and helping hands: New approaches to urban policing. *Public Affairs Comment*, 35, 1–9.

Stambaugh, H., Beaupre, D.S., Icove, D.J., Baker, R., Cassady, W., & Williams, W.P. (2001). *Electronic Crime Needs Assessment for State and Local Law Enforcement, National Institute of Justice*. Washington, DC: National Institute of Justice.

Stone, J. (2015). Popcorn time sites knocked offline by UK Court ruling, but the torrent streamer isn't dead yet. *International Business Times*, April 29. www.ibtimes.com/popcorn-time-sites-knocked-offline-uk-court-ruling-torrent-streamer-isnt-dead-yet-1901237.

Sullivan, R.J. (2013). The US adoption of computer-chip payment cards: Implications for payment fraud. *Economic Review*. Federal Reserve Bank of Kansas City.

Sullivan, R.J. (2014). Controlling security risk and fraud in payment systems. *Economic Review*. Federal Reserve Bank of Kansas City. www.kc.frb.org/publicat/econrev/pdf/14q3Sullivan.pdf.

Surowiecki, J. (2013). Why did criminals trust liberty reserve. *The New Yorker*, 31 May. www.newyorker.com/online/blogs/newsdesk/2013/05/why-did-criminals-trust-liberty-reserve.html.

Symantec Corporation (2014). *Symantec Internet Security Threat Report, Volume 18*. www.symantec.com/threatreport/.

Taylor, P. (1999). *Hackers: Crime in the Digital Sublime*. London: Routledge.

Tyler, T.R. (2006). Restorative justice and procedural justice: Dealing with rule breaking. *Journal of Social Issues*, 62, 307–326.

Tyler, T.R., Callahan, P.E., & Frost, J. (2007). Armed and dangerous (?): Motivating rule adherence among agents of social control. *Law and Society Review*, 41, 457–492.

Verrier, R. (2013). MPAA backs anti-piracy curriculum for students. *LA Times*, November 11. articles.latimes.com/2013/nov/11/entertainment/la-et-ct-piracy-education-20131111.

Wall, D.S. (2001). Cybercrimes and the Internet. In D.S. Wall (Ed.), *Crime and the Internet* (pp. 1–17). New York: Routledge.

Wall, D.S. (2007). *Cybercrime: The Transformation of Crime in the Information Age*. Cambridge: Polity Press.

Willison, R., & Siponen, M. (2009) Overcoming the insider: Reducing employee computer crime through situational crime prevention. *Communications of the ACM*, 52, 133–137.

Wilson, S. (2012). Calling for a uniform approach to card fraud offline and on. *Journal of Internet Banking and Commerce*, 17, 1–5.

Wolak, J., Finkelhor, D., & Mitchell, K. (2012). *Trends in Law Enforcement Responses to Technology-facilitated Child Sexual Exploitation Crimes: The Third National Juvenile Online Victimization Study (NJOV-3)*. Durham, NH: Crimes Against Children Research Center.

Wolfe, S.E., Higgins, G.E., & Marcum, C.D. (2007). Deterrence and digital piracy: A preliminary examination of the role of viruses. *Social Science Computer Review*, 26, 317–333.

Ybarra, M.L., Mitchell, K.J., Finkelhor, D., & Wolak, J. (2007). Internet prevention messages: Targeting the right online behaviors. *Archives of Pediatrics and Adolescent Medicine*, 161, 138–145.

Young, K.S., & Case, C.J. (2004). Internet abuse in the workplace: New trends in risk management. *CyberPsychology & Behavior*, 7, 105–111.

Zetter, K. (2010). "Google" hackers had ability to alter source code. *Wired*. www.wired.com/threatlevel/2010/03/source-code-hacks/82.

6 The future of cybercrime, technology, and enforcement

Chapter goals

- Explore the possibility of future cybercrime trends
- Consider technology, including disruptive technologies, that will shape our future
- Examine how the Internet and social media in particular will affect future social movements and radicalization
- Contemplate the regulation of online spaces and off-line behavior
- Assess possible future solutions to improve the global enforcement of cybercrime

The prior chapters of this work have documented the current landscape of cybercrime research, with an emphasis on both the strengths and limitations of this scholarship. Such an assessment is necessary to understand where our knowledge of cybercrime currently lies. This information also provides a basis to consider how the types of cybercrimes may change in the near future, along with how they are committed. Technology changes frequently, and so does the behavior of offenders. The motivations and underlying causes of offending may remain (see Chapter 3), but the means and practicalities of an offense may change dramatically. In this respect, many forms of cybercrime are somewhat distinct from other forms of street crime where offender behaviors may change incrementally in response to target hardening strategies (e.g. Copes & Cherbonneau, 2006; Mativat & Tremblay, 1997).

This chapter seeks to speculate on the future of cybercrime by identifying areas for future research based on our current knowledge of different phenomena. The discussion is meant to truly probe the boundaries of our knowledge and provide direction for scholarship that will expand the scope of the field and challenge our assumptions about the nature of cybercrime. We urge readers to take the arguments and ideas presented in this chapter as an initial discussion toward the shape of the future of the discipline rather than finalized conclusions. Only through recognizing what we know and do not know can we begin to improve our basis for study. Otherwise, we will simply continue to replicate established research findings and maintain the existing cybercrime research paradigm rather than transform it into something greater.

Considering the future of cybercrime

As scholarship on cybercrime increases, our knowledge of the applicability of traditional theories of crime to various forms of cybercrime has expanded as well. The current literature demonstrates that there are some consistent patterns in the predictors of both cybercrime offending and the risk of cyber victimization (Holt & Bossler, 2014), which may lead to predictions regarding cybercrime trends. That is not to conclude that any crime trend, on or off-line, is likely to continue; rates of various offenses are notoriously difficult to predict (e.g. Blumstein & Wallman, 2005).

The prediction of future cybercrime trends is particularly challenging because the adoption and abandonment rates of technologies are not well understood. For example, some current applications such as Facebook have massive user populations today. Studies suggest this population will shrink within the next five years (Cannarella & Spechler, 2014; PiperJaffray, 2014). In fact, Facebook may continue to be used by parents and guardians while teens have begun to transition to other social media services like Snapchat (Madden et al., 2013). Against this backdrop, we discuss some prospective trends that may continue over the next five years based on current criminological research and trend analyses from various cybersecurity vendors.

One of the most likely cybercrimes to continue without abatement is **malware infections**. Victim populations have great difficulty determining when an infection has occurred (Holt & Bossler, 2013; Pew Charitable Trust, 2005). In addition, the success of antivirus tools appears limited in minimizing the risk of victimization (Bossler & Holt, 2009; Holt & Turner, 2012; Ngo & Paternoster, 2011). As a result, there is no reason why cybercriminals would abandon a successful attack tool. The continuing stability of botnets and other economically oriented forms of malware suggests that hackers are continuing to generate revenue by infecting new systems and maintaining them over time (e.g. Cole, Mellor, & Noyes, 2007; de Graaf, Shosha, & Gladyshev, 2013; Holt, 2013; Motoyama et al., 2011).

Recent forms of malware illustrate that the use of software tools to gain access to computer systems and networks will continue in the foreseeable future and evolve into more complex and effective forms. For example, there are new forms of malware called **ransomware** which require victims to pay fees in order to regain access to system files and data (Ferguson, 2013). CryptoLocker, a form of ransomware, spreads via attachments in emails or as downloadable malware online, and once executed, encrypts data on any hard drives attached to the infected system (Ferguson, 2013). The key to decrypt the file is maintained by an attacker who can send the key via a command-and-control structure to the victim machine. The key is only made available after the victim provides the hacker with a US$300 payment through various electronic currencies. If payment is not made, the key for the victim machine will be deleted, which is often extremely difficult to repair or decrypt through other means (Ferguson, 2013).

The devices that malware writers and hackers target will likely change moving into the future as well. As mobile devices, including smartphones, tablets, and other handheld devices, garner more of the market from desktops and laptops, it is sensible that they will be targeted for malware infections. Current evidence from various security vendors suggests that mobile malware is experiencing the largest growth over all other forms of malware generally (McAfee Labs, 2014; Panda Security, 2013).

There is also evidence that criminals are specifically targeting the Android operating system for infections over all other mobile platforms (Panda Security, 2013). Evidence from F-Secure suggests that 97 percent of all mobile malware created from 2000 to 2013 exclusively targeted Android devices. From a situational crime-prevention standpoint, attackers have the greatest access to victim populations through this operating system because it places fewer restrictions on the ways that users can download programs. An Android operating system allows users to download applications through either the Google application (app) store or third-party markets that are less regulated. Devices, like the iPhone, that use other operating systems only allow users to purchase apps through their own store which minimizes the likelihood that malware can be made available. As a consequence, hackers can design an app that appears legitimate and make it available in various marketplaces for Android users. In the event that malware is identified by the Google store, it will be removed, but it will still be available in other markets.

This pattern will no doubt continue until such time as cell phone users recognize the threat they face and take steps to secure their systems through antivirus software and regular updates. It is unclear how this will happen, as antivirus tools are not immediately included in the operating system. Though security apps are available through various stores, the need for these tools is not clearly communicated to users. Some app designers have even made the argument that no security tools are needed on mobile devices so long as the software is kept up to date (Williams, 2014). Such an assertion is not likely to be true, as virtually every device has inherent flaws that can be exploited by attackers in order to gain access to computer systems. At this time, there is no *criminological* inquiry, to our knowledge, as to the risk factors associated with cell phone malware victimization, let alone the proportion of cell phone users who have experienced an infection. There is also minimal research considering any differences in the perceived security of mobile devices relative to traditional PCs. Such basic research is needed in order to improve our knowledge of the relationships between victimization on mobile devices and traditional laptops and desktops.

Just as malicious software and hacking threats evolve, so too will identity fraud and theft victimization trends. The number of large-scale data breaches occurring in the US in different sectors (e.g. financial, commercial, health, education, etc.) over the last decade demonstrates that personal information is a clear target for cybercriminals (Collins et al., 2011; Higgins, 2014; McAfee Labs, 2014). The concurrent growth of online data markets where this information is sold for a profit also reflects the economic interests of these actors (e.g. Franklin et al., 2007; Holt, 2013; Holt & Lampke, 2010; Yip et al., 2013). As a consequence, researchers must begin to understand the ways that the behaviors of victims and offenders are changing the minimizing of risks and the maximizing of rewards.

A small number of studies have identified risk factors for identity theft victimization, primarily through a routine activity framework (e.g. Holt & Turner, 2012; Reyns, 2013). These studies are helpful, though they do not provide information on the extent to which individuals are victimized through various avenues in order to gain personally identifiable information. For instance, Ngo and Paternoster (2011) found that 54.8 percent of a sample of college students received phishing emails. The study did not identify whether respondents actually provided information in response to the email, only that they received such a message. This type of measurement issue may explain why the only significant predictor of phishing in the study was an individual's participation in online deviance (Ngo & Paternoster, 2011).

By contrast, Holt and Turner (2012) found that respondents whose bank or financial information was acquired by someone electronically did not regularly update various protective software programs installed on the computer they use most often. Such a finding demonstrates the potential association between malicious software threats and identity theft, though future study is needed with various refinements not only for the measurement of victimization but for the guardianship factors that may impact the likelihood of victimization.

Since identity theft and fraud may occur as a result of circumstances beyond the control of an individual, such as a massive data breach, there is a need to understand how legislation and/or accreditation requiring improved network security within certain sectors and the reporting of data breaches may decrease future data breaches and their impact on victims. For example, Collins et al. (2011) found that the passage of data breach reporting legislation was associated with an increase in the number of incidents reported in the healthcare sector; they found, however, that there was a decrease in incidents reported by educational institutions. Additional research is needed to further examine the effects of legislation on not only the improved reporting of breaches but whether requiring institutions to report breaches will encourage them to better protect their systems and decrease breaches in the long term. This research could also examine whether differences in reporting legislation could help provide additional insight into why certain sectors are more vulnerable than others.

Related to the issue of how institutions react to data breaches is how citizens respond after they are informed that their personal data may have been stolen. There are now various identity theft services that are available to alert consumers in the event that their personal information is misused. Several questions have been left unanswered about these services in general, their impact on consumer behavior, and their effectiveness. For instance, it is unclear if individuals generally pay for these services before or after experiencing victimization. In addition, there has been no empirical assessment of the efficacy of these services in protecting consumers. It is also unknown how consumer behaviors change after mass breaches. Although consumers are often told to monitor their bank accounts for purchases they did not make and contact major credit bureaus to establish fraud alerts associated with their identity, it is unknown how many actually take these steps. These are just a few areas that must be addressed if we are to improve our knowledge of identity theft and fraud victimization.

There is also a need for research considering the practices of offenders who acquire and sell these data. Though studies have identified the scope of personal information sold, and the advertised prices for data (Franklin et al., 2007; Holt & Lampke, 2010; Holz et al., 2009; Honeynet Research Alliance, 2003; Motoyama et al., 2011; Wehinger, 2011), few have been able either to identify the total number of transactions completed or the total profits made by data sellers and buyers (see Holt, Smirnova, & Chua, 2013). Thus, economic analyses are needed with data acquired from active forums and data sources to understand the scope of harm caused by the sale of personal information.

In addition, research is needed with data from various markets operating worldwide in order to improve our knowledge of the practices and diversity of actors. Current studies draw primarily from either limited samples of active forums (e.g. Holt, 2013; Motoyama et al., 2011), or forum communities that were closed due to law enforcement interventions (Yip et al., 2013). A small body of research has begun to draw from registration-only Russian- and English-language forums (Holt & Smirnova, 2014; Holt, Smirnova, Chua, & Copes, 2015), which may improve our knowledge of the practices of market actors. Evidence suggests these markets are increasingly transitioning to more secured and vetted access where actors must pay a fee in order to observe advertisements (e.g. Holt & Smirnova, 2014). Thus, researchers must find ways to access these communities without affecting the practices of the market or engaging in overtly illegal behavior themselves.

There is also a need for research assessing the real and perceived impact of law enforcement interventions in online forums to understand the efficacy of online intervention techniques. This would require innovative research methodologies, including direct engagement with law enforcement, forum participants, and observations of market activities before, during, and after any intervention. In turn, this may inform our knowledge of the impact of the Internet on the risk-reduction strategies of data thieves in response to threats from other actors and law enforcement generally. The findings could also improve our understanding of the influence of technology on the nature of crime and deviance in the twenty-first century.

It is also likely that person-based cybercrimes such as bullying, harassment, and stalking will continue to increase over the next decade (Nobles et al., 2014; Reyns et al., 2011). Evidence from various data sources demonstrates that victimization is increasingly common among youth and college samples (see Chapter 2 for discussion). As youth populations continue to gain access to technology at earlier ages, it is plausible that opportunities for both offending and victimization will increase. The development of various social media apps such as Snapchat, Vine, and Instagram easily allow youth to post personal information and connect with people they may or may not know. In turn, this enables individuals to send hurtful messages via text or send and receive sexual images.

Though research on person-based cybercrimes has increased dramatically over the last decade, there are still several questions that must be addressed. For instance, research has found a strong relationship between verbal, physical and cyberbullying victimization (Arseneault et al., 2006; Hinduja & Patchin, 2009; Holt et al., 2013; Kowalski & Limber, 2007; Nansel et al., 2001; Turner et al. 2013; Ybarra & Mitchell, 2004). Numerous studies have focused on individual-level predictors of bullying victimization on and off-line, though virtually no research has considered macro-level predictors associated with these experiences. Limited study has considered the association between neighborhood conditions and physical bullying, demonstrating that disorder increases the risk of bullying victimization (Bowes et al., 2009; Bradshaw, Sawyer, & O'Brennan, 2009; Nansel et al., 2001). Only one study to date has examined the relationship between neighborhood disorder, physical bullying, and cyberbullying victimization (Holt, Turner, & Exum, 2014). This study found that youth living in disordered communities were more likely to experience all forms of bullying victimization. This preliminary evidence suggests that neighborhood conditions may affect online behavior as well as real-world experiences, though additional research is needed to replicate this finding.

There is also a need for research considering the effects of individual behavioral and personality characteristics on different types of cyberbullying and stalking experiences. Scholars have recently explored the impact that individual factors, such as childhood adversity and psychiatric disorders, have on physical bullying (Vaughn, Fu, Beaver, DeLisi, Perron, & Howard, 2011; Vaughn, Fu, Bender, DeLisi, Beaver, Perron, & Howard, 2010). There is, however, virtually no research assessing these dynamics with respect to cyberbullying. The majority of cyberbullying and stalking research is also cross-sectional in nature, limiting our ability to understand the theoretical dynamics affecting both offending and victimization. Furthermore, there is no real longitudinal research examining the short- and long-term factors associated with cyberbullying victimization and subsequent participation in offending.

Evidence also suggests that the communications and economic infrastructure afforded by technology will continue to encourage the commission of traditional crimes to move into online spaces. For example, research has demonstrated the ways that prostitution and paid sex work is transforming because of the development of forums and the web. The customers of prostitutes now utilize the Internet as a vehicle to communicate with one another, review the services of sex workers, and discuss the practices of law enforcement which may facilitate displacement (Holt, Blevins, & Kuhns, 2008). At the same time, sex workers now utilize web pages and email as a means to directly advertise their services to the public, arrange meetings, and validate their clients' identities prior to an encounter (Cunningham & Kendall, 2010). These developments appear to have a transformative impact on the illicit sex trade by reducing the need for some sex workers and customers to openly solicit in public spaces. This may reduce the risks of physical violence and minimize the likelihood of arrest or public outcry by moving paid encounters entirely behind closed doors.

A similar transformation appears to be in progress with respect to the sale of illicit drugs through the development of online marketplaces that enable individuals to buy and sell narcotics through various mechanisms internationally. Individuals advertise their products on sites operating on the encrypted **Tor network**, which helps to anonymize individual identities and reduce the likelihood of identification by law enforcement. Tor operates via the use of specialized encryption software and browser protocols which hide users and their locations. This network also enables the creation of websites and content hosted on Tor which are similarly encrypted, minimizing the possibility for law enforcement to identify where they are hosted. Payments for products are also made electronically through **crypto-currencies**, particularly **Bitcoin**, which is a relatively anonymous form of electronic currency that can be delivered directly between two parties without the need to engage traditional financial institutions (Franklin, 2013).

These **cryptomarkets** hosted on Tor quickly drew attention from law enforcement and the media, particularly the Silk Road which began operation in 2011 (Franklin, 2013; Martin, 2014). The site was created to enable individuals to buy various materials ranging from computer equipment to clothing, though sellers offered various narcotics and paraphernalia to manufacture and distribute drugs. Since it opened, the Silk Road has enabled over 1 million transactions worth an estimated $1.2 billion in revenue (Barratt, 2012). Law enforcement agencies in both the US and Australia soon began undercover operations against buyers in the market, leading to the eventual arrest of the site administrator in 2013 and the dismantling of the market (Gibbs, 2013). A number of other markets soon emerged to take its place, however, including a second and third version of the original Silk Road, operated by different actors (Dolliver, 2015).

The emergence of the Silk Road demonstrates that cyberspace will increasingly be used by real-world criminal actors to facilitate offending. The distributed nature of the Internet and the ability to hide one's identity and flow of money makes it an ideal environment for illicit economies of all stripes. Research on virtual drug markets is in its infancy, with the few published studies utilizing samples of ads from the market to assess the scope of the economy and products offered (Dolliver, 2015; Martin, 2014; Phelps & Watt, 2014). Such information is helpful to demonstrate trends in services offered and variations in user behavior as markets expand and close.

There is a need for additional study moving beyond the scope of the market to consider how and why these markets flourish, and the extent to which they actually impact the behavior of buyers and sellers. An initial study has attempted to address this issue using survey data collected from an international sample. Barratt, Ferris, and Winstock (2014) found that 35 percent of a sample of 9,470 drug-using respondents in Australia, the UK, and the US had consumed drugs purchased from the Silk Road. A much larger proportion of respondents had heard of the market, but had yet to use products from its vendors. Of those who had made a purchase through the Silk Road, the majority had purchased MDMA or cannabis, and indicated that they felt the market had a better range of products, of higher quality, and that it was easier to access and determine legitimate sellers (Barratt et al., 2014). Additionally, respondents in Australia and the US were statistically more likely to purchase products through the Silk Road because of lower prices and less fear of being caught.

The findings from this study provide a valuable demonstration of the extent to which these markets may displace traditional illicit markets in the real world. Greater research is needed to replicate these findings and consider how buyer behaviors change as greater law enforcement attention is placed on these markets. In addition, research is needed on the vendors operating within these markets to identify any differences in the demographic composition of actors who engage in virtual markets relative to those in the real world. Though technological access is increasingly normalized across economic and demographic groups in the US (e.g. Moore, 2011), it is unclear to what extent individuals who would otherwise participate in street corner drug sales are aware of cryptomarkets. For example, although Pyrooz, Decker, and Moule (2015) found that street gang members may be more likely to use the Internet for criminal purposes, such as to illegally download media, sell drugs, and search social network sites to steal, than non-gang respondents and former gang members, they argue that the Internet is used more for symbolic purposes (e.g. self-promotion) by gangs than for furthering their instrumental goals. Thus, additional research is needed to understand the extent to which low-level dealers or mid-level distributors are active in both simple and complex online markets. In turn, we may be able to better understand the impact of virtual markets on the practices of open-air markets in the real world.

Disruptive technologies

The creation of online markets, such as the Silk Road, is built on encryption software and hosting services which are technologies that have been around for some time. The implementation of these tools to facilitate real-world offending, however, is quite novel and demonstrates the extent to which technology can affect criminality. In a broader context, the development and release of new hardware and software can dramatically change the behavior of humans. Products such as the iPhone are an excellent example of an extremely simple design with an intuitive user interface (i.e. swiping to move from screen to screen), along with a unique way for the device to engage with software platforms through the use of apps. Such innovation in technology can be referred to as a **disruptive technology**, in that it creates a new market and network for products which supplants or disrupts an existing market space (Bower, 2002; Zeleny, 2009). In other words, a disruptive technology creates its own product category which will draw users away from an existing market, and potentially replace it over time.

It is extremely difficult to know when a potentially disruptive technology will hit the market, or what its impact may be on society. Technology companies often keep the design and features of products secret until the last possible moment, and attempt to dazzle the world through media campaigns and product launches. Not all devices may be accepted by the general public, regardless of how innovative or potentially transformative they may be. For instance, the **Google Glass** wearable technology released in 2011 failed to catch on with early adopters and the general public (Wohlsen, 2014). These thin glasses incorporate a wearable computer providing a heads-up display within the glass frame that is voice activated and controlled by the user's eye movements. Though individuals could surf the web, check email, and record events from a first-person perspective hands-free, it was a commercial and critical failure that Google has largely shelved in favor of new innovations.

Despite this lack of success, there is a range of **wearable devices** that are Internet enabled and have become popular and are beginning to gain market share. Devices like the Fitbit and various smart watches, which can be connected to cell phones via Bluetooth, provide the ability to track daily habits, exercise, heart rate, and even sleep cycles. These data are presented to the user via apps that can help assess health and calorie intake and provide a degree of behavior management for those looking to lose weight or improve health. The devices themselves do not present a disruptive technology, because they must typically work with other devices such as laptops or cell phones in order to provide visual representations of data to the user. Thus they will not replace any existing product category as they serve as peripheral devices to current technologies commonly used.

The information collected by wearable devices may, however, serve a disruptive function for data collection and information aggregation. On the surface, such a point may seem banal and have generally no impact on criminological concerns or deviant behavior generally. This perception ignores the broader implications regarding the massive quantities of personal information that may be captured, questions as to individual privacy, and the inherent security of the devices at play.

For instance, the Fitbit and other health-tracking wearable technologies are being integrated into corporate health and wellness plans. This information can then be linked to company health insurance plans (Olson, 2014). By capturing the health practices of employees, companies may be able either to reduce healthcare plan costs by encouraging employees to exercise and maintain healthier lifestyles, or in some cases sanction employees for poor health choices (Olson, 2014). This seems like a rational, but highly invasive, use of technology, even if employees are given the opportunity to opt out if they are uncomfortable with attempts to monitor their private lives.

The use of such data-collection methods creates massive opportunities for data breaches affecting health-based application services (Collins et al., 2011). As noted previously, data breaches have become a common problem, leading to the loss of consumer financial information. Criminals can readily monetize credit and debit card data because it can be used to engage in various forms of fraud and theft. There is increasing concern about the potential for breaches of healthcare data, as demonstrated by a major incident affecting US citizens in 2014. Anthem Health Care was compromised by hackers who were able to acquire personal information on as many as 80 million Americans, including names, dates of birth, social security numbers, addresses, employer information, and income (Abelson & Creswell, 2015).

Though this breach is among the largest in the industry, 18 healthcare providers lost sensitive data in 2014 due to some form of hacking (Ponemon Institute, 2015). The recognition among hackers as to the value of health data, coupled with increasing connections between wearable devices and healthcare provider data sources, may create opportunities for data theft and harm that exceeded prior possibilities. In fact, research on wearables by Pricewaterhouse Cooper found that 86 percent of a sample of 1,000 industry experts worried that wearable technology would increase their risk of data breaches (Pricewaterhouse Cooper, 2014).

In much the same way, companies and utilities providers are encouraging consumers in the US and UK to adopt thermostats and home security systems that are connected to and managed via the Internet (see Curtis, 2013). These devices allow consumers to easily manage their energy use and view goings-on in their home with great ease through mobile apps and web browsers. These devices, along with the wearable technologies mentioned above, create an **Internet of Things**, consisting of all the non-computing devices that are connected together via the Internet (Curtis, 2013). The convenience afforded by these technologies cannot be understated, but they are not likely to be a disruptive technology as they are not currently on track to replace existing thermostat and HVAC (heating, ventilation and air-conditioning) technologies in the larger consumer population in the near future.

Their potential security implications, however, serve as a massive disruption point for both criminals and nation-state actors. At the individual level, having applications run through a smartphone or tablet turns that device into a set of house keys or a remote control (Curtis, 2013). The security of an individual's home and infrastructure are then entirely dependent on how well they manage the device. If their phone or tablet is not password protected, anyone would be able to gain control if they were able to acquire it. The same is true for the passwords used to secure and manage the systems in their home. If an individual uses a simple password, it could easily be guessed or compromised. In fact, a study by HP found that ten common smart devices sold to the general public, including smart thermostats, had common vulnerabilities that could be easily hacked to gain access to and control of the equipment (HP, 2014). Also, many of these devices captured personal information about the user which could be subject to data breaches if compromised. Given that many in the general public do not recognize or understand the need to apply basic security protocols to their devices, there are now tremendous opportunities for offenders to compromise these devices.

While it may seem that such concerns are only a technological problem regarding the development of better security protocols or procedures to mitigate attacks, the human element of cybercrime offending and victimization cannot be understated. Hackers and malicious actors engage in problem-solving behaviors to find paths of least resistance to gain access to otherwise hardened targets. One scenario, for instance, could involve hackers targeting states during heatwaves or extreme cold snaps and remotely shutting off heating and cooling services. The email address associated with that device could then be sent a message spoofing the manufacturer's information and indicate that the recipient must pay a fee in order to have their devices turned back on. Such scams are regularly used with success in various malware and phishing schemes, and would require only slight adjustments on the part of attackers in order to be effective. At a more insidious level, the same techniques could be used by extremist groups or nation-state hackers to directly affect the population of an enemy nation to cause fear or disrupt services.

As a whole, criminological research can be inherently valuable to complement computer science research in this space through identifying the behavioral and attitudinal dynamics of hackers who might target these devices. Research could also prove valuable to understand how end users recognize threats to their equipment and identify strategies to improve security awareness and potential recognition of attacks. To date, there is minimal published criminological research considering attacks against critical infrastructure that can be managed in part through remote devices. Specifically, Rege (2013) examined threats to the industrial control systems used to manage critical infrastructure in power and sewer systems through a situational crime prevention framework. This work gives interesting context as to the ways that virtual targets may be hardened from attack and potential ways to minimize the likelihood of success on the part of attackers.

The lack of research in this space demonstrates a critical and inherent challenge that has yet to be addressed in criminology as a discipline. There is a deficit of technological expertise on the part of researchers in the field regarding how cyber-attacks operate and the ways that data can be effectively captured through various mechanisms in the wild. Though criminology is an historically interdisciplinary field of study, there is generally little collaboration between computer scientists, engineers, and social science researchers. There are few current criminologists with any technical training (formal or otherwise), and minimal interdisciplinary programs for university students which incorporate both social and technical science expertise. Instead, areas of inquiry are furthered based on incremental knowledge gains made by the few individuals who identify one another across the disciplines and are able to find points of collaboration.

This knowledge gap must be filled if we are to improve our knowledge on both the reasons why individuals engage in cybercrime and the process of offending and securing targets. There are a few, but inadequate, attempts to link the research communities together through either interdisciplinary research conferences or a few new journals designed to promote scholarship developed by researchers in different fields. These examples are the exception rather than the rule. These patterns must change and scholars must force themselves to become more informed of the technical processes involved in cybercrime offending and the ways that various devices actually operate. Only then can we truly push our knowledge of cybercrime forward and improve the validity of our research findings to practical scenarios in the field, rather than hypothetical examples on survey instruments.

Social movements, social media, and radicalization

Access to technology not only creates threats to electronic targets, but it also enables potential real-world threats to be actualized and more clearly communicated. The role of social media in our day-to-day lives is quite pertinent to the relationship between online activity and real-world action. Social media have become a pivotal resource in political expression worldwide, whether as part of general social discourse in democratic nations or as a tool to express dissent or show the realities of life in totalitarian regimes (see DiMaggio et al., 2001; Van Laer, 2010).

A growing concern over the last decade that will likely continue is the role of the Internet in general, and social media specifically, in communicating radical ideas and fomenting terrorism in various parts of the world. In fact, the National Institute of Justice has dedicated millions of dollars in grant funds to the study of **radicalization**, with at least two multi-year projects funded in 2014 exploring these issues. As young people use social media for all facets of their personal lives, exposure to messages of violence and aggression may attract some individuals toward radicalization (e.g. Freilich et al., 2013; Neer & O'Toole, 2014). Groups such as the Islamic State of Iraq and Syria (ISIS) have been able to craft extremely strong messages of radical Islam targeted through social media to promote their agenda and potentially attract recruits to their cause (Neer & O'Toole, 2014).

There is, however, a limited body of empirical research on the role of the Internet and online discourses in the radicalization process to violent ideologically motivated activity (Corb, 2011; Tsfati & Weimann, 2002; Weimann, 2011). There is evidence that a range of websites and online content is used by members of both the Far Right and Islamic extremist movements to promote their ideologies through mass-media (Denning, 2011; Freiburger & Crane, 2011; Holt, 2010, 2012; Weimann, 2011). Social media provide an avenue to spread news stories that may enrage individuals toward radical agendas (Corb, 2011). The Internet also provides an outlet to coordinate real-world events across multiple areas and facilitate social relationships (Erez, Weimann, & Weisburd, 2011; Simi & Futrell, 2010). Research suggests that individuals who engaged in extremist behaviors either maintained or visited websites hosting radical group content (Chermak, Freilich, & Simone, 2010; Freilich et al., 2013).

There is, however, no substantive research at this time assessing the extent to which online experiences actually factor in to an individual's process to radicalization. Scholarship on the process of radicalization has identified a range of structural and individual factors, though they recognize radicalization cannot be explained by any one factor (Borum, 2011a, 2011b; Horgan, 2005; McCauley & Moskalenko, 2008; Taylor & Horgan, 2006). One of the most influential frameworks (McCauley & Moskalenko, 2008) identifies 12 mechanisms affecting radicalization spanning the individual, group, and mass levels. They define radicalization as the process of "[i]ncreasing extremity of beliefs, feelings, and behaviors in directions that increasingly justify inter-group violence and demand sacrifice in defense of the in group" (McCauley & Moskalenko, 2008: 416).

Individual attitudes and experiences are critical when examining an individual's radicalization into violence in support of extremist beliefs. Individuals who are emotionally vulnerable, whether because of feelings of anger, alienation, or disenfranchisement, are more likely to make the transition to morally justifying violence as an alternative in obtaining political or social goals (McCauley & Moskalenko, 2008; Taylor & Horgan, 2006). Several models of radicalization identify the importance of cognitive openings, where a personal crisis or sense of longing leaves individuals receptive to new world views, as key to initiating the radicalization process (McCauley & Moskalenko, 2008; Simi & Futrell, 2010; Taylor & Horgan, 2006; Wiktorowicz, 2004). Those who are exposed to radicalized messages during this period may be more willing to accept and justify value systems of an extremist movement and the use of violence as a political strategy (McCauley & Moskalenko, 2008; Simi & Futrell, 2010). Thus, the Internet may be a key venue in exposing individuals to viewpoints that justify the use of violence.

In addition, access to the Internet may be essential in the process of radicalization due to the potential social stigma associated with certain ideologies or movements. Individuals who indicate they are beginning to accept white nationalist or neo-Nazi value systems to others in the real world may experience social rejection from peers and employers (Blee, 2002; Dobratz & Shanks-Meile, 1997) and cultural isolation generally (Freilich et al., 2013; Simi & Futrell, 2010). In online environments, however, individuals can freely associate with those who share their beliefs and discuss their viewpoints and ideas without fear of reprisal (Simi & Futrell, 2010; Weimann, 2011). In addition, individuals use the Internet as a means to identify others within their geographic location and arrange meetings and events in the real world (Simi & Futrell, 2010). This may further integrate individuals into social networks that support the acceptance of a radical identity.

There is a need for scholarship clearly addressing this issue as it will undoubtedly improve our understanding of the process of radicalization and the role of technology in the process. It would also be valuable to compare the behaviors of members of the Far Right and the *jihadi* community in order to identify any similarities in the process of radicalization. Further study is also needed assessing the extent to which differences are present in the radicalization process for those who may choose to engage in non-violent behavior relative to violent extremists. There may be clear differences in the drivers of this process on and off-line, which can only be explored through the use of on and off-line data.

There is also a need for empirical research examining what impels individuals to engage in politically motivated forms of cyber-attack. Non-nation-state hackers increasingly target government and industry resources based on their individual political, nationalistic, and religious motives (Holt, 2009; Kilger, 2011; Woo, Kim, & Dominick, 2004). Research indicates that between 10 and 20 percent of college populations engage in simple forms of hacking, like password guessing and adding files to/deleting files from a system. There is minimal research considering what factors would lead an individual to engage in those behaviors in support of a particular ideology or nation-state (see Holt & Kilger, 2012). One of the few studies examining this behavior found a significant relationship between willingness to engage in physical protest behaviors, such as attending rallies, writing letters, or even engaging in acts of violence, and willingness to engage in cyber-attacks (Holt & Kilger, 2012). This is an interesting finding, pointing to the potential for cyber-attacks from extremist groups as well. The extremely limited body of research demands expansion in order to improve our knowledge of the growing threats present online.

Regulation of online spaces and off-line behavior

As noted throughout this book, social media increasingly play a role in all facets of both deviant and non-deviant behavior. Indications of drinking, drug use, and violent tendencies can all be derived from the photos and messages individuals post on Facebook, Twitter, and other forms of social media. Whether this will translate into actual deviant or criminal behavior is unclear, though many law enforcement agencies are monitoring social media to identify threats before they can occur (see Chapter 1 for discussion of Yik Yak arrests). This is a unique challenge for law enforcement, as it requires an understanding of both online behavior and application of traditional investigative techniques.

Such innovation is necessary in order for law enforcement to find ways to better investigate cybercrime and real-world crimes enabled by technology. Historically, law enforcement agencies at all levels have responded to cybercrime through improved digital evidence collection and analysis techniques (Brenner, 2008; Hinduja, 2007; McQuade, 2006; Stambaugh et al., 2001), virtual stakeouts and stings, and reducing opportunities for crime in a situational crime-prevention framework (Newman & Clarke, 2003; Grabosky, 2007; Wall & Williams, 2007).

Evidence explored in Chapter 4 demonstrated that local agencies do not perceive cybercrimes to fall within their investigative purview. These agencies are likely to be the first point of contact for citizens in the event they observe a cybercrime or believe they have been victimized in some way. As a result, there is a need to identify techniques that could improve collaborations with non-law enforcement agencies, entities, and citizens who already "police" (i.e. monitor) the Internet, or provide security to various extents, or both (e.g. Brenner, 2008; Hinduja, 2007; Wall, 2007). One of the best options is the creation of targeted programs that incorporate Internet users, or online citizens, into policing strategies since they constitute the largest group of individuals online and are able to observe criminality (Wall, 2001; Wall & Williams, 2007). They are more adept at identifying deviance and can quickly report inappropriate behavior to authorities, Internet service providers, or both (Wall, 2001).

One way to achieve an effective collaboration between the public and police may be through the use of principles derived from community-oriented policing used to combat traditional crimes. Community policing has shaped modern police practices over the last 30 years through innovative programs that not only identify but address local problems through community-based partnerships (Skogan, 2006). While the actual techniques employed by police agencies vary based on the size of the population and the police force, there are three consistent components observed in community policing. Specifically, they include: (1) a responsibility shared by the community and police to address crime through non-arrest proactive strategies (Adams et al., 2002; Bayley, 1998; Mastrofski et al., 1995; Skogan, 2006; Skogan & Hartnett, 1997); (2) solutions to problems considered the greatest concerns of the community (Miller, 1999); and (3) organizational changes which support partnerships in the public and private sectors (Braga, 2008; McGarrell et al., 2006).

Due to national headlines of recent police aggressive practices in the US, there has been an increased awareness of poor police–minority community relationships. These issues may lead police forces to transition back to community-oriented practices over the next several years (see President's Task Force on 21st Century Policing, 2015). The resurgence of community policing in the real world may also encourage a movement toward online community policing techniques.

Both scholars and police administrators have begun to recommend that some type of **online community-oriented policing programs** be developed (Brenner, 2008; Forss, 2010; Jones, 2007; Wall & Williams, 2007). The International Association of Chiefs of Police (2009) advocated for the implementation of online community policing programs to decrease cybercrimes. There are few examples of such programs in action. Although there is no specific single model for use, there is evidence that agencies in the Netherlands, UK, and US use social media to request information from the general public to generate investigative leads from major crimes and to provide alerts from agencies to the public on criminal incidents in progress (e.g. Heverin & Zach, 2010; Wang & Doong, 2010).

The Dutch government has also rolled out a nationwide strategy called the **Burgernet** (or Citizennet), which involves an app that citizens can download to their smartphone or tablet (CGI Group, Inc., 2014). When a call for service is received by a police control room, particularly for either burglaries or missing children, an alert is then sent via text or voicemail to Burgernet users giving a detailed description of the suspect or victim. If an individual sees anything that may be of value related to the incident, they can then use the app to contact police, who will then update the incident information and provide these data to officers in the area. Once the incident is resolved, a message is sent to all participants indicating what occurred and how information led to a specific outcome (CGI Group, Inc., 2014). This project has over 1.5 million participants across the country, and includes approximately 400 incidents per month. Evidence suggests that approximately 10 percent of incidents pushed through this system led to the direct arrest of suspects or recovery of lost or stolen items or persons (EDPOL, 2015).

The success of this program is also indirectly responsible for the development of another Dutch program called the Community Protection Network (Compronet), which combines information acquired through various sensor technologies, including calls for service, gunshot detection microphones, alarm systems, and data mining via social media platforms (deJonge & Mente, 2011). These disparate sources are aggregated through a software program that identifies unique incidents which are then processed by analysts to gather additional information through various open and closed sources. For instance, if a shooting is thought to have occurred based on shot sensor data and calls for service, an analyst can then push requests through social media feeds for photos and information from citizens near the scene while simultaneously dispatching officers to the incident (deJonge & Mente, 2011). As information develops, the data are aggregated and provided to responding officers and call center operators to ensure all necessary agents have appropriate situational information (deJonge & Mente, 2011).

These two platforms present interesting models to potentially integrate citizens into policing initiatives through the use of technology. The power of these programs lies in the fact that citizens can actively participate or opt out, depending on their level of interest. Applying this sort of framework to cybercrime investigations may prove fruitful, as citizens who were interested in participating could immediately and surreptitiously engage in the program without the need for face-to-face interaction with police. This might be an advantageous way to incorporate the online community by increasing reports of cybercrime and developing direct intelligence on offenses generally (Brenner, 2008; Jones, 2007; Wall, 2001; Wall & Williams, 2007). Engaging participants in online communities can expand the scope of police investigative resources because of their Internet knowledge, particularly in areas of the dark web or proxy-supported networks that require technical proficiency to access (Wall, 2001, 2007; Wall & Williams, 2007). This partnership may lead to actionable intelligence to improve successful investigations and prosecutions while also increasing clearance rates of particular types of cybercrime.

In addition to social media engagement, there is a need to find ways to integrate more traditional mechanisms of community policing into the response to cybercrime. For example, convening public workshops where police and the community come together to learn what the citizens are concerned about is paramount to traditional models of community policing. Identifying the immediate concerns of the population served is vital to develop holistic strategies to best benefit the community. Since many in the general public may not recognize the threats they face or understand the mechanics of cybercrime, holding educational workshops to educate them on these issues may be a pivotal first step. Explaining basic forms of cybercrime and how individuals may become a victim could help the public understand why cybercrime is not an abstract threat. Communicating what to do if an individual becomes a victim and basic security measures to minimize risk would also prove invaluable to ensure that actual crimes (rather than the receipt of a single spam email) are brought to the attention of law enforcement.

Workshop environments would also prove useful to inform citizens as to how they can become effective sources for information on cybercrimes they see online. For instance, explaining what to do when a person observes threatening messages posted on social media sites or the presence of child pornography on a website could increase the quantity of leads developed from the general public. Developing targeted programs for youth populations would prove inherently valuable as they spend substantial time on various social media platforms and websites that law enforcement agencies may not yet know. Furthermore, this may encourage youth to recognize that there are clear guidelines for online behavior and to consider the impact of their behavior on others.

The implementation of educational programs and community engagement as prescribed by community policing programs has often been resisted by patrol officers in the field. The notion that officers engage the community through direct interactions outside calls for service has made officers to both feel uncomfortable and consider these encounters undesirable (Adams et al.,

2002; Pelfrey, 2004; Skogan & Hartnett, 1997). In addition, providing educational experiences for the community goes against the model of police as "crime fighters" which may be unattractive to some officers (Adams et al., 2002; Miller, 1999; Reuss-Ianni, 1983). Developing programs that require community engagement through real and virtual environments may appear extremely difficult and problematic to line officers.

Since there is a clear need for community engagement to effectively deal with cybercrime, there is a need for research examining the ways that community policing initiatives and similar programs are implemented in the field. At present, two studies (Bossler & Holt, 2013, 2014) have considered local officers' attitudes toward and support for online community policing. Bossler and Holt (2013), using a sample of officers from Savannah, GA, and Charlotte, NC, found that nearly 40 percent of officers agreed that principles of community policing could be used in virtual settings; most, however, were unsure. A majority of respondents (63.3 percent) felt that their department should hold information workshops for the public to educate them regarding cybercrime risks and prevention efforts. Finally, 60 percent of respondents felt that it was important to work with online citizens to "police" the Internet (Bossler & Holt, 2013).

Bossler and Holt (2013) also found that officers who supported traditional community policing practices were more likely to support all three of these strategies to combat cybercrime. In addition, officers who believed that cybercrimes were underreported were more likely to want to work with the public through information workshops. An expansion of this study by Bossler and Holt (2014) found that officers who viewed cybercrime as a drain on agency resources were less likely to support online community policing strategies. Those officers who believed that cybercrimes would alter policing overall were more likely to support the use of information workshops for the public. Individuals who supported the use of online stakeouts were more likely to support working with online citizens to police the Internet (Bossler & Holt, 2014).

These studies are only potential indicators of the relationships between officers and their willingness to implement community policing in online spaces. Much greater research is needed to understand managerial interest in such programs, as well as identify funding sources to implement them in the field. Process and outcome evaluations are also needed to understand the factors affecting the success of online community policing programs as well as their impact on citizens' perceptions of and willingness to report cybercrimes to police. In turn, our knowledge of how the police support innovative practices to address cybercrime can improve dramatically.

The global enforcement of cybercrime

As noted in Chapter 4, law enforcement at the transnational level is extremely complicated in some cases due to a lack of parity in legislation and criminal statutes and virtually impossible in others because of a lack of extradition relationships between nations. Those nations with large criminal hacker populations such as Russia and the Ukraine do not have an extradition treaty with the US, making any prosecutions unlikely to succeed unless the suspects are caught while traveling abroad. There have been several noteworthy examples of such instances occurring, though the odds that all cybercriminals from these nations will be arrested while on a vacation or business trip are slim. As a consequence, there are few ways to deter actors in these nations from targeting the US and other countries with which no formal extradition treaties exist.

These challenges have led some to call for additional legislation that increases punishments and extends existing legislation to cover more offenses that may occur. For instance, the consistent data breaches occurring in the US have increased the potential risks for identity theft and fraud as a result of data purchased in cybercrime markets. The current legislative language in the Federal Computer Fraud and Abuse Act (CFAA) allows prosecutors to pursue charges against cybercriminals who engage in data breaches or attempt to misuse credit card data while using systems within the US. If the actor does not actually engage US computer systems in order to make purchases or in any way acquire the data, then there are few legal mechanisms that can be employed to pursue action against that person. Thus, the Department of Justice has begun to lobby Congress to revise or create new legislation in order to criminalize the sale, purchase, or possession of credit/ debit card information issued from a US bank, no matter where in the world a transaction takes place (Tucker, 2014).

While this may seem unnecessary, such legislation may serve a vital role in sentencing enhancements to increase the punitive sanctions a hacker may receive in the event that they are arrested. This is exemplified by the recent case against Vladislav Horohorin, a hacker with citizenship in Russia, Israel, and the Ukraine (Department of Justice, 2013). He advertised stolen credit and debit cards through underground forums under the handle "BadB" and was thought to have been involved in the theft of over $9 million from a credit card processor in Atlanta, Georgia (Department of Justice, 2013). Horohorin was initially indicted by a federal grand jury in November 2009 on charges under the CFAA, and was separately indicted again in August 2010 on charges of wire fraud, conspiracy to commit wire fraud, and violations of the CFAA (Department of Justice, 2013).

Through a collaborative investigation by the US Secret Service and French law enforcement, Horohorin was arrested in Nice, France, while attempting to fly to Moscow in 2010. At the time of his arrest, he was in possession of 2.5 million stolen credit and debit card numbers but there was no way to pursue further charges for the possession of these materials (Department of Justice, 2013). Instead, he was extradited to the US in 2012 and prosecuted for his existing charges. He was found guilty on two counts of CFAA violations and conspiracy to commit wire fraud and sentenced to 88 months in prison and a fine of $125,739 (Department of Justice, 2013). Had there been a way also to charge him for the possession of the additional stolen data, he may have received a more severe sentence befitting the scope of his crimes.

The demand for legislative revisions is not easy for lawmakers due in part to the constant changes evident in technology use and its application in criminal behavior. Legislators may neither recognize the way that a piece of technology may be misused nor can they predict how well any one device or application will be accepted and used. As a result, legislation must be designed to be broadly applicable to various circumstances while also providing enough deterrent value to potentially affect the decision-making processes of offenders. This is especially challenging, and has led US legislative efforts at both the state and federal levels to be largely reactive to emergent cybercrime threats rather than proactively designed to apply to various offense types.

This phenomenon is exemplified in the recent development of **sexting**, or the use of camera or video features of smartphones and Internet-enabled devices to send and receive sexually suggestive photos or videos through text messages or applications like Snapchat (Mitchell, Finkelhor, Jones, & Wolak, 2012). Camera and video technologies have been integrated into cell phones and various devices for over a decade, though legislation and attempts to prosecute sexting developed in 2008 and 2009. Much of the focus was on the potential for minors to be coerced into the creation of nude images which may facilitate the dissemination of child pornography (Jones et al., 2012). There are also concerns that once a person sends a sext, they lose control of the image because recipients can easily forward the image to others or post it on social media and websites without permission from the image creator (Mitchell et al., 2012).

These concerns have led to a law enforcement response that is somewhat surprising relative to the scope of other forms of cybercrime. For instance, police agencies at both the local and federal levels investigated 3,477 cases of sexting in 2008 and 2009 alone (Wolak, Finkelhor, & Mitchell, 2012). The sexting images involved in these incidents went to almost as many youth as they did adults (31 percent to 36 percent), though adults were more likely to be arrested as a result of their involvement (62 percent to 36 percent). The sheer quantity of cases also calls into question the value of such a response, as these incidents may overburden forensic investigators and draw time from more serious cases. In addition, if a young person is arrested on charges related to child pornography, this may have serious negative consequences well beyond what may otherwise be seen as a normal form of sexual experimentation (Jones et al., 2012). If the number of arrests related to sexting cases is held up as an example of criminal justice and legislative success, this may only embolden the use of knee-jerk policy responses rather than tempered responses on the basis of the potential impact of new laws on the system as a whole.

At a global level, there is also a need for improved international mechanisms to help combat serious financial and hacking-related cybercrimes. The current gap in this area is beginning to be filled by private industry groups engaging in partnerships with law enforcement agencies in various nations. This strategy may prove fruitful for some forms of cybercrime, though it may also lead to long-term degradation of the perceived legitimacy of many law enforcement mechanisms and affect the perception of industry sources generally. Legitimacy with respect to law enforcement is a critical issue which has been found to be as important as deterrence in promoting compliance with the law (Garland, 1996; Sunshine & Tyler, 2003; Tyler, 2004). When a law, policy, or agency is seen as overstepping its bounds, this can reduce the public's trust in the state, and question the authority and legitimacy of the state as a whole.

The general public may already have doubts as to the ability of law enforcement agencies to arrest cybercriminals (e.g. Furnell, 2002). If industry sources become a primary vehicle to disrupt international cybercrime networks, this may lead some to perceive that they have overstepped their role as a service provider into order maintenance. The public may question the legitimacy of such a change, given that industry sources are not mandated by constitutions or the community to play such a role (Sunshine & Tyler, 2003; Tyler, 2004). This may increase individual willingness to engage in cybercrimes due to a perception that the mechanisms used to enforce the law are unjust, unsanctioned, and being run for profit. Thus, there is a need for substantive questioning of the movement of industry sources into more direct engagement in law enforcement efforts and enforcement strategies in the future (e.g. Brenner, 2008).

If policies can be developed to strengthen international cooperation between agencies and foster greater power in state-based law enforcement mechanisms, this may be a better strategy than relinquishing partial control to industry agents. One potential way to increase not only the perceived legitimacy of enforcement efforts, but also sanction transnational offenders, is through the creation of an **international criminal tribunal for cyberspace** (Schjolberg, 2012). The United Nations (UN) has proposed that the International Criminal Court (ICC) could serve as an appropriate venue for prosecution of cybercrimes that have a substantive impact on multiple nations (Schjolberg, 2012). Currently, the ICC has jurisdiction over international offenses including genocide, crimes against humanity, and war crimes. Extending its authority to cybercrime may be feasible since many nations across the world have begun to harmonize their cybercrime laws based on model legislation like the European Union's Convention on Cybercrime (CoC). This provides an opportunity for an international body to serve victims from nations that recognize the authority of the court to prosecute offenders based on consistent laws and international treaties such as the Rome Statute.

In order for the ICC to develop a Tribunal on Cybercrime, it must be established at the UN by a Resolution of the Security Council in accordance with all UN Charter rules (Schjolberg, 2012). Such a condition may not be possible, as the permanent member nations of the Security Council are China, France, Russia, the UK, and the US. These nations have a vested interest in retaining existing relationships regarding extradition and jurisdictional authority within their own justice systems, rather than extending power to a body that may disadvantage their citizens. In fact, model resolution language has been available for the last few years, though it has not been moved forward or acted upon by the Security Council.

If a Tribunal could be established, it might also be disadvantaged by the fact that some countries would not be represented or participate in the court. Only those states that have ratified the **Rome Statute**, which recognizes the authority of the ICC, can take part in its activities (Schjolberg, 2012). At present, the ICC has 123 member nations, including most of Europe, Australia, South America, and portions of Africa. The US and Russia have signed, but not ratified, the Rome Statute. China, India, Pakistan, and various nations in the Middle East and Southeast Asia are considered non-state parties which do not recognize the authority of the court. If these nations do not have any role in or recognize the authority of the ICC, then they may become safe havens for international cybercriminals to operate with impunity. Based on these conditions, it is not clear if the ICC may ever be able to play a role in the global enforcement and prosecution of cybercrimes.

Though it is helpful to speculate on mechanisms to pursue justice against cybercriminals, there are myriad fundamental research questions that must be addressed to improve our knowledge of the global limits and perceptions of cybercrime enforcement generally. To date, one of the few studies to directly compare cybercrime prosecutions and system responses cross-nationally was published by Smith, Grabosky, and Urbas (2004). This study compared arrests and prosecutorial outcomes for cybercrime cases in North America, Australia, and the UK. The findings are now over a decade old, and only hint at potential divergences between these nations in a modern context. For instance, 75 percent of US cases referred to federal prosecutors between 1992 and 2001 were declined because of a lack of evidence (Smith et al., 2004). It is possible that this figure may have decreased with improvements in both evidence handling and prosecutorial awareness of cybercrime. Empirical investigation is essential in order to improve our knowledge of these fundamental questions with respect to the processing of cybercrime cases by judicial systems across the world.

Summary and conclusions

This work has demonstrated that cybercrime scholarship is truly a work in progress. The literature contains more limitations and questions than it does solid empirical findings, creating ample opportunities for informed research. To do so, scholars must expand their knowledge of not only human behavior, but of the devices that we use to enable our online experiences. In addition, researchers must move beyond geographically limited convenience samples and begin to develop more robust generalizable sample populations. Such techniques would improve both our knowledge of the prevalence of both victimization and offending as well as theoretical relationships between variables.

Research is also needed evaluating the utility of policing strategies and deterrent techniques to reduce offending. Though the criminal justice literature has been built on process and outcome evaluations of various policing initiatives, such research is absent in the cybercrime literature. Similarly, there is virtually no research on the experiences of cybercriminals in the court system or correctional process. These cases may comprise a small proportion of all prosecutions, though it would be invaluable to understand how they are viewed by judges, prosecutors, and the extent to which offenders are treated differently by street criminals while inside prisons.

A final and perhaps more fundamental question must also be addressed by researchers moving forward: Should we stop using the term "cybercrime" and refer to these acts as simply "crime"? In other words, should we stop thinking of cybercrime as fundamentally different from many forms of street crime? As our lives increasingly involve and blend on and off-line experiences, individuals who are wronged in one environment often experience consequences in the other. Cybercrime victimization may have an impact on the behaviors of individuals on and off-line, whether in changing shopping habits or engagement in social media. In particular, person-based cybercrimes may push some individuals out of online spaces entirely over fear of subsequent victimization and lead to social isolation in the real world as well (Baum et al., 2009; Nobles et al., 2014).

Considering all offenses simply as crimes rather than cyber versus street crimes may also aid law enforcement agencies by removing potential stigma from the notion of "cybercrimes" as offenses they cannot or should not investigate. Designating all offenses as crimes may also engender victim reporting by eliminating confusion over whether it is a local or federal incident. Instead, first responders can provide the necessary triage for a case and push it up to a higher agency if necessary.

The likely answer to the question is "no." Cybercrime as a designation will remain in place moving forward. Budget limitations and managerial concerns over specialized roles in law enforcement agencies will undoubtedly require that cybercrimes be uniquely identified in order to ensure all necessary resources can be acquired to investigate these offenses. Similarly, computer security vendors and service providers have a vested interest in cybercrimes remaining the purview of both industry and law enforcement. Contemplating what would happen if the answer were "yes" creates opportunities to speculate as to how the criminal justice system at all levels could improve its response to various forms of cybercrime. Such exercises are essential to the growth of the field, and may help push cybercrime research from the periphery to the center of the research community.

Key terms

Bitcoin
Burgernet
Crypto-currencies
Cryptomarkets
Disruptive technology
Google Glass
International criminal tribunal for cyberspace
Internet of Things
Malware infections
Online community-oriented policing programs
Radicalization
Ransomware
Rome Statute
Sexting
Tor network
Wearable devices

Discussion questions

1   Do you agree with the authors' predictions for future cybercrime trends?
2   Which of the possible cybercrime trends may have the greatest impact on our lives? On the economy? For the criminal justice system?
3   How much will online markets move open-air illicit markets (e.g. prostitution, drug sales) to less public spaces?
4   What does the history of the Silk Road tell us about online illicit markets and the demand for certain products?
5   Can you imagine a future in which you have to pay with Bitcoin on a more regular basis?
6   What type of product, device, or technology do you think will be the next disruptive technology? What impact will this new technology have on crime?
7   Do the benefits related to the Internet of Things outweigh the potential risks?
8   Is online community policing a viable policing strategy to address cyber-crimes and various forms of cyber-deviance? Are there additional pitfalls to online community policing in comparison to that of community policing in the physical world?
9   What strategies discussed in this chapter have the most promise in improving our global response to cybercrime?
10   Should cybercrimes be categorized separately from traditional offenses? Should we stop thinking of cybercrime as fundamentally different from many forms of street crime?
11   The chapter provided a plethora of research questions that will improve our knowledge regarding cybercrime and technology. Which two research questions do you think scholars should focus upon the most? Why?

References

Abelson, R., & Creswell, J. (2015). Data breach at Anthem may forecast a trend. *The New York Times*, February 6. www.nytimes.com/2015/02/07/business/data-breach-at-anthem-may-lead-to- others.html?_r=0.

Adams, R.E., Rohe, W.M., & Arcury, T.A. (2002). Implementing community-oriented policing: Organizing change and street officer attitudes. *Crime and Delinquency*, 48, 399–430.

Arseneault, L., Walsh, E., Trzesniewski, K., Newcombe, R., Caspi, A., & Moffitt, T.E. (2006). Bullying victimization uniquely contributes to adjustment problems in young children: A nationally representative cohort study. *Pediatrics*, 118, 130–138.

Barratt, M.J. (2012). Silk Road: eBay for drugs. *Addiction*, 107, 683.

Barratt, M.J., Ferris, J.A., & Winstock, A.R. (2014). Use of the Silk Road, the online drug marketplace, in the United Kingdom, Australia, and the United States. *Addiction*, 109, 774–783.

Baum, K., Catalano, S., Rand, M., & Rose, K. (2009). *Stalking Victimization in the United States*. Bureau of Justice Statistics, US Department of Justice. www.ovw.usdoj.gov/docs/stalking-victimization.pdf.

Bayley, D.H. (1998). *What Works in Policing*. New York: Oxford University Press.

Blee, K. (2002). *Inside Organized Racism: Men and Women in the Hate Movement*. Berkley, CA: University of California Press.

Blumstein, A., & Wallman, J. (2005). *The Crime Drop in America*. Cambridge University Press.

Borum, R. (2011a). Radicalization into violent extremism I: A review of social science theories. *Journal of Strategic Studies*, 4, 7–36.

Borum, R. (2011b). Radicalization into violent extremism II: A review of conceptual models and empirical research. *Journal of Strategic Security*, 4, 37–62.

Bossler, A.M., & Holt, T.J. (2009). On-line activities, guardianship, and malware infection: An examination of routine activities theory. *International Journal of Cyber Criminology*, 3, 400–420.

Bossler, A.M., & Holt, T.J. (2013). Assessing officer perceptions and support for online community policing. *Security Journal*, 26, 349–366.

Bossler, A.M., & Holt, T.J. (2014). Further examining officer perceptions and support for online community policing. In C. Marcum & G. Higgins (Eds.) *Social Networking as a Criminal Enterprise* (pp. 167–196). London: Taylor & Francis.

Bower, J. (2002). Disruptive change. *Harvard Business Review*, 80, 95–101.

Bowes, L., Arseneault, L., Maughan, B., Taylor, A., Caspi, A., & Moffitt, T. (2009). School, neighborhood, and family factors associated with children's bullying involvement: A nationally representative longitudinal study. *Journal of the American Academy of Child and Adolescent Psychiatry*, 48, 545–553.

Bradshaw, C.P., Sawyer, A.L., & O'Brennan, L.M. (2009). A social disorganization perspective on bullying-related attitudes and behaviors: The influence of school context. *American Journal of Community Psychology*, 43, 204–220.

Braga, A.A. (2008). Pulling levers focused deterrence strategies and the prevention of gun homicide. *Journal of Criminal Justice*, 36, 332–343.

Brenner, S.W. (2008). *Cyberthreats: The Emerging Fault Lines of the Nation State*. New York: Oxford University Press.

Cannarella, J., & Spechler, J.A. (2014). Epidemiological modeling of online social network dynamics, unpublished paper.

CGI Group, Inc. (2014). *Burgernet, Netherlands: Case Study.* www.cgi.com/sites/defa ult/files/pdf/Burgernet-gets-citizens-involved-police-work- Netherlands.pdf.

Chermak, S.M., Freilich, J.D., & Simone, Jr., J. (2010). Surveying American state police agencies about lone wolves, far-right criminality, and far-right and Islamic jihadist criminal collaboration. *Studies in Conflict and Terrorism*, 33, 1019–1041.

Cole, A., Mellor, M., & Noyes, D. (2007). Botnets: The rise of the machines. *Proceedings on the 6th Annual Security Conference*, 1–14.

Collins, J.D., Sainato, V.A., and Khey, D.N. (2011). Organizational data breaches 2005–2010: Applying SCP to the Healthcare and Education Sectors. *International Journal of Cyber Criminology*, 5, 794–810.

Copes, H., & Cherbonneau, M. (2006). The key to auto theft: Emerging methods of auto theft from the offenders' perspective. *British Journal of Criminology*, 46, 917–934.

Corb, A. (2011). *Into the Minds of Mayhem: White Supremacy, Recruitment and the Internet.* A report commissioned for Google Ideas.

Cunningham, S., & Kendall, T. (2010). Sex for sale: Online commerce in the world's oldest profession. In T.J. Holt (Ed.), *Crime On-line: Correlates, Causes, and Context* (pp. 40–75). Raleigh, NC: Carolina Academic Press.

Curtis, S. (2013). Home invasion 2.0: How criminals could hack your house. *Tele-graph*August 2. www.telegraph.co.uk/technology/internet- security/10218824/Hom e-invasion-2.0-how-criminals-could-hack-your-house.html.

de Graaf, D., Shosha, A.F., & Gladyshev, P. (2013). Bredolab: Shopping in the cyber-crime underworld. In M. Rogers & K.C. Seigfried-Spellar (Eds.), *Digital Forensics and Cybercrime.* Fourth International Conference, ICDF2C 2013 (pp. 302–313). Racine, WA: Springer. ulir.ul.ie/handle/10344/2896.

deJonge, E., & Mente, R. (2011). Law enforcement's newest weapon: Internet scanning and use of social media for in-progress crime. *The Police Chief*, 78, 28–29.

Denning, D.E. (2011). Cyber-conflict as an emergent social problem. In T.J. Holt & B. Schell (Eds.), *Corporate Hacking and Technology-Driven Crime: Social Dynamics and Implications* (pp. 170–186). Hershey, PA: IGI-Global.

Department of Justice (2013). International credit card trafficker sentenced to 88 months in prison. Department of Justice Office of Public Affairs, April 5. www.justice.gov/opa/pr/international-credit-card-trafficker-sentenced-88-m onths-prison.

DiMaggio, P., Hargittai, E., Neuman, W.R., & Robinson, J.P. (2001). Social implications of the Internet. *Annual Review of Sociology*, 27, 307–336.

Dobratz, B.A., & Shanks-Meile, S. (1997). *"White Power, White Pride!" The White Separatist Movement in the United States.* New York: Twayne.

Dolliver, D.S. (2015). Evaluating drug trafficking on the Tor Network: Silk Road 2, the sequel. *International Journal of Drug Policy.*

EDPOL (2015). Citizen participation: The Netherlands, Burgernet. ed-pol.eu/site/? page_id=1014.

Erez, E., Weimann, G., & Weisburd, A.A. (2011). *Jihad, Crime, and the Internet: Content Analysis of Jihadist Forum Discussions.* Washington, DC: National Institute of Justice. www.ncjrs.gov/pdffiles1/nij/grants/236867.pdf.

Ferguson, D. (2013). CryptoLocker attacks that hold your computer to ransom. *The Guardian*October 19. www.theguardian.com/money/2013/oct/19/cryptolocker-atta cks-computer-ransomeware.

Forss, M. (2010). Virtual community policing. www.slideshare.net/fobba/virtual-comm unity-policing-3938294.

Franklin, O. (2013). Unravelling the Dark Web. *British GQ*. www.gq-magazine.co.uk/comment/articles/2013-02/07/silk-road-online-drugs- guns-black-market/viewall.

Franklin, J., Paxson, V., Perrig, A., & Savage, S. (2007). An inquiry into the nature and cause of the wealth of Internet miscreants. Paper presented at CCS07, October 29–November 2, in Alexandria, VA.

Freiburger, T., & Crane, J.S. (2011). The Internet as a terrorist's tool: A social learning perspective. In K. Jaishankar (Ed.), *Cyber Criminology: Exploring Internet Crimes and Criminal Behavior* (pp. 127–138). Boca Raton, FL: CRC Press.

Freilich, J.D., Chermak, S.M., Belli, R., Gruenewald, J., & Parkin, W.S. (2013). Introducing the United States Extremist Crime Database (ECDB). *Terrorism and Political Violence*, 25, 1–13.

Furnell, S. (2002). *Cybercrime: Vandalizing the Information Society*. London: Addison-Wesley.

Garland, D. (1996). The limits of the sovereign state. *The British Journal of Sociology*, 36, 445–471.

Gibbs, S. (2013). Silk Road underground market closed—but others will replace it. *The Guardian*, October 3. www.theguardian.com/technology/2013/oct/03/silk-road-underground-market- closed-bitcoin

Grabosky, P. (2007). *Electronic Crime*. Trenton, NJ: Pearson Education.

Heverin, T., & Zach, L. (2010). Twitter for city police department information sharing. *Proceedings of the American Society for Information Science and Technology*, 47, 1–7.

Higgins, K.J. (2014). Target, Neiman Marcus data breaches tip of the iceberg. *Dark Reading*, January 13. www.darkreading.com/attacks-breaches/target-neiman-marcus-data-breaches-tip-o/240165363.

Hinduja, S. (2007). Computer crime investigations in the United States: Leveraging knowledge from the past to address the future. *International Journal of Cyber Criminology*, 1, 1–26.

Hinduja, S., & Patchin, J.W. (2009). *Bullying Beyond the Schoolyard: Preventing and Responding to Cyberbullying*. New York: Corwin Press.

Holt, T.J. (2009). The attack dynamics of political and religiously motivated hackers. In T. Saadawi & L. Jordan (Eds.) *Cyber Infrastructure Protection* (pp. 161–182). New York: Strategic Studies Institute.

Holt, T.J. (2010). Exploring strategies for qualitative criminological and criminal justice inquiry using on-line data. *Journal of Criminal Justice Education*, 21, 300–321.

Holt, T.J. (2012). Exploring the intersections of technology, crime and terror. *Terrorism and Political Violence*, 24, 337–354.

Holt, T.J. (2013). Examining the forces shaping cybercrime markets online. *Social Science Computer Review*, 31, 165–177.

Holt, T.J., Blevins, K.R., & Kuhns, J.B. (2008). Examining the displacement practices of johns with on-line data. *Journal of Criminal Justice*, 36, 522–528.

Holt, T.J., & Bossler, A.M. (2013). Examining the relationship between routine activities and malware infection indicators. *Journal of Contemporary Criminal Justice*, 29, 420–436.

Holt, T.J., & Bossler, A.M. (2014). An assessment of the current state of cybercrime scholarship. *Deviant Behavior*, 35, 20–40.

Holt, T.J., Chee, G., Ng, E., & Bossler, A.M. (2013). Exploring the consequences of bullying victimization in a sample of Singapore youth. *International Criminal Justice Review*, 23, 25–40.

Holt, T. & Kilger, M. (2012). Examining willingness to attack critical infrastructure on and off-line. *Crime and Delinquency*, 58, 798–822.

Holt, T.J., & Lampke, E. (2010). Exploring stolen data markets on-line: Products and market forces. *Criminal Justice Studies*, 23, 33–50.

Holt, T.J., & Smirnova, O. (2014). *Examining the Structure, Organization, and Processes of the International Market for Stolen Data*. Washington, DC: US Department of Justice. www.ncjrs.gov/pdffiles1/nij/grants/245375.pdf.

Holt, T.J., Smirnova, O., & Chua, Y.T. (2013). An exploration of the factors affecting the advertised price for stolen data. *eCrime Researchers Summit (eCRS)*, 1–10.

Holt, T.J., Smirnova, O., Chua, Y.T., & Copes, H. (2015). Examining the risk reduction strategies of actors in online criminal markets. *Global Crime*, 16, 81–103.

Holt, T.J., & Turner, M.G. (2012). Examining risks and protective factors of on line identity theft. *Deviant Behavior*, 33, 308–323.

Holt, T.J., Turner, M.G., & Exum, M.L. (2014). The impact of self control and neighborhood disorder on bullying victimization. *Journal of Criminal Justice*, 42, 347–355.

Holz, T., Engelberth, M., & Freiling, F. (2009). Learning more about the underground economy: A case-study of keyloggers and dropzones. In M. Backes & P. Ning (Eds.), *Computer Security-ESCORICS* (pp. 1–18). Berlin and Heidelberg: Springer.

Honeynet Research Alliance (2003). *Profile: Automated Credit Card Fraud*. Know Your Enemy Paper series. www.honeynet.org/papers/profiles/cc fraud.pdf.

Horgan, J. (2005). The social and psychological characteristics of terrorism and terrorists. In T. Bjørgo (Ed.), *Root Causes of Terrorism: Myths, Reality and Ways Forward* (p.44). London: Routledge.

HP (2014). Internet of Things research study, 2014 report. www.hp.com/h20195/V2/GetPDF.aspx/4AA5-4759ENW.pdf.

International Association of Chiefs of Police (2009). 2008 IACP Community Policing Awards: Presented at the 115th Annual IACP Conference. *The Police Chief*, 77(3). policechiefmagazine.org/magazine/index.cfm?fuseaction=display_arch&article_id=1749&issue_id=32009.

Jones, B.R. (2007). Comment: Virtual neighborhood watch: Open source software and community policing against cybercrime. *Journal of Criminal Law and Criminology*, 97, 601–630.

Jones, L.M., Mitchell, K.J., & Finkelhor, D. (2012). Trends in youth Internet victimization: Findings from three youth Internet safety surveys 2000–2010. *Journal of Adolescent Health*, 50, 179–186.

Kilger, M. (2011). Social dynamics and the future of technology-driven crime. In T.J. Holt & B. Schell (Eds.), *Corporate Hacking and Technology Driven Crime: Social Dynamics and Implications* (pp. 205–227). Hershey, PA: IGI-Global.

Kowalski, R.M., & Limber, P. (2007). Electronic bullying among middle school students. *Journal of Adolescent Health*, 41, 22–30.

McAfee Labs (2014). McAfee Labs 2014 threat prediction. www.mcafee.com/us/resources/reports/rp-threats-predictions-2014.pdf.

McCauley, C., & Moskalenko, S. (2008). Mechanisms of political radicalization: Pathways toward terrorism. *Terrorism and Political Violence*, 20, 415–433.

McGarrell, E.F., Chermak, S., Wilson, J.M., & Corsaro, N. (2006). Reducing homicide through a "lever-pulling" strategy. *Justice Quarterly*, 23, 214–231.

McQuade, S. (2006). Technology-enabled crime, policing and security. *Journal of Technology Studies*, 32, 32–42.

Madden, M., Lenhart, A., Cortesi, S., Gasser, U., Duggan, M., Smith, A., & Beaton, M. (2013). Teens, social media, and privacy. www.pewinternet.org/2013/05/21/teens-social-media-and-privacy/.

Martin, J. (2014). Lost on the Silk Road: Online drug distribution and the crypto-market. *Criminology and Criminal Justice*, 14, 351–367.

Mastrofski, S.D., Worden, R.E., & Snipes, J.B. (1995). Law enforcement in a time of community policing. *Criminology*, 33, 539–563.

Mativat, F., & Tremblay, P. (1997). Counterfeiting credit cards: Displacement effects, suitable offenders, and crime wave patterns. *British Journal of Criminology*, 37, 165–183.

Miller, S. (1999). *Gender and Community Policing: Walking the Talk*. Boston: Northeastern University Press.

Mitchell, K.J., Finkelhor, D., Jones, L.M., & Wolak, J. (2012). Prevalence and characteristics of youth sexting: A national study. *Pediatrics*, 129, 13–20.

Moore, K. (2011). *71% of Online Adults Now Use Video-sharing Sites*. Pew Internet and American Life Project. pewinternet.org/Reports/2011/Video-sharing-sites.aspx.

Motoyama, M., McCoy, D., Levchenko, K., Savage, S., & Voelker, G.M. (2011). An analysis of underground forums. *IMC'11*, 71–79.

Nansel, T.R., Overpeck, M., Pilla, R.S., Ruan, W.J., Simmons-Morton, B., & Scheidt, P. (2001). Bullying behavior among U.S. youth: Prevalence and association with psychosocial adjustment. *Journal of the American Medical Association*, 285, 2094–2100.

Neer, T., & O'Toole, M.E. (2014). The violence of the Islamic State of Syria (ISIS): A behavioral perspective. *Violence and Gender*, 1, 145–156.

Newman, G., & Clarke, R. (2003). *Superhighway Robbery: Preventing e-Commerce Crime*. Cullompton: Willan.

Ngo, F.T., & Paternoster, R. (2011). Cybercrime victimization: An examination of individual and situational level factors. *International Journal of Cyber Criminology*, 5, 773–793.

Nobles, M.R., Reyns, B.W., Fox, K.A., & Fisher, B.S. (2014). Protection against pursuit: A conceptual and empirical comparison of cyberstalking and stalking victimization among a national sample. *Justice Quarterly*, 31, 986–1014.

Olson, P. (2014). Wearable tech is plugging into health insurance. *Forbes*, June 19. www.forbes.com/sites/parmyolson/2014/06/19/wearable-tech-health-insurance/.

Panda Security (2013). *Annual Report Pandalabs 2013 Summary*. press.pandasecurity.com/wp-content/uploads/2010/05/Annual Report PandaLabs 2013.pdf.

Pelfrey, W.V. (2004). The inchoate nature of community policing: Differences between community policing and traditional police officers. *Justice Quarterly*, 21, 579–601.

Pew Charitable Trust (2005). *Pew Internet and American Life Project*. www.pewinternet.org/Reports/2009/10 Home_Broadband_Adoption-2009.aspx.

Phelps, A., & Watt, A. (2014). I shop online—recreationally! Internet anonymity and Silk Road enabling drug use in Australia. *Digital Investigation*, 11, 261–272.

PiperJaffray (2014). *PiperJaffray 27th Semi-Annual Taking Stock With Teens Survey Spring, 2014*. www.piperjaffray.com/private/pdf/TSWT%20Infographics.pdf.

Ponemon Institute (2015). *2014 Cost of Cyber Crime Study*. Traverse City, MI: Ponemon Institute.

President's Task Force on 21st Century Policing (2015). *Interim Report*. www.cops.usdoj.gov/pdf/taskforce/interim_tf_report.pdf.

Pricewaterhouse Cooper (2014). *The Wearable Future*. Consumer Intelligence Series. www.pwc.com/us/en/industry/entertainment- media/publications/consumer-intelligence-series/.

Pyrooz, D.C., Decker, S.H., & Moule, R.K. (2015). Criminal and routine activities in online settings: Gangs, offenders, and the Internet. *Justice Quarterly*, 32, 471–499.

Rege, A. (2013). Industrial control systems and cybercrime. In T.J. Holt (Ed.), *Crime On-line: Causes, Correlates, and Context*. Second edition (pp.191–218). Raleigh, NC: Carolina Academic Press.

Reuss-Ianni, E. (1983). *The Two Cultures of Policing: Street Cops and Management Cops*. New Brunswick, NJ: Transaction Books.

Reyns, B. (2013). Online routines and identity theft victimization: Further expanding routine activity theory beyond direct-contact offenses. *Journal of Research in Crime and Delinquency*, 50, 216–238.

Reyns, B.W., Henson, B., and Fisher, B.S. (2011). Being pursued online: Applying cyberlifestyle-routine activities theory to cyberstalking victimization. *Criminal Justice & Behavior*, 38, 1149–1169.

Schjolberg, J. (2012). *Recommendations for Potential New Global Legal Mechanisms Against Global Cyberattacks and Other Global Cybercrimes*. EastWest Institute (EWI) Cybercrime Legal Working Group. www.cybercrimelaw.net/documents/ICTC.pdf.

Simi, P. & Futrell, R. (2010). *American Swastika: Inside the White Power Movement's Hidden Spaces of Hate*. New York: Rowman and Littlefield Publishers.

Skogan, W.G. (2006). *Police and Community in Chicago: A Tale of Three Cities*. New York: Oxford University Press.

Skogan, W.G., & Hartnett, S.M. (1997). *Community Policing. Chicago Style*. New York: Oxford University Press.

Smith, R.G., Grabosky, P., & Urbas, G. (2004). *Cyber Criminals on Trial*. Cambridge: Cambridge University Press.

Stambaugh, H., Beaupre, D.S., Icove, D.J., Baker, R., Cassady, W., & Williams, W.P. (2001). *Electronic Crime Needs Assessment for State and Local Law Enforcement*. Washington, DC: National Institute of Justice, NCJ 186276.

Sunshine, J., & Tyler, T.R. (2003). The role of procedural justice and legitimacy in shaping public support for policing. *Law & Society Review*, 37, 513–548.

Taylor, M., & Horgan, J. (2006). A conceptual framework for addressing psychological process in the development of a terrorist. *Terrorism and Political Violence*, 18, 585–601.

Tsfati, Y., & Weimann, G. (2002). www.terrorism.com: Terror on the Internet. *Studies in Conflict and Terrorism*, 25, 317–332.

Tucker, E. (2014). One simple legal fix could help fight overseas credit card fraud, claims DOJ. *PBS Newshour*. www.pbs.org/newshour/rundown/one-simple-legal-fix-help-justice-department-fight-overseas-credit-card-fraud/.

Turner, M.G., Exum, M.L., Brame, R., and Holt, T.J. (2013). Bullying victimization and adolescent mental health: General and typological effects across sex. *Journal of Criminal Justice*, 41, 53–59.

Tyler, T.R. (2004). Enhancing police legitimacy. *The Annals of the American Academy of Political and Social Science*, 593, 84–99.

Van Laer, J. (2010). Activists online and offline: The Internet as an information channel for protest demonstrations. *Mobilization: An International Journal*, 15, 347–366.

Vaughn, M.G., Fu, Q., Beaver, K., DeLisi, M., Perron, B., & Howard, M. (2011). Effects of childhood adversity on bullying and cruelty to animals in the United States: Findings from a national sample. *Journal of Interpersonal Violence*, 26, 3509–3525.

Vaughn, M.G., Fu, Q., Bender, K., DeLisi, M., Beaver, K.M., Perron, B.E., & Howard, M.O. (2010). Psychiatric correlates of bullying in the United States: Findings from a national sample. *Psychiatric Quarterly*, 81, 183–195.

Wall, D.S. (2001). Cybercrimes and the Internet. In D.S. Wall (Ed.), *Crime and the Internet* (pp. 1–17). New York: Routledge.

Wall, D.S. (2007). *Cybercrime: The Transformation of Crime in the Information Age.* Cambridge: Polity Press.

Wall, D.S., & Williams, M. (2007). Policing diversity in the digital age: Maintaining order in virtual communities. *Criminology and Criminal Justice*, 7, 391–415.

Wang, H.C., & Doong, H.S. (2010). Does government effort or citizen word-of-mouth determine e-Government service diffusion? *Behaviour & Information Technology*, 29, 415–422.

Wehinger, F. (2011). The Dark Net: Self-regulation dynamics of illegal online markets for identities and related services. *Intelligence and Security Informatics Conference*, 209–213.

Weimann, G. (2011). Cyber-fatwas and terrorism. *Studies in Conflict and Terrorism*, 34, 1–17.

Wiktorowicz, Q. (2004). *Islamic Activism: A Social Movement Theory Approach.* Bloomington, IN: Indiana University Press.

Williams, W. (2014). Do Android users really need malware protection? *Betanews*. beta news.com/2014/07/07/do-android-users-really-need-malware-protection/.

Wohlsen, M. (2014). Failure is the best thing that could happen to Google Glass. *Wired*, April 15. www.wired.com/2014/04/failure-is-the-best-thing-that-could-happen-to-google-glass/.

Wolak, J., Finkelhor, D., & Mitchell, K. (2012). *Trends in Law Enforcement Responses to Technology-facilitated Child Sexual Exploitation Crimes: The Third National Juvenile Online Victimization Study (NJOV-3).* Durham, NH: Crimes against Children Research Center.

Woo, H., Kim, Y., & Dominick, J. (2004). Hackers: Militants or merry pranksters? A content analysis of defaced web pages. *Media Psychology*, 6, 63–82.

Ybarra, M.L., & Mitchell, J.K. (2004). Online aggressor/targets, aggressors, and targets: A comparison of associated youth characteristics. *Journal of Child Psychology and Psychiatry*, 45, 1308–1316.

Yip, M., Webber, C., & Shadbolt, N. (2013). Trust among cybercriminals? Carding forums, uncertainty, and implications for policing. *Policing and Society*, 23, 1–24.

Zeleny, M. (2009). Technology and high technology: Support net and barriers to innovation. *Advanced Management Systems*, 1, January, 8–21.

Glossary

Absence of a capable guardian Variable in routine activity theory that references the lack of physical, personal, or social protection that can minimize harm to a target.

Actor-network theory (ANT) A social science research approach which treats objects, including computer systems, as a part of larger social networks and gives agency to those devices in the same way as human actors.

Advance fee fraud messages A scheme where a spam mail sender requests a small amount of money upfront from the recipient in order to share a larger sum of money later.

Advanced Persistent Threats (APT) A series of computer attacks that are relatively concealed and constant, involving nation-states targeting businesses and organizations around the world. This term is sometimes associated with attacks originating from China.

Anomaly detection The process of classifying events within large data sets that are unusual or deviations from general trends and patterns. Typically used in computer security processes to flag unusual user behaviors that may be malicious.

Antivirus software Software program designed to detect, block, and remove malicious software from computer systems on the basis of known signatures for various forms of malware.

Biometric security A form of access control based on physiological or behavioral characteristics of humans, including fingerprint scans, voice recognition, and retina scans.

Bitcoin A relatively anonymous form of electronic currency used by a range of actors to pay for goods. Increasingly used in underground markets to pay for drugs and cybercrime services.

Blogs A web log, abbreviated to blog, which is used to display personal details and information.

Botnet A form of malware that combines aspects of Trojan Horse programs and viruses and allows an infected computer to receive commands and be controlled by another user through Internet Relay Chat channels or the web via HTTP protocols.

Bulletin Board Systems (BBS) A computer server that runs a unique software program allowing individuals to access the system, upload and download information, make posts, and exchange private messages.

Burgernet A mobile phone application developed by law enforcement in the Netherlands which enables citizens to provide information directly to the police regarding known crimes or suspicious incidents.

Burnout The experience of long-term exhaustion associated with chronic stressors, typically observed and associated with workplace experiences.

California Security Breach Notification Act of 2003 The first state law in the US that requires any state agency or business that maintains computerized personal data to notify potential victims in the event that their information is acquired by an unauthorized person through a data breach.

Cease and desist letter A document sent to an individual or business to stop a specific act that may be unlawful and insist that they do not engage in the behavior again or meet other demands, under penalty of lawsuit.

Celerity Swiftness, in the context of deterrence theory.

Certainty Refers to how likely it is that the individual will be caught and punished for an offense within deterrence theory.

Child pornography The real or simulated depiction of sexual or sexualized physical abuse of children under 16 years of age, or who appear to be less than 16, that would offend a reasonable adult.

Chip and PIN Brand name used by banks in the UK and Ireland that provide a credit or debit card with an integrated circuit or computer chip that authenticates a transaction at the point of sale terminal or automatic teller machine (ATM).

Classical School Criminological perspective that argues human behavior, and criminal activity, stem from individual decisions made through rational choices and the weighing of costs and benefits for any action.

Code-based obfuscation Techniques to hide the meanings in activities used to search and operate data queries which make it difficult for an attacker or insider to determine the functions needed to actually use data maintained in a repository.

Computer-assisted crimes A crime where a computer is used in a supporting role, such as the use of email as a means either to send fraudulent messages or carry out scams.

Computer crime Crime in which the perpetrator uses special knowledge about computer technology to commit the offense.

Computer Emergency Response Team (CERT) An agency that serves as a coordinating point for responses to major network emergencies.

Computer-focused crimes Crime that cannot exist without computer technology, such as hacking into a sensitive computer network.

Computer-mediated communications (CMCs) The various forms of technology that enable interpersonal communications, including text, email, instant messaging, and other programs.

Corporate security personnel   Officers who are tasked with the protection and management of assets within their organization and serve as gatekeepers to law enforcement agencies in the event of a compromise.

Crime scripts   A method of examining criminality from the offender's perspective in order to identify the process of a given act from start to finish in sequential order.

CrowdStrike   A company that provides endpoint protection and intelligence on targeted attacks against computer networks and corporations.

Crypto-currencies   A type of alternative currency that operates online which utilizes cryptography to secure transactions.

Cryptomarkets   Online communities operating on the Tor network which are used to sell various illicit materials, including drugs, firearms, and personal data.

Cyberbullying   The use of computer-mediated communications to send mean or threatening messages about another person through text or video files.

Cybercrime   Crime in which the perpetrator uses special knowledge of cyberspace.

Cyber-deception/theft   All the ways that individuals may illegally acquire information or resources online.

Cyber-deviance   The use of technology to engage in behavior that may not be illegal, but violates norms and beliefs of the larger culture.

Cyber-porn   The range of sexually expressive content online.

Cyberterrorism   The premeditated, methodological, and ideologically motivated dissemination of information, facilitation of communication, or attack against physical targets, digital information, computer systems, and/or computer programs, intended to cause social, financial, physical, or psychological harm to noncombatant targets and audiences for the purpose of affecting ideological, political, or social change; or any utilization of digital communication or information that facilitates such actions directly or indirectly.

Cyber-trespass   The act of crossing boundaries of ownership in online environments.

Cyber-violence   The ability to send or access injurious, hurtful, or dangerous materials online.

Cyberwar   Term used to describe the use of cyber-attacks in support of conflict between nation-states.

Cyberwarfare   The use of cyber-attacks in support of conflict between nation-states.

DarkMarket   A stolen data market operating out of Europe that was eventually penetrated and taken down through an undercover operation by the Federal Bureau of Investigation (FBI).

Data breach notification   Legal mandate requiring a company or organization to notify consumers in the event that their personal data has been lost due to the illegal acquisition of mass quantities of information through hacking techniques.

Data masking Techniques used to conceal or encrypt data stored in large online repositories.

Data obfuscation Techniques used to conceal or encrypt data stored in large online repositories.

Definitions One of the four principal components of Akers's social learning theory, suggesting that the way an individual views a behavior will affect their willingness to engage in that activity.

Deindividuation Psychological theory which some apply to the Internet to account for involvement in cybercrime by being freed from common behavioral norms, enabling them to behave in any way they see fit.

Deterrence theory This perspective argues that humans will be deterred from choosing to commit crime if they believe that punishments will be certain, swift, and proportionately severe.

Differential association One of the four principal components of Akers's social learning theory, arguing that who we associate with influences our willingness to engage in crime and our exposure to definitions supporting offending.

Differential reinforcement One of the four principal components of Akers's social learning theory, arguing that the punishments or positive reinforcement we receive after engaging in crime will influence our willingness to perform that act again.

Digital drift Criminological theory developed by Goldsmith and Brewer which suggests that the Internet enables individuals to feel disconnected from society and removes a sense of responsibility from societal norms enabling crime on or off-line.

Digital evidence Information that is either transferred or stored in a binary form.

Digital immigrants Those born before the creation of the Internet and digital technologies.

Digital natives Youths who were born into a world that was already digital, spend large amounts of time in digital environments, and utilize technological resources in their day-to-day lives.

Disruptive technology An innovative technology that creates a new market for a product that supplants existing technologies.

e-Gold An online payment platform that utilized its own currency backed by the price of gold or other precious metals, which was suspended due to its involvement in illegal transactions.

Europay, MasterCard, and Visa (EMV) A global standard for the connection of chip cards at point of sale terminals and ATMs to authenticate debit and credit card transactions.

External attacker Actors who attempt to infiltrate networks which they have neither physical nor user credentials to access.

Fair and Accurate Credit Transactions Act of 2003 The US law that provides multiple protections to help reduce the risk of identity theft and assist victims in repairing their credit in the event of identity theft.

Fair Use Policies A set of guidelines and rules given to individuals regarding the appropriate use of computers, networks, and Internet access, as well as any penalties that may occur for violating these terms of use.

First responder An employee of an emergency service (including police, fire, and medical professionals) who are typically the first individuals to be called to the scene of an accident, crime, disaster, terrorist incident, or other emergency.

Folkways Sociological term used to refer to norms that guide routine behaviors and casual interactions.

Forums An online discussion medium where people can communicate through posts to one another.

Fusion center An information-sharing center designed to promote the exchange of information between federal and state agencies across the US which began in 2003 under the US Department of Homeland Security and Department of Justice.

General strain theory An individual-level theory developed by Robert Agnew that discusses the role of frustrations leading to negative emotions which, if not addressed appropriately, can lead individuals to engage in crime as a response.

General theory of crime Gottfredson and Hirschi's theory which argues that crime stems from low self-control and opportunities to offend.

Google Glass A form of wearable technology created by the company Google. These thin glasses come with a wearable computer featuring a heads-up display that is voice-activated and controlled. Users can do a variety of things while wearing Glass, including taking photos and videos, searching the Internet, checking email, and several other activities that are evolving through the creation of new applications.

Government-controlled organizations A group or agency that is owned and operated by a government or state entity.

Guardians of Peace (GoP) A hacker collective that claimed responsibility for attacks against Sony Pictures in 2014 and demanded the cancellation of the release of the film "The Interview."

Health Insurance Portability and Accountability Act (HIPAA) The US federal law created in 1996 with the goal of making it easier for people to keep health insurance, reduce the costs of healthcare administration, and protect the confidentiality and security of healthcare information.

Honeypots A computer system that acts as a decoy to entice actors to gain unauthorized access so that their activities can be monitored and tracked through various software.

Imitation One of the four principal components of Akers's social learning theory, suggesting that an individual's first act of deviance or criminality is an attempt to model the behavior of their peers and imitate others.

Internal attacker Individuals with access to system resources on a network who attempt to extend their credentials beyond what they have been given permission to use or access.

International criminal tribunal for cyberspace A potential truly international court that could represent victim nations and offenders and could be a valuable tool to pursue cases where multiple nations are affected by a group of actors.

Internet Crimes Against Children (ICAC) task forces US-based local task forces that provide a mechanism for coordination between local, state, and federal law enforcement, as well as prosecutors, to combat child sex offenses.

Internet of Things All non-computing devices connected together via the Internet, including thermostats, refrigerators, and other appliances.

Internet service provider (ISP) An organization that provides services for access and use of the Internet, which may be commercial, non-profit, or privately owned businesses.

Internet Use Policy (IUP) A series of rules and guidelines given to individuals regarding the appropriate use of computers, networks, and Internet access, as well as any penalties that may occur for violating these terms of use.

Internet users (From Wall's typology of groups policing the Internet) The individuals who use the Internet who comprise the largest population of potential actors policing the Internet.

Intrusion Detection System (IDS) A software application that monitors network activity for malicious action or policy violations and reports this information to a management station for action of some type.

Malware infections The activation and execution of malicious software, including viruses, worms, and Trojan Horse programs, on a computer system.

Motivated offender Variable within routine activity theory that constitutes any individual or group who has both the inclination and ability to commit crime.

National Crime Victimization Survey (NCVS) A US-based survey with a nationally representative sample of respondents which serves as the nation's primary source of information on criminal victimization.

National Incident-Based Reporting System (NIBRS) The US-based incident-reporting system used by law enforcement agencies to collect and report data on crime.

Newsgroups A type of computer-mediated communication acting as a repository where messages can be posted for others to see using a system called Usenet.

Non-governmental organization (NGO) An organization that is neither a governmental agency nor run as a for-profit business but instead involves a number of volunteers and has a specific goal or task.

Online community-oriented policing programs An online adaptation of a well-known program used by law enforcement agencies to connect with citizens and identify key crime problems that can be addressed through collaborative methods.

Online payment systems   The various Internet-based platforms and services used to send and receive payments in some denomination or currency between individuals and/or organizations.

Open source repository   A publicly accessible site where information can be shared with others and informed by the general public.

Operation Aurora   The name given to a series of cyber-attacks against various major corporations to steal sensitive intellectual property information, which appeared to originate in China.

Password   A word or phrase using a combination of letters, numbers, and symbols that an individual enters in order to gain access to sensitive resources and information.

People's Liberation Army (PLA)   The name of the Chinese military.

Personal Identification Number (PIN)   The four-digit number used as a password to secure access to bank accounts at ATMs.

Phishing   Using email messages to try to acquire personal information, including banking details, from potential victims.

Pornography   The representation of sexual situations and content for the purposes of sexual arousal and stimulation.

Positivist perspective   Criminological paradigm which argues that crime is the result of factors internal or external to an individual, and can include biological, economic, or social forces.

Privacy Rights Clearinghouse   A California-based non-profit organization focusing on consumer information and advocacy to assist the general public.

Pump and dump email   A form of spam-enabled fraud that attempts to manipulate the value of corporate stocks.

Radicalization   The process by which an individual or group adopts extreme political, social, or ideological ideas, associated with neo-Nazi groups and *jihad*.

Ransomware   Malware that demands that the operator of the infected system pay in order to have their system's functionality restored.

Rational choice theory   Criminological theory which argues that criminals are rational actors who make decisions on the basis of the risks of detection versus the potential rewards and benefits of offending.

Rome Statute   Abbreviated name for the treaty that established the International Criminal Court, adopted at a diplomatic conference.

Routine activities theory   Theory created by Cohen and Felson which argued that direct-contact predatory victimization occurs with the convergence in both space and time of three primary components: (1) a motivated offender; (2) a suitable target; and (3) the absence of a capable guardian.

Secondary trauma   The stress resulting from helping or working with an individual who is traumatized in some way or suffering. Sometimes referred to as vicarious trauma due to the exposure to others' traumatic life events.

Self-control   The ability to constrain one's own behavior through internal regulation.

Severity Involves the intensity of the punishment relative to the harm caused by the crime in the context of deterrence theory.

Sexting The practice of sending photos or videos of individuals in provocative outfits or engaging in sexually suggestive activities through text messaging.

ShadowCrew A criminal group that operated an online forum where individuals bought and sold personal information and other cybercrime services, which was taken down by a multi-agency investigation in 2004.

Situational crime prevention (SCP) Criminological theory developed from tenets of rational choice, routine activities, and crime pattern analysis used to deter crime through various mechanisms that affect both the offender's decision-making process, and the behaviors of both potential victims and place managers.

Social engineering The use of tactics that try to fool or convince people to provide information which can be used to access different resources.

Social learning theory Criminological theory created by Ron Akers which argues that the learning process of any behavior, including crime, includes four principal components: (1) differential association; (2) definitions; (3) differential reinforcement; and (4) imitation.

Space-transition theory Theory created by K. Jaishankar which argues that people behave differently while online than they otherwise would in physical space.

Spam Unsolicited email sent to large groups.

Stress The physical and psychological response individuals have to working demands when they are not matched to their abilities, which also challenges their ability to cope with these experiences in a positive way.

Subcultural perspective A framework in which scholars examine any group having differentiating values, norms, traditions, and rituals that set them apart from the dominant culture.

Suitable target A variable in routine activity theory referring to a person or object that has traits making him/her/it attractive to the offender on a wide range of factors.

Target hardening The process of applying various techniques to minimize the likelihood that an individual, product, or building will be targeted by criminals, whether through the use of social or technical guardians or other means.

Task force A unit or group established to work on a single activity, which may include members from various groups or organizations.

Technicways Term referring to the ways that behavior patterns change in response to, or as a consequence of, technological innovations.

Theoretical integration The process of merging two or more distinct criminological theories to create a new theory. There are various models of integration, depending on the knowledge and perspectives of the authors.

Tor network An anonymous and encrypted network used by individuals to hide their physical location.

UK Action Fraud   The UK national agency that handles complaints of Internet-based fraud and theft.

Undercover operations   Law enforcement operations in which agents act covertly in order to infiltrate criminal groups, gain trust, and eventually disrupt their activities.

Uniform Crime Report (UCR)   The primary US reporting mechanism used by law enforcement agencies to collect and report data on crimes made known to the police.

US Internet Crime Complaint Center (IC3)   A collaborative effort of the National White Collar Crime Center (NW3C) and the FBI operating for crime victims, consumers, and researchers to understand the scope of various forms of online fraud. Victims can contact the agency through an online reporting mechanism that accepts complaints for a range of offenses.

Virtual communities of hate   Term used to describe the various websites, forums, and other forms of computer-mediated communication used by extremists and terrorist groups to spread messages related to bias and hate of groups based on race, ethnicity, religion and other differences.

Virtual Global Taskforce (VGT)   Established in 2003, an alliance of agencies and private industry that works together in order to identify, investigate, and respond to incidents of child exploitation.

Wearable devices   Any sort of Internet-enabled device that can be worn by a person, such as a watch or pair of glasses.

Web defacements   An act of online vandalism wherein an individual replaces the existing HTML code for a web page with an image and message that they create.

Index

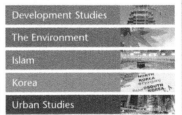

Lightning Source UK Ltd.
Milton Keynes UK
UKOW05n1823051016

284576UK00015B/129/P

9 781138 024168